# D. Barton Johnson

# Worlds in Regression: Some Novels of Vladimir Nabokov

Ardis, Ann Arbor

D. Barton Johnson, *Worlds in Regression: Some Novels of Vladimir Nabokov*
Copyright© 1985 by Ardis Publishers
All rights reserved under International and Pan-American Copyright Conventions.
Printed in the United States of America

Ardis Publishers
2901 Heatherway
Ann Arbor, Michigan 48104

**Library of Congress Cataloging in Publication Data**

Johnson, Donald B. (Donald Barton), 1933—
    Worlds in Regression.

    1. Nabokov, Vladimir Vladimirovich, 1899-1977—
Criticism and interpretation. I. Title.
PG3476. N3Z696   1985    813'.54    84-28359
ISBN 0-88233-908-7

For Sheila

# CONTENTS

# ACKNOWLEDGMENTS

Portions of this book have appeared in different versions in various journals and collections. Acknowledgments are as follows: the chapters in Section One appeared as "Synesthesia, Polychromatism and Nabokov" in *A Book of Things about Vladimir Nabokov*, ed. Carl Proffer (Ann Arbor, 1974), pp. 84-103 and "The Alpha and Omega of Nabokov's Prisonhouse of Language: Alphabetic Iconicism in *Invitation to a Beheading*" in *Russian Literature*, (Amsterdam) VI, 4, pp. 347-369; those in Section Two as "The Scrabble Game in *Ada* or Taking Nabokov Clitorally" in *Journal of Modern Literature*, IX, 2, pp. 291-303 and "The Index of Refraction in Nabokov's *Pale Fire*" in *Russian Literature Triquarterly*, XVI, pp. 33-49; Section Three—"Text and Pre-Text in Nabokov's *Defense*" in *Modern Fiction Studies*, XXX, 2, pp. 278-287 and "The Key to Nabokov's *Gift*" in *Canadian-American Slavic Studies*, XVI, 2, pp. 190-206; Section Four—"The Labyrinth of Incest in Nabokov's *Ada*" forthcoming in *Comparative Literature* and "Inverted Reality in Nabokov's *Look at the Harlequins!*" in *Studies in Twentieth Century Literature*, VIII, 2, pp. 293-309; Section Five—"Spatial Modeling and Deixis: Nabokov's *Invitation to a Beheading*" in *Poetics Today*, (Tel Aviv) III, 1, pp. 81-98 and "The Ambidextrous Universe of Nabokov's *Look at the Harlequins!*" in *Critical Essays on Vladimir Nabokov*, ed. Phyllis Roth (Boston, 1983), pp. 202-215; Section Six—"'Don't Touch My Circles': The Two Worlds of Nabokov's *Bend Sinister*" in *Delta* (Montpellier), 17, pp. 33-52 and "Vladimir Nabokov's *Solus Rex* and the 'Ultima Thule' Theme" in *Slavic Review*, XXXX, 4, pp. 543-556.

The present book also contains scattered information drawn from other of my articles as follows: "The Role of Synesthesia in the Work of Vladimir Nabokov" in *Melbourne Slavonic Studies*, IX-X, pp. 125-139; "Nabokov's *Ada* and Pushkin's *Eugene Onegin*" in *Slavic and East European Journal*, XV, 3, pp. 316-323; "Nabokov as a Man-of-Letters: The Alphabetic Motif in his Work" in *Modern Fiction Studies*, XXV, 3, pp. 397-412; "A Guide to Vladimir Nabokov's *Putevoditel' po Berlinu*" in *Slavic and East European Journal*, XXIII, 3, pp. 353-361; and "Belyj and Nabokov: A Comparative Overview" in *Russian Literature*, IX, 2, pp. 379-402. Also see my "Eyeing Nabokov's *Eye*" in the special forthcoming Nabokov issue of *Canadian-American Slavic Studies* (1984) and "The Books Reflected in Nabokov's *Eye*" to appear in *Slavic and East European Journal* in 1985.

The following Nabokov editions are cited in the study. All citations and references in the text are identified by abbreviations, e.g., (SO 37): *Ada* [A] (New York, 1969); *Bend Sinister* [BS] (New York, 1964); *The Defense* [Df] (London, 1964) & *Zashchita Luzhina* [ZL] (Berlin, 1930); *Despair* [D] (New York, 1966) & *Otchaianie* [O] (Berlin, 1936); *The Gift* [G] (New

York, 1963) & *Dar* (Ann Arbor, 1975); "A Guide to Berlin" in *Details of a Sunset and Other Stories* (New York, 1976) & *"Putevoditel' po Berlinu"* in *Vozvrashchenie Chorba* (Ann Arbor, 1976); *Invitation to a Beheading* [IB] (New York, 1965) & *Priglashenie na kazn'* [PK] (Paris, 1966); *King, Queen, Knave* [KQKn] (New York, 1968) & *Korol', dama, valet* [KDV] (New York, 1969); *Lolita* [L] (New York, 1958) and *Lolita* [L] (Russ. trans.) (New York, 1967); *Look at the Harlequins!* [LATH] (New York, 1974); *Pale Fire* [PF] (New York, 1966); *Pnin* [P] (New York, 1957); *Poems and Problems* [PP] (New York, 1970); *The Real Life of Sebastian Knight* [SK] (Harmondsworth, 1964); *"Solus Rex"* in *Sovremennye zapiski* (Paris), LXX (1940) & *A Russian Beauty and Other Stories* (New York, 1973); *Speak, Memory* [SM] (New York, 1960 & 1966) & *Drugie berega* [DB] (New York, 1954); *Stikhi* (Ann Arbor, 1979); "Terror" in *Tyrants Destroyed and Other Stories* (New York, 1973) & *"Uzhas"* in *Vozvrashchenie Chorba* (Ann Arbor, 1976); "Ultima Thule" in *A Russian Beauty . . .* & in *Vesna v Fial'te i drugie rasskazy* (New York, 1956); *Transparent Things* (New York, 1972); "The Vane Sisters" in *Tyrants Destroyed. . . .* In the Notes, which are placed at the end of each section, references to the cited editions are by title only.

I would like to acknowledge the assistance of the Research Committee of the Academic Senate of the University of California in meeting the expenses entailed in the preparation of the manuscript. More personal thanks are the due of Carl and Ellendea Proffer who encouraged a linguist to turn to literary criticism. Most of all, my thanks to Sheila Golburgh Johnson who took time from her own writing to help with mine.

# INTRODUCTION

> "...what I would welcome at the close of a
> book of mine is a sensation of its world
> receding in the distance and stopping
> somewhere there, suspended afar like a
> picture in a picture: *The Artist's Studio* by
> Van Bock."
>
> *Strong Opinions* (72-3)

Many of Vladimir Nabokov's novels end with this sense of a receding world inset within the world of Van Bock's studio. It is, however, the picture of a real Flemish master that provides another essential ingredient of Nabokov's aesthetic cosmology. In Jan van Eyck's *Giovanni Arnolfini and His Bride*, the newlyweds appear to be alone in their bridal chamber, but reflected in a circular wall mirror we see the miniature image of the painter and a female onlooker peering into the room.[1] The two paintings, Van Bock's *The Artist's Studio* and Van Eyck's *Giovanni Arnolfini and His Bride*, one imaginary and one real, constitute a concise paradigm of Nabokov's art: *ut pictura poesis*.[2]

'Mirroring,' 'doubling,' 'inversion,' 'self-reflexiveness,' 'pattern,' 'coincidence,' 'involution' are all frequently used to describe Nabokov's novels. All are apt. Less obvious is that their aptness proceeds from a consistent aesthetic cosmology that dominated Nabokov's work for nearly half a century. This vision is hinted in the author's remark that all of his novels have an air "not quite of this world, don't you think?".[3] The figure occurs again in *Speak, Memory*, when Nabokov (in the guise of an anonymous critic) describes the Russian novels of Sirin as "windows giving on a contiguous world" (280). We shall see that these comments are simple statements of fact. Many, if not all, of Vladimir Nabokov's novels contain more than one world in varying degrees of presence. This is not merely a stock literary metaphor: the world of the novel versus the world of the novelist. At the very least, what appears to be the world of the novelist is that of an author-persona who, within the framework of the novel, creates and occasionally intrudes upon the world of his characters. Author Nabokov stands at still greater remove. An analogy with Van Eyck's wedding scene is illuminating. The small figure in the world of the mirror is not the artist but his persona, while the artist who creates the whole remains outside the frame. Each Nabokov novel contains at least two fictive worlds. This "two world" model accounts (in a formal sense) for much of what happens in many Nabokov novels. It describes their underlying cosmology. The patterns, the webs of coincidence that pervade the world of the characters, are but an imperfect mirroring of events on a second, controlling world. Although the characters of a given universe regard the intuited next higher world as the ultimate, all-defining one, it in turn stands in the same subordinate position vis-à-vis a still more all-encompassing world.

Nabokov's autobiography, with its recurrent theme of the author's "colossal efforts to distinguish the faintest of personal glimmers in the impersonal darkness on both sides of (his) life" (20), suggests that the aesthetic cosmology that governs the novels was not without significance for his personal life. Nabokov's concern with the "hereafter," with the other world, has been well established, and it seems possible that the cosmology we have outlined for his novels is a projection of a personal cosmology.[4] It must be conceded, however, the reverse is equally possible: the aesthetic cosmology may provide a personal cosmology. In either case, Nabokov saw himself and his world in much the same way some of his fictional favorites come to see their own. Cincinnatus of *Invitation to a Beheading* and Adam Krug of *Bend Sinister* sense in the secret patterns surrounding them signs of an encompassing world and, at the moment of death, enter that other world. If we blend Nabokov's fictional cosmology with his presumed personal cosmology, we find an infinite succession of regressive worlds: the fictional world inside that of the author-persona who in turn aspires to that of his author (the real one from our point of view) who stands in the same relationship to *his* author *ad infinitum*: worlds in infinite regression.

The reader may well have recognized the philosophical prototype of Nabokov's regressive worlds, for they bear a marked resemblance to the model of the universe advanced by Neoplatonism. A summary statement of a few of the major tenets of Neoplatonism brings this out: 1) "There is a hierarchy of reality, a plurality of spheres of being arranged in descending order..." 2) "Each sphere of being is derived from its superior" and "is established in its own reality by turning back toward its superior in a movement of contemplative desire, which is implicit in the original creative impulse...that it receives from its superior." 3) "Each sphere of being is an image or expression on a lower level of the sphere above it, and each individual reality an image or expression of a corresponding reality in a higher sphere. The relationship of archetype and image runs through the whole of the Neoplatonic universe."[5] We shall see, especially toward the end of our study, how closely the worlds of Nabokov and his novels conform to this philosophical cosmology.

Neoplatonism and Gnosticism were central ingredients of the Russian Symbolist movement in the early years of the century[6] and as Nabokov once reminded his friend Edmund Wilson, "I am a product of that period, I was bred in that atmosphere."[7] Nabokov was not, of course, part of the Symbolist movement, but his aesthetic and philosophical views owe much to the Symbolist tradition.[8]. Russian Symbolism was a movement of great complexity and little internal agreement. There was consensus on only two central points. The first is that there exists, beyond the scope of the intellect, another, more real world, and that what man sees before him is but a shadow and echo of that true reality. The second is that art reveals the truth of that higher order beyond our shadow world. In addition to these areas of philosophical accord, Nabokov shares the pronounced aestheticism of many of the Symbolist writers. In particular we would note his highly developed sense of formal structure and his overriding concern with language and style. Further, much Symbolist writing was distinguished by a sense of whimsy and intellectual play that lies outside the mainstream of Russian literature. These Symbolist tenets and practices underlie the Nabokovian two-world cosmology which is developed at length in the essays.

The following chapters treat eight of Nabokov's novels and the autobiography with occasional side-glances at other works. The novels are equally divided between Nabokov's Russian and English periods and show, among other things, the remarkable continuity of certain ideas in his work. The basic theme of our study is Nabokov's two worlds, and the individual essays show in greater or lesser degree the presence of the two (or more) worlds and illustrate the interrelations between them. The six sections fall into three thematic groups: 1) letters and word games (I&II), 2) chess problems and mazes (III&IV), and 3) the riddle of the universe (V&VI).

Nabokov has often been criticized as a mere game player, and games do indeed play a large and important role in his work. Much recent Nabokov criticism, such as Ellen Pifer's *Nabokov and the Novel* and W.W. Rowe's *Nabokov's Spectral Dimension* are in part directed toward defending Nabokov from such charges which, at least in the eyes of the accuser, diminish his literary stature. Nabokov's work does, of course, have a moral dimension, although it is happily latent rather than explicit. As useful as these and other such critical studies are, the game aspect of Nabokov should not be down played, for Nabokov's games, in addition to the sheer fun and delight that they introduce into his novels, have a "serious" purpose. Nabokov's games are a prominent part of the intricate web of allusion, coincidence, and pattern that mark the presence of the other world in the novels. They are a critical aspect of Nabokov's two-world aesthetic cosmology. The games often mirror in miniature the themes and subthemes of the novels. This thesis is argued and illustrated in detail in the following pages.

The opening section, "Nabokov as Man of Letters," unlike its successors, does not deal with games in any strict sense but rather with the world of alphabetic symbols. Alphabetic symbols are shown to be Nabokov's master motif as a writer and, more importantly for our thesis, to be emanations from another world. The second section, "Nabokov as Anagrammist," moves directly into the world of word games. Section III turns to the use of chess in two of the novels, while the following section, "Nabokov as Maze Maker," traces the labyrinth of incest in a pair of late novels. Section V, "Nabokov as Literary Cosmologist," moves away from games and into an exposition of the two-world model underlying so much of Nabokov's fiction. The final section, "Nabokov as Gnostic Seeker," explores the themes of consciousness and death in the context of Nabokov's regressive worlds. The essays and their themes progress from the highly specific and concrete to the more general and abstract.

Each essay is developed in the thematic context of its section but, in most cases, the essays also offer fairly wide-ranging interpretations of particular novels. In consequence, they often contain material that might seem as well suited to a different section. The groupings are not mutually exclusive. The material on letter play and anagrams in *Invitation to a Beheading* treated in Section V could have equally well been used in Section II. Similarly, the treatment of letter play in *Bend Sinister* might have been incorporated in one of the game sections rather than in "Nabokov as Gnostic Seeker." Such sacrifices to thematic homogeneity would needlessly fragment the analysis of the novels. Three of the novels are, however, treated in two separate essays set in different sections. Certain game aspects of *Invitation to a Beheading*, *Ada*, and *Look at the Harlequins!* are examined as specialized subjects while more general interpretations of these books are offered in later sections.

The essays exhibit a variety of critical approaches depending on what seemed most appropriate to the subject matter. Some, such as "The Two Worlds of *Invitation to a Beheading*" are explicitly structuralist in orientation. Few of the essays stray very far from their texts, although "The Labyrinth of Incest in *Ada*" is in part a venture into comparative literature, and "Text and Pre-text in *The Defense*" moves into the extra-literary world of chess history. Most of the studies fall within the tradition of classical *explication de texte*. All are "close readings" and tend to be strongly language-oriented.

Many of the essays contain a great deal of detail. In closing I should like to refer to two Nabokov quotations on the subject. The first is: "In high art and pure science detail is everything" (SO 118). The second is Nabokov's definition of reality:

> Reality is a very subjective affair. I can only define it as a kind of gradual accumulation of information; and as specialization. If we take a lily, for instance, or any other kind of natural object, a lily is more real to a naturalist than it is to an ordinary person. But it is still more real to a botanist. And yet another stage of reality is reached with that botanist who is a specialist in lilies. You can get nearer and nearer, so to speak, to reality; but you never get near enough because reality is an infinite succession of steps, levels of perception, false bottoms, and hence unquenchable, unattainable (SO 10-11).

NOTES

Introduction

1. Van Eyck's picture may be found in H.W. Janson, *History of Art* (Englewood Cliffs, NJ, 1967), pp. 290-92.

2. Nabokov's metaphor of the writer as painter is not an idle one. The writer once reminisced "I think I was born a painter . . . and up to my fourteenth year . . . I was supposed to become a painter . . ." (*Strong Opinions*, p. 17). Many painterly effects and allusions color Nabokov's works—perhaps most prominently in *Ada* with its numerous *tableaux vivants*, as Alfred Appel, Jr., has called them ("*Ada* Described," *Triquarterly*, 17 [Winter, 1970], p. 161). Among the many art teachers of the young Nabokov, the most prominent was M.V. Dobuzhinski to whom the writer renders tribute both in *Speak, Memory* and in his 1926 poem "Ut pictura poesis," which is a verbal evocation of the painter's St. Petersburg scenes (*Stikhi* [Ann Arbor 1979], p. 101).

3. Andrew Field, *Nabokov: His Life in Part* (New York, 1977), p. 87.

4. The most succinct statement of this concern is in Vera Nabokov's "Foreword" to the posthumous publication of her husband's collected Russian poems, *Stikhi*.

5. "Neoplatonism," *Encyclopedia Britannica*, 1959 edn., vol. XVI, p. 216.

6. These schools of thought found their major Russian embodiment in the writings of the mystic philosopher and poet Vladimir Solovyov (1852-1900), who was a major influence on Alexander Blok, Andrei Bely and other avatars of Russian Symbolism. For a concise survey of his work, see D.S. Mirsky, *A History of Russian Literature*, ed. Frances J. Whitfield (New York, 1958), pp. 362-68.

7. *The Nabokov-Wilson Letters: Correspondence between Vladimir Nabokov and Edmund Wilson 1940-1971*, edited, annotated and with an introductory essay by Simon Karlinsky (New York, 1979), p. 220. Nabokov's ties with Gnosticism as exemplified in *Invitation to a Beheading* are developed at length in Sergei Davydov's "*Teksty-Matreshki Vladimira Nabokova*" (München, 1982), pp. 100-82.

8. For a discussion of Nabokov and the Russian Symbolists, see my "Bely and Nabokov: A Comparative Overview," *Russian Literature*, IX, 2, pp. 379-402.

# SECTION ONE

# NABOKOV AS MAN OF LETTERS

The hallmark of Nabokov's style is an intricate integration of theme, plot and motif. The theme that in a general sense is embodied by a novel's plot is caught in miniature by a motif which neatly sums up the whole. The novel *Despair* may serve as an example. Its plot involves a schizoid, nearly bankrupt, chocolate manufacturer who, on finding a tramp whom he considers to be his look-alike, decides to switch identities with the wanderer, kill him and have his wife collect the insurance so they may start life anew. The flaw apparent to everyone except the first person narrator is that the tramp does not resemble him in the least. Hermann, the anti-hero, views his grisly accomplishment and his literary reincarnation of it as a genial work of art, although the scheme itself is threadbare and its telling is riddled with echoes of the double theme from the Russian classics.[1] The motif that Nabokov has chosen as the emblem for his novel is, classically, mirrors. A more subtle integration of theme, plot and motif may be found in *Laughter in the Dark* (originally and more aptly entitled *Kamera obskura*) whose central figure, an impercipient art connoisseur, dreams of bringing the work of old masters to life through a motion picture cartooning process. His marriage and his life are destroyed when, as a result of his love affair with an avaricious, screen-struck teen-ager, he loses his vision in a car catastrophe. The book's intentionally hackneyed plot is conceived entirely in terms of cinematic technique—presumably as a thematic metaphor for flawed perception. Here again Nabokov introduces a motif that resonates with theme and plot—frames: door frames, window frames, mirror frames, picture frames; i.e., the lens frame of the camera obscura through which the viewer follows the story. In *The Defense*, Nabokov's first fully formed novel, Grandmaster Luzhin proposes and disposes in his abstract chess kingdom. On the board of life, however, Luzhin fares less well in his chess-like battle with insanity as it is mirrored in the motif pattern of light and dark squares scattered throughout the book.

The above examples all involve themes and motifs of specific novels. Beyond such individual themes, Nabokov's *oeuvre* exhibits certain broader themes that figure in greater or lesser degree in almost all of his writings. Such a central theme was remarked as early as the nineteen thirties by Nabokov's most astute Russian critic, Vladislav Khodasevich: "The life of the artist and the life of the device in the consciousness of the artist—this is Sirin's theme."[2] The continued validity of this insight is affirmed by Andrew Field who adds that "this view provides a universal key which 'works' in almost all of the Nabokov's fiction."[3] Reformulating

7

Khodasevich's statement, we may say that Nabokov's central theme is that of the act, the process, of literary creation, Just as each of Nabokov's works contains a particularized theme with a motif carefully selected and modulated to that theme, Nabokov's master theme also has its own distinctive motif. The motif figure that Nabokov chose to articulate his master theme is the alphabetic symbol, the letter.

Nabokov's use of alphabetic signs as emblematic motifs of the theme of literary creativity is found in various dimensions throughout his works. Not surprisingly, it is in the three works in which the theme of literary creativity is particularly prominent that we see the most explicit and diverse manifestations of the letter motif. The autobiography, *Speak, Memory*, is a compendium of Nabokovian themes and motifs, and it is here that we find an account of the establishment of the emblematic bond between the motif of the letter and the theme of literary creation. In the summer of 1905, Nabokov's father found that his six-year-old son could read and write English but not Russian and engaged the village schoolmaster to give Russian spelling lessons to the boy. On the spelling master's first day he presented his pupil with "a box filled with tremendously appetizing blocks with a different letter painted on each side; these cubes he handled as if they were infinitely precious things, which, for that matter, they were..." (28). The spelling master reappears in the summer of 1914 when "in the course of the languid ramble that accompanied the making of my first poem, I ran into the village schoolmaster.... (I welcome his image again.)" It is not by chance that the young Nabokov just then encounters the very man who taught him his first Russian letters and presented him with those precious colored alphabet blocks (218-219).

The symbolic role of the alphabet as a token of literary creativity is equally manifest in *The Gift*. When the young writer Fyodor Godunov-Cherdyntsev is asked about the genesis of his gift, he replies, "When my eyes opened to the alphabet" (68). That his reply is more than metaphoric is attested by the remainder of the conversation. A similar association of first awareness of the alphabet and of the writer's creative gift is to be seen in Nabokov's *Invitation to a Beheading*. The artist-protagonist, Cincinnatus, whose gift makes him different and hence criminal in the totalitarian dream-world of the novel, recalls the day when he first realized his criminality, "I must have just learned to make letters since I remember myself wearing on my fifth finger the little copper ring that was given to children who already knew how to copy... model words..." (96).

These books in which the nature of the creative process is central, all make extensive use of the alphabetic motif. Nabokov's choice of the alphabet symbol for what we might call his signature motif is apt, for what could be more uniquely apposite to the dominant theme of his *oeuvre*, the creative process of the verbal artist, the writer? The two essays that follow examine works in which alphabetic motif systems play important roles and demonstrate how that motif both integrates the text and symbolizes the central theme. In Nabokov's autobiography, *Speak, Memory*, alphabetic chromesthesia, which appears to be an incidental curiosity, is shown to be the basis of an elaborate metaphor describing the author's creative life. In *Invitation to a Beheading* the covert stylistic device of alphabetic iconicism proves to be the key to the relationship of the two worlds in this most obscure and difficult of Nabokov's novels.

## THE ALPHABETIC RAINBOWS OF *SPEAK, MEMORY*

*Speak, Memory* is described by its author as "a systematically correlated assemblage of personal recollections..." (9). This is a curiously precise description, for the book is not a traditional autobiography but a highly selective series of chapter-memoirs, each devoted to a particular theme. Many of the themes have associated motifs—sometimes evanescent, sometimes pervading whole chapters. Butterflies, one of the reigning passions of Nabokov's life, are the subject of one such chapter. They are one of the thematic series that unify, give shape and meaning to the author's life from a morning on the family's summer estate circa 1906 through the butterfly expeditions in Colorado nearly fifty years later. A country bog in Northern Russia imperceptibly blends into the alpine meadows of Colorado as the two locales and times are linked in pursuit of an escaped Swallowtail. Space and time are telescoped by a coalescence of related images. It is the beginning of the sequence that we shall touch on here: Nabokov's first butterfly. "The original event had been banal enough. On the honeysuckle, overhanging the carved back of a bench just opposite the main entrance, my guiding angel (whose wings, except for the absence of a Florentine limbus, resemble those of Fra Angelico's Gabriel) pointed out to me a rare visitor, a splendid, pale-yellow creature with black splotches, blue crenels, and a cinnabar eyespot above each chrome-rimmed black tail. ... my desire for it was one of the most intense I have ever experienced" (120). The event may have been banal enough, but the latent comparison is breathtaking in its hyperbole. Gabriel, to whose wings those of the swallowtail are likened, appears in Fra Angelico's *L' Annunciazione* in which the herald angel announces to the Virgin Mary the incarnation of Christ. The leap from the swallowtail's wing to Gabriel's coalesces the two events and implicitly compares the boy's awakening to the marvel of butterflies to that of the Virgin Mary's momentous enlightenment. Both experience epiphanies. To be sure, Nabokov's use of hyperbole here is not without an element of the grotesque, but more to the point is that it is based upon a finely observed detail which unites the two visions. It is the recurrent detail that yields pattern and hence meaning to Nabokov's art and life.

A more extended example of a motif that is used to integrate a thematic series is the magic lantern figure that underlies Nabokov's chapter on his successive tutors. One of the longer surviving tutors, Lenski, arranged a series of educational magic lantern shows for his reluctant charges and their friends. At the first performance home-made colored slides illustrating scenes from Lermontov's *Mtsyri* were shown while Lenski recited the long poem. Nabokov draws upon the magic lantern figure as a framework for recounting the sequence of tutors that graced his youth and ends the chapter with a marvellously detailed, sensuous scene of a family picnic in which at the place of the tutor there is a succession of fade-ins and fade-outs—a reprise of the chapter's theme. It is only in retrospect that the reader realizes that the pseudonym "Lenski," the creator of the magic lantern show, derives from the "lens" of the magic lantern show of memory.

Perhaps the most remarkable thing about Nabokov's "autobiography" is what it seems not to include. Two topics are conspicuously absent: the author's marriage and his literary career. In the foreword, Nabokov dismisses his writings by referring the reader to the introduction of his translated Russian novels which, he says, "give a sufficiently detailed, and racy, account of the creative part of my European past" (14-15). The biography includes only an evocation of Nabokov's first poem and his youthful efforts to become a poet. Later, in his description of the Russian literary scene in exile, he devotes a paragraph to the brilliant if often misunderstood talents of one Sirin who vanished from the émigré scene as mysteriously as he had come. It is for the reader to know that "Sirin" is reborn in the United States as Nabokov. It is, all in all, a very strange autobiography for a writer. We shall see, however, that in spite of its overt absence the theme of Nabokov's creative life is repeatedly symbolized throughout the memoir in the form of a synesthetic rainbow. Just as many of the autobiography's chapters have their own motifs, *Speak, Memory* as a whole is unified by the master motif of the synesthetic rainbow.

Synesthesia, to which Nabokov is "inordinately prone," is one of the more exotic byways of human experience. It is defined as "a sensation produced in one modality when a stimulus is applied to another modality, as when the hearing of a certain sound induces the visualization of a certain color."[4] The intersensorial blend may involve any mixture of the sense modalities: touch/smell, taste/sight, sound/taste, touch/sight/sound, and so on. One of the most commonly cited examples is that of a man, congenitally blind, who, when asked to describe his impression of the color scarlet, likened it to the blare of a trumpet.[5] This example represents a type of synesthesia known as chromesthesia in which a given sound simultaneously evokes a consistent and automatic color response in the hearer. It is also referred to as *audition coloree* or colored hearing. Chromesthesia is noted fairly commonly among children, but tends to die out before adolescence.[6] Occasionally, however, the phenomenon survives into adulthood. The Russian composers Rimsky-Korsakov and Scriabin both possessed colored hearing, and the latter wrote a symphonic poem, *"Prometheus: Poem of Fire,"* for which he orchestrated an accompanying light show based on his synesthetic sound/color correspondences.[7] Roman Jakobson tells of a thirty-two-year-old Czech, gifted in both music and painting, who exhibited a complete set of color correspondences for all of the Czech vowels and consonants.[8] Psychological synesthesia is a well-documented phenomenon with a clinical history of nearly three hundred years.[9]

Literary (as opposed to psychological) synesthesia is a metaphor in which words and images normally appropriate to the description of one type of sense perception are applied to the description of some other type of sense perception. A familiar example is Rudyard Kipling's "the dawn comes up like thunder," in which the cataclysmic violence and abruptness of a natural sound phenomenon is imputed to the tropical sunrise, a visual phenomenon. Literary synesthesia is at least as old as Western literature (it is found in Homer) and, doubtless, a great deal older.[10]

Literary synesthesia became a subject of intense interest late in the last century largely through its cultivation by the French Symbolists. The most famous exemplification of literary *audition coloré*e is Arthur Rimbaud's 1871 sonnet "Voyelles" which begins:

A noir, E blanc, I rouge, U vert, O bleu: voyelles,
Je dirai quelque jour vos naissances latentes:
A, noir corset velu des mouches éclantes
Qui bombinent autour des puanteurs cruelles....

The following stanzas give a set of colored images evoked by the remaining vowel sounds. Critics attacked the device of literary synesthesia with a ferocity that now seems amusing. The German critic Max Nordau, for example, asserted that synesthesia is:

...an evidence of diseased and debilitated brain activity, if consciousness releases the advantages of the differentiated perceptions of phenomena, and carelessly confounds the reports conveyed by the particular senses. It is a retrogression to the very beginning of organic development. It is a descent from the height of human perfection to the low level of the mollusc. To raise the combination, transposition and confusion of the perceptions of sound and sight to the rank of a principle of art, to see futurity in this principle, is to designate as progress the return from the consciousness of man to that of the oyster.[11]

This passage, although more strident in tone, is typical of many critics' reaction to synesthesic transfer in at least two ways. Firstly, the author sees synesthesia as a diseased condition—which it is not—and, secondly, he fails to distinguish between synesthesia as a psychological phenomenon and synesthesia as a purely literary artifice—simply another type of metaphor which is in no way dependent upon its psychological counterpart. Intersensorial metaphors, at least in their less extravagant forms, are far from uncommon in everyday usage. In many cases they have become standard figures of speech or clichés in which we no longer see their synesthetic basis. We describe, for example, the sound of the human voice in visual terms (silver, golden), kinesthetic terms (heavy), tactile (velvety, soft, warm), or even in gustatory terms (bitter). We habitually speak of loud colors and dull pain. The universality of this phenomenon has been summed up by the eminent psycholinguist Roger Brown with his observation that "Many, perhaps all, languages make metaphorical extentions of their vocabularies of sensation."[12]

In *Speak, Memory*, the author discusses his own synesthetic gifts at some length.[13] Nabokov first became aware of his own chromesthetic gift while playing with a set of colored alphabet blocks presented to him by the village schoolmaster. In the course of building a tower with the new blocks, the boy remarked to his mother that the colors for the various letters were "all wrong." It turned out that his mother also had letter (sound)/color associations and that some of the toy block letters had the same hues for her as for her son (but different from those assigned by the toy manufacturer) (35).[14] Once aware of the boy's synesthetic gift she encouraged his sensitivity to visual stimulation in various ways. An amateur painter, she showed him the magical results of blending colors. At bedtime the child was allowed to play with masses of her jewelry which seemed to him hardly inferior to "the illumination in the city during imperial fêtes..." (36). Drawing and painting lessons were part of his early home education.

As Nabokov notes, colored hearing is not an entirely apt name in his case since the concurrent color response is not keyed exclusively to a sound unit. He remarks that "the color sensation seems to be produced by the very act of my orally forming a given letter while I imagine its outline" (34). This suggests that in addition to the sound the physiological facts of articulation are an element in the process. Other comments show the child was particularly sensitive to the physical shape of letters—both written and printed. In describing his new French dictation notebook, he recounts "...delighting in every limb of every limpid letter ... with exquisite care I would inscribe the word *Dictée*..." (105). Or in speaking of his first English primer he recalls how its four protagonists "now drift with a slow-motion slouch across the remotest backdrop of memory; and akin to the mad alphabet of an optician's chart, the grammar-book lettering looms again before me" (80). It is of interest that Nabokov describes the relationship between the later Russian and the earlier English variants of his memoirs as that of capital letters to cursive (*DB* 8). The influence of letter shapes is also mentioned by Nabokov in discussing his reaction to them in different languages. He notes that the slightest difference in the physical shape of a letter representing the same sound in different languages also alters its color impression. In particular, Russian letters representing the same sound but formed differently from their Latin counterparts are generally distinguished by their duller tone (*DB* 26-27). Thus the Russian *П* is described as "gouache" green whereas the Latin P is characterized as "unripe apple" green—a brighter shade. This particular example is also instructive in that it shows that sound rather than letter shape is the primary determinant of hue since the Cyrillic *П* and Latin P have basically the same color (green), although the letter shapes are quite different. That still other sense modalities are involved in the correspondences is suggested in the Russian variant of Nabokov's autobiography; in reference to Cyrillic letters he notes that their "color sensation is formed by palpable, labial, almost gustatory means. In order to determine thoroughly the hue of a letter, I have to savor the letter, let it swell and radiate in my mouth while I imagine its visual design" (*DB* 26). Nabokov's sound (letter)/color correspondences are clearly dependent on a variety of factors: sound, articulatory physiology, letter shape, and perhaps taste. All contribute in some measure to his color responses. In his memoirs, Nabokov lists in detail his color associations for each sound and/or symbol of the two alphabets, English and Russian. Since the English material is readily available, I shall give only the Russian correspondences by way of example:[15] the black-brown group contains a rich lusterless *A*, a rather smooth *P* (r), hard rubber *Г* (g),a bitter chocolate *Ж* (zh), and a polished dark brown *Я* (ya); the whitish group—a vermicelli-colored *Л* (1), a Smolensk-kasha-colored *H* (n), a milk-of-almonds *O*, a dry roll *(sukhoi khleb)* *X* (kh), and an *Э* (eh), Swedish bread; an intermediate gray group includes a clysteral *Ч* (ch), the fluffy gray *Ш* (sh),and the similar *Щ* (shch) which, however, has a yellowish tinge. The spectral colors include: a red group with a cherry brick *Б* (b), a pinkish flannel *M*, and a pinkish flesh-colored *B* (v); a yellow group with an orange *Ё* (yo), an ochrous *E* (ye), a pale yellow *Д* (d), a light pale yellow, straw-colored *И* (ee), a golden *У* (u), and a brassy *Ю* (yu);a green group with a gouache *П* (p), a dusty alder *Ф* (f), a pastel green *T*; a dark blue through violet group with a tin *Ц* (ts), a moist sky-blue *C* (s), a bilberry-colored *K*, and a lustrous lilac *З* (z). Much can be said about the linguistic and structural aspects of Nabokov's alphabetic chromesthesia, but here we shall focus on the more literary aspects of the phenomenon, i.e., its aesthetic and thematic implications and its role in his creative psychology.

Nabokov's work provides a number of synesthetic images based on alphabetic symbols. One of the most extended examples occurs in the poem *An Evening of Russian Poetry*.[16] The speaker, Nabokov, is giving a talk on Russian poetry to an American women's group:

> My little helper at the magic lantern,
> insert that slide and let the colored beam
> project my name or any such-like phantom
> in Slavic characters upon the screen.
> The other way, the other way. I thank you.

On mellow hills the Greek, as you remember,
fashioned his alphabet from cranes in flight;
his arrows crossed the sunset, then the night.

Our simple skyline and a taste for timber,
the influence of hives and conifers,
reshaped the arrows and the borrowed birds.
Yes, Sylvia? "Why do you speak of words
when all we want is knowledge nicely browned?"
Because all hangs together—shape and sound,
heather and honey, vessel and content.

Not only rainbows—every line is bent,
and skulls and seeds and all good worlds around
like Russian verse, like our colossal vowels:
those painted eggs, those glossy pitcher flowers
that swallow whole a golden bumble bee,
those shells that hold a thimble and the sea.

The chromesthetic representation is so explicit as to be almost clinical—the projection of the Cyrillic characters by the colored light beam, the discussion of the mythical origins of the letter shapes, and, finally, the rainbow-curved colored vowels, those painted eggs. Nabokov's name in colored letters also occurs in his memoir where he records his delight on finding his surname in "golden Slavic characters" on a mural in the American Museum of Natural History in commemoration of his uncle's presence at the signing of the peace treaty ending the Russo-Japanese War (61). Another English poem, *"Voluptates Tactionum,"* which is built on sound/touch interplay, introduces the amusing notion of Braille synesthesia: "When you turn a knob, your set / Will obligingly exhale / Forms, invisible and yet / Tangible—a world in braille." Nabokov goes on to explore the erotic potentialities of his invention. *Bend Sinister*, the first American novel, also contributes an example. Its hero, the anguished philosopher Adam Krug, tells an uncomprehending listener that "the word 'loyalty' phonetically and visually reminds him of a golden fork lying in the sun on a smooth spread of yellow silk" (76). This bit of synesthetic imagery rests upon the author's chromesthetic perception of the two 'Y's as "bright golden yellow" as well as the fork-like shape of the letters themselves. Where Nabokov details his sound/color correspondence in *Speak, Memory*, we find more extensive use of the device. In *Drugie berega*, the Russian version of the autobiography, we read of a twilight foray for hawkmoths. Nabokov stands waiting before a lilac bush while "the young *'Ю'* -colored moon hung in a 'B' -colored aquarelle sky" (*molodaia luna tsveta ' ю ' visela v akvarel'nom nebe tsveta* 'B') (124). The earlier chromesthesia account informs us that the letter *'Ю'* (pronounced 'you') is brass-colored while 'B' ('v' as in 'very') is pinkish flesh-colored. Not only are the chromesthetic colors of the Cyrillic letters appropriate to the objects depicted, but their sound values echo those of the key words, i.e., the *u* of *luna* and *v* of *akvarel'nom*. In a less explicit case of a chromesthetic alphabetic symbol the moon is evoked as "that great heavenly 'O'" (61). The use of the letter symbol is even more appropriate than it might seem for the chromesthetic color of the letter 'O' is a shade described by Nabokov as "milk of almonds" (27).

Tamara, Nabokov's first teen-age love, is also drawn into the chromesthetic motif that pervades *Speak, Memory*. Her appearance is preceded by the letters of her name scrawled on a pavilion door. Nabokov introduces her with the words: "When I first met Tamara—to give her a name concolorous with her real one—she was fifteen, and I was a year older" (229). There is reason to suspect that the term 'concolorous' is to be taken literally here, although phonetic similarity also plays its part. The color sequence corresponding to the Cyrillic form of Tamara is T—pale green, A—dull black, M—rose flannel, A—dull black, R—smooth black, and A—dull black. The predominant color is black with initial and medial flares of green and pink. It is not by chance that the Cyrillic form of Maria is also predominantly black and shares a flash of pink. The names are indeed concolorous and it is of interest that Nabokov's first novel, an autobiographically tinged account of his first love affair, is eponymously called *Mashen'ka*, a Russian diminutive of Maria.

Sirin, the pseudonym Nabokov adopted during his Cambridge years from the name of a fabulous bird of mythology and which he used until his departure from Europe, was apparently selected in a somewhat similar way. To Andrew Field's inquiry as to how he picked his *nom de plume*, Nabokov replied "I saw Sirin with an 's' being a very brilliant blue, a light blue, the 'i' golden, the 'r' a wriggly black, and the 'n' yellow." Nabokov's Russian pen name, unlike "Tamara," is not, incidentally, "concolorous" with his real name which (in Cyrillic) is N-yellow, A-black, B-brick red, O-whitish, K-bluish-black, and V-flesh pink.

Still other synesthetic associations of letters and colors may be found.[17] Perhaps the most wide-spread manifestation of the chromatic letter motif is in the rippling, jewel-like electrical signs that ornament his work. In some sense these images find their origin in the author's childhood memory of illuminations during imperial fêtes when "in the padded stillness of a frosty night, giant monograms, crowns, and other armorial designs made of colored electric bulbs—sapphire, emerald, ruby—glowed with a kind of charmed restraint" (36). In Nabokov's first novel, *Mary*, the hero Ganin unexpectedly learns that his first love is alive and is coming to Berlin to join her husband. As Ganin, dazed at the news, walks the night streets, he sees

"letters of fire which poured out one after another along a black roof..."
(26-27). It is of course an electric advertising sign, but in Ganin's exalted
state he takes it for a "glow of human thought; a sign, a summons; a question
hurled into the sky and suddenly getting a jewel-bright enraptured answer."
In *Invitation to a Beheading* we see "a good million light bulbs of diverse
colors..., artfully arranged in such a way as to embrace the whole nocturnal
landscape with a grandiose monogram" (162). In his nocturnal wanderings
Fyodor, the young poet-hero of *The Gift* sees an "illuminated music hall sign
in which the flashing lights run up the steps of vertically placed letters,
which go out all together, and the light again scrambles up: what Babylonian
word would reach the sky?...a compound name for a trillion tints:
diamonddimlunalilithlilasafieryviolentviolet and so on—and how many
more" (337). Fyodor's Babylonian word harks back to the synesthetic
alphabet blocks with which Nabokov started his own Tower of Babel in
early childhood (SM 35). Similar imagery occurs in Nabokov's poetry. In a
1939 poem written in Paris the author visualizes "an electric sign's tears on
the opposite bank; through the mist the stream of its emeralds running." A
note identifies the "tears" as "the streaming emeralds of an aspirin
advertisement on the other side of the Seine" (PP 94).

Alphabetic chromesthesia is a striking stylistic device, and it is easily
understood why Nabokov occasionally draws on it—especially given his
own synesthetic endowment. Its exotic nature also explains its inclusion in
the author's autobiography. *Speak, Memory* is, however (as Nabokov
himself notes), an extremely selective, "systematically correlated
assemblage of recollections". Almost every detail is intricately interwoven
into one of the book's thematic patterns. Topics that do not fit into one of
these patterns are ruthlessly (and artistically) suppressed. What then of
Nabokov's rather apologetic exegesis on his colored hearing?[18] Why is it
included? What does it mean within the context of the whole? The answers
to those questions are not to be found in the autobiography, but in
Nabokov's novel *The Gift*, where we find an explicit statement of a
relationship between chromesthesia and literary creativity. This occurs in
an imaginary dialogue between the protagonist Fyodor Godunov-
Cherdyntsev, a young writer, and the poet and critic Koncheyev. Their talk
ranges over much of Russian literature. In passing, Godunov-Cherdyntsev
observes that Leskov, although a second-rank writer, "has a Latin feeling for
blueness: *lividus*. Lyov Tolstoy, on the other hand, preferred violet
shades..." (84). Finally Koncheyev asks Fyodor:

How did it begin with you?

When my eyes opened to the alphabet. Sorry, that sounds pretentious, but the fact is,
since childhood I have been afflicted with the most intense and elaborate *audition colorée*.

So that you too, like Rimbaud, could have—

> Written not a mere sonnet but a fat opus, with auditive hues he never dreamt of. For instance, the various numerous *'a'*s of the four languages which I speak differ for me in tinge, going from lacquered-black to splintery-gray—like different sorts of wood. I recommend to you my pink flannel *'m.'* I don't know if you remember the insulating cotton wool which was removed with the storm windows in spring? Well, that is my Russian *'y,'* or rather *'ugh'*, so grubby and dull that words are ashamed to begin with it.[19] If I had some paints handy I would mix burnt-sienna and sepia for you so as to match the color of a gutta-percha *'ch'* sound; and you would appreciate my radiant *'s'* if I could pour into your cupped hands some of those luminous sapphires that I touched as a child ... when my mother ... allowed her perfectly celestial treasures to flow out of their abyss into her palm, out of their cases onto black velvet ... and if one turned the curtain slightly..., one could see, along the receding riverfront, facades in the blue-blackness of the night, the motionless magic of an imperial illumination, the ominous blaze of diamond monograms, colored bulbs in coronal designs....
>
> *Buchstaben von Feuer*, in short.[20]

Although in the foreword to the English translation of *The Gift*, Nabokov specifically warns the reader against identifying Fyodor with the book's author, this particular passage is undeniably drawn from Nabokov's own psychological landscape. In almost every detail the passage corresponds to the information in *Drugie berega* where Nabokov discusses his own synesthetic gift (27-28). Thus the very genesis of literary creativity is attributed to alphabetic chromesthesia.

If we accept this as an explanation of why alphabetic chromesthesia is discussed in *Speak, Memory*, we are still left with the question of how it relates to the whole. *Speak, Memory* is shot through with descriptions utilizing color complexes. Many of these, while not involving synesthesia in a strict sense, employ a wide range of sensory data in addition to the visual. Perhaps the most frequent complex color image in the autobiography is the rainbow, both natural, and artificial as refracted through a prism. The magic lantern show staged by Lensky ends with a color slide illustrating Lermontov's lines: "Blue, green and orange, wonderstruck / With its own loveliness and luck, / Across a crag a rainbow fell / And captured there a poised gazelle" (165). Other examples: in Nabokov's last glimpse of his childhood love, Colette "... there was, I remember, some detail in her attire ... that reminded me of the rainbow in a glass marble. I still seem to be holding that wisp of iridescence ..." (152). This image is evoked again in "a colored spiral in a small ball of glass. This is how I see my own life" (275). Elsewhere, we read of "... a pleasantly supercilious, although plainly psychopathic, rotatory sprinkler, with a private rainbow hanging in its spray above gemmed grass" (304). Of his father, Nabokov writes, "I viewed his activities through a prism of my own, which split into many enchanting colors the rather austere light my teachers glimpsed" (186). Even more frequent are descriptions of rainbow-like color spectra—although often without explicit reference to the underlying rainbow image. The young Nabokov's governess showed him the art of selecting autumn maple leaves and arranging them into "an almost complete spectrum (minus the blue—a big disappointment!), green shading into lemon, lemon into orange and so on through the reds and purples, purplish browns, reddish again and back through lemon to green..." (97). Similarly, he tells of his mother's passion for hunting the "tawny *edulis,* brown *scaber,* red *aurantiacus,*" mushrooms which were spread out on a white garden bench "while the sun cast a lurid gleam just before setting..." (44). The color spectrum occurs again in a passage on: "Colored pencils. Their detailed spectrum advertised on the box but never completely represented by those inside" (100).[21]

In Nabokov's Victorian, albeit Russian, childhood, upper class homes made lavish use of stained-glass window decoration and Nabokov often mentions particular color patterns in describing such dwellings. One of the most persistent color motifs in *Speak, Memory* (and not uncommon in Nabokov's other works) is that of stained-glass window-panes. The family town house front door had stained glass with a tulip design (92). A more significant occurrence of the stained glass motif describes Mademoiselle O's French readings to the Nabokov children on the glass-enclosed veranda of their country house. Nabokov writes of the pleasure of listening to Mademoiselle O "distilling her reading voice from the still prism of her person" (105).

> But the most constant source of enchantment during those readings came from the harlequin pattern of colored panes inset in a whitewashed framework on either side of the veranda. The garden when viewed through these magic glasses grew still and aloof. If one looked through blue glass, the sand turned to cinders while inky trees swam in a tropical sky. The yellow created an amber world infused with an extra strong brew of sunshine. The red made the foliage drip ruby dark upon a pink footpath. The green soaked greenery in a greener green. And when, after such richness, one turned to a small square of normal, savorless glass, with its lone mosquito or lame daddy longlegs, it was like taking a draught of water when one is not thirsty (106).

The memoir's stained glass motif culminates in a passage about a pavilion located on the family country estate. The pavilion sits midway on a small bridge which rises over a ravine "like a coagulated rainbow" and has "wine-red, bottle-green, and dark blue lozenges of stained glass" that "lend a chapel-like touch" (215). This pavilion plays a key role in Nabokov's artistic and emotional development in that it serves as the point of genesis for two of the ruling passions of his life and is closely connected with a third: literature, love and lepidoptera. Nabokov's first venture into literature was as a poet:

In order to reconstruct the summer of 1914, when the numb fury of verse-making first came over me, all I really need is to visualize a certain pavilion . . . I dream of my pavilion at least twice a year. As a rule, it appears in my dreams quite independently of their subject matter, which, of course, may be anything, from abduction to zoolatry. It hangs around, so to speak, with the unobtrusiveness of an artist's signature. I find it clinging to a corner of the dream canvas or cunningly worked into some ornamental part of the picture (215).

It was in this pavilion that the young Nabokov waited out a brief but violent wind and rainstorm: "Beyond the park, above streaming fields, a rainbow slipped into view; the fields ended in the notched dark border of a remote fir wood; part of the rainbow went across it, and that section of the forest edge shimmered most magically through the pale green and pink of the iridescent veil drawn before it: a tenderness and a glory that made poor relatives of the rhomboidal, colored reflections which the return of the sun had brought forth on the pavilion floor. A moment later my first poem began" (216-17).

The pavilion is also the scene of Nabokov's initial meeting with his first love, Tamara. Thirty-three years later Nabokov describes their first meeting as taking place on "August 9, 1915, to be Petrarchally exact, at half-past four of that season's fairest afternoon in the rainbow-windowed pavilion" (230). The pavilion has still other strong associations for Nabokov. His early butterfly collecting was centered on the grounds of the country estate where the pavilion stood. It is certainly not without significance that Nabokov comments on the etymological relationship between "pavilion" and *papilio,* the Latin word for butterfly (216). The pavilion also functions on a more abstract, purely aesthetic plane in the formal structure of the autobiography. It is in the pavilion that the numerous polychromatic images (e.g., the imperial illuminations with their jewel-like monograms and designs of colored lights, the colored pencils, the autumn leaves, the mushrooms, the stained-glass windows, etc.) all blend back into the rainbow motif whence they originated. The pavilion is the end of Nabokov's aesthetic rainbow.

We initiated our discussion of color spectra by suggesting a connection with synesthesia. There is, of course, no necessary tie between the two phenomena. The association is justified only insofar as we can show them to be linked in Nabokov's mind. The expanded 1966 English version of Nabokov's memoirs (but not the earlier English or Russian variants) has an index which is, at certain points, as much aesthetic as practical.[22] In addition to the factual entries for names, places, and books, there are also a few general thematic entries. We find, among others, the following: Colored hearing, Stained glass, Jewels, and Pavilion, as well as Magic lantern and Mushrooms. Most of the constituent elements which enter into the rainbow motif are given, although there is no index entry for Rainbow. The connection between most of these polychromatic entries and Colored hearing is patent. The reader who consults Colored hearing is referred to Stained glass and thence to Jewels and Pavilion. The Jewels entry, via a cross reference, leads the reader back to Stained glass. In other words, Colored hearing (alphabetic chromesthesia) is the primary entry and takes the reader to associated secondary topics. The latter do not, however, point back to Colored hearing. The associational chain establishes the connection between the elements of the rainbow motif and synesthesia.

The rainbow motif is still more important in another context for it plays a key role in confirming synesthesia, specifically alphabetic chromesthesia, as Nabokov's master metaphor for his creative consciousness. English-speaking children sometimes learn the colors of the rainbow and their sequence by a simple mnemonic device: the nonce name Roy G. Biv—an acronym formed from red, orange, yellow, green, blue, indigo, violet.[23] The primary rainbow displays these seven colors with red at the top and violet at the bottom. The standard acronym is obtained by reading the initial letters of the color names from top to bottom. Nabokov, however, coins his own acronymic names for his Russian and English rainbows, but does so in the context of his own synesthetic color/sound correspondences. For Nabokov, the first (i.e., topmost) rainbow color, red, is correlated with the Russian letter 'B' (v); the second rainbow color, orange, with 'Ë' (yo); the third, yellow, with 'E' (ye); green, with 'П' (p); blue with 'C' (s); indigo with 'K' (k); and violet with '3' (z). On the basis of these chromesthetic correspondences, Nabokov makes up his own Russian rainbow acronym *вёепск3* (pronounced *vyoyepskz*). The discussion of the colors of the Russian letters and sounds and the derived Russian rainbow 'word' is in the Russian version of his autobiography, *Drugie berega* (26-27). The parallel English acronym, KZSPYGV, is found in *Speak, Memory* (34-35). The English acronym is formed in the same way as its Russian counterpart, but in reverse order: violet is 'K'; indigo, 'Z'; blue, 'S'; green, 'P'; yellow, 'Y'; orange, 'G'; and red, 'V'. The relationship between the two rainbow words is more clearly demonstrated in the following:

| *Russian* | *English* |
|---|---|
| B Ë E П C K 3 | K Z S P Y G V |
| R O Y G B I V | V I B G Y O R |
| e r e r l n i | i n l r e r e |
| d a l e u d o | o d u e l a d |
| n l e e i l | l i e e l n |
| g o n   g e | e g   n o g |
| e w   o t | t o   w e |

The most curious thing brought out by this juxtaposition is that the Russian and English rainbow acronyms are in reverse order vis-à-vis each other: Russian *ВËЕПCK3* (ROYGBIV) and English KZSPYGV (VIBGYOR).[24] They are, within the limits imposed by the somewhat different sound/color correspondences of the two languages, inverted mirror images of each other. Why should the Russian chromatic rainbow acroynm reflect the color sequence: red, orange, yellow... violet, whereas its English counterpart displays the backward ordering: violet, indigo, blue... red? If there is any single aspect of Nabokov's work that is indisputable it is that his constructs are never random. It is not by chance that the colors reflected in his Russian and English rainbow words are antithetically ordered.

Nabokov in addition to being a man of letters, was also a natural scientist of some repute. His interest in nature and his acuity of observation are evident in his work. It is here that we must seek an explanation of the mirror image rainbows. There are, in nature, two kinds of rainbows—primary and secondary. A primary rainbow is one in which the rays are refracted on entering each drop, reflected from its interior surface, and refracted again on emerging. The red is seen on the top of the bow. A secondary rainbow is one that is above, concentric with, and somewhat larger and fainter than a primary rainbow. Red is seen on the bottom edge of the rainbow.[25] Nabokov's Russian rainbow acronym *ВËЕПCK3*( red, orange, yellow, etc.) corresponds to the bright primary rainbow with red at the top, whereas his English KZSPYGV corresponds to the larger, fainter secondary rainbow with red (i.e., V) at the bottom. The arrangement and relationship of the mirror image rainbows is illustrated in the accompanying figure.

The rainbow motif runs throughout Nabokov's work but only in the autobiographies does it assume a sharply defined meaning. In *The Gift* we argued that Nabokov identified his literary creativity with his alphabetic chromesthesia. The mirror-image chromesthetic rainbows of *Speak, Memory* are a projection of this master metaphor and one that confirms the initial inference. The primary rainbow word *ВËЕПCK3* represents Nabokov's literary creation in his native Russian, and the secondary rainbow word, KZSPYGV, his English language writing. Many readers now think of Nabokov primarily as an English-language writer, but when the first English and Russian versions of the autobiography were being written he had published only two English novels versus nine in Russian. Neither *The Real Life of Sebastian Knight* (1941) nor *Bend Sinister* (1947) display the verbal artistry of the last Russian novels such as *Dar* (*The Gift*, 1937), nor the subsequent stylistic virtuosity of the later English works starting from *Lolita* (1955). In the forties and early fifties Nabokov was very much concerned with bringing the level of his English prose style to that of his Russian. The latter part of his period was that of the writing of *Lolita* and in his postscript

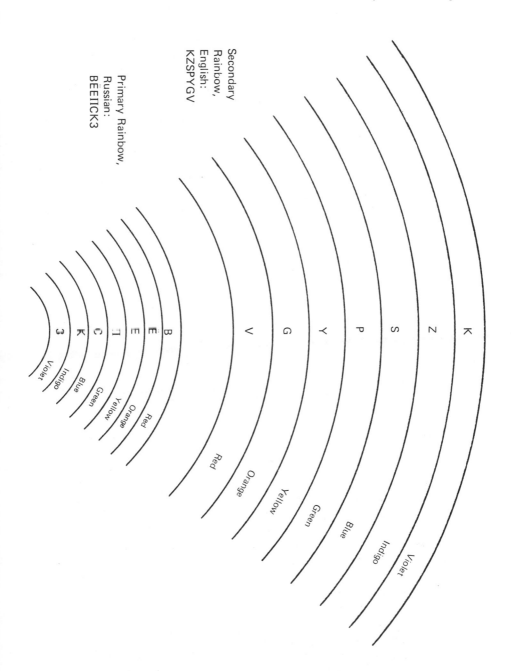

Secondary
Rainbow,
English:
KZSPYGV

Primary Rainbow,
Russian:
ВЁЕПСКЗ

to the novel Nabokov touches on this problem. After summarizing *Lolita* as
the record of his love affair with the English language, the author goes on to
say "My private tragedy . . . is that I had to abandon my natural idiom, my
untrammeled, rich and infinitely docile Russian tongue for a second-rate
brand of English, devoid of any of those apparatuses—the baffling mirror,
the black velvet backdrop, the implied associations and traditions—which
the native illusionist, frac-tails flying, can magically use to transcend the
heritage in his own way" (318-19). The English reader cannot agree that
Nabokov's change of language was a tragedy. Indeed, Nabokov suggests in
the postscript to his own Russian translation of *Lolita* that the confrontation
of the two texts at last disabused him of the notion that his Russian style is
vastly superior to that of his English (296).[26] Appropriately, it is the cover
of Nabokov's Russian *Lolita* that offers further confirmation of our
interpretation of *Speak, Memory*'s dual chromesthetic rainbows. The title
word, *Lolita*, is printed on the cover in the following fashion:

$$\overline{\text{Л О Л И Т А}}$$
$$\text{Ɐ Ɫ И Ꞁ О Ꞁ}$$

The block letters are rainbow-hued with the top title displaying the primary
rainbow colors (starting from the middle with the green on the spine and
with the initial LO of *Lolita* completing the spectrum), while the bottom,
inverted title displays the same colors but in reverse order. In addition to
miming the auto-translation process, the inverted alphabetic rainbows again
reflect Nabokov's bilingual creative career. The confirmation of Nabokov's
mirror-image rainbows as an emblematic analogue to the two languages of
his literary creation brings us back to the source of the double rainbows—
their chromesthetic origin in the Russian and English alphabets.

The chromesthesia-based twin rainbows are consciously elaborated
symbols of Nabokov's creative process. It is, however, possible to argue that
the basis of this emblematic imagery is literary rather than psychological
synesthesia. That is, Nabokov may indeed possess psychological synesthesia
and use it as the basis for a metaphor describing his art. The use of
synesthesia as the basis of the art metaphor does not, however, necessarily
mean that synesthesia is an active agency in Nabokov's creative process. It
could simply be a convenient, very apt vehicle for the metaphor symbolizing
his creative processes. The question is whether the relationship between
Nabokov's synesthesia and his art is purely metaphorical (i.e., literary) or
psychological (i.e., inherent). The answer may well lie somewhere between
these polarities. Memory is a dominant theme in Nabokov's writing. It is, in
his view, man's line of defense against death and oblivion. This theme is
explicit in the autobiography, and it is not by chance that its final title is the

imperative injunction *Speak, Memory!* The memory theme is also prominent in *Ada* whose hero, Van, counts his life span not from the day of his birth but from his first memory 195 days later (535-36). It is of related significance that Nabokov's account of his own earliest recollections is cast in the form of a synesthetic image: "In probing my childhood...I see the awakening of consciousness as a series of spaced flashes, with the intervals between them gradually diminishing until bright blocks of perception are formed, affording a memory a slippery foothold" (20). One of the brightest of these "blocks of perception" is the "recollection of my crib...which brings back...the pleasures of handling a certain beautiful, delightfully solid, garnet-dark crystal egg left over from some unremembered Easter; I used to chew a corner of the bedsheet until it was throroughly soaked and then wrap the egg in it tightly, so as to admire and relick the warm ruddy glitter of the snugly enveloped facets that came seeping through with a miraculous completeness of glow and color. But that was not yet the closest I got to feeding upon beauty" (24). Synesthetic perception is characteristic of childhood, and this is perhaps in part why synesthetic metaphors seem prevalent in Nabokov's early recollections. It is, however, in *Ada,* that we find a discussion of the interrelations of synesthesia and memory.

*Ada,* like *Speak, Memory,* is a memoir, albeit a fictional one, written by the octagenarian Van in celebration of his life-long affair with his sister Ada. Memory and its adjunct, time, are central themes. "Time is but memory in the making," Van says (559). It is the subject of the extended essay "The Texture of Time" which constitutes Part IV of the novel, and this same title was at one point Nabokov's tentative title for the novel as a whole (*SO* 91). The title phrase is of particular interest in that it is itself a synesthetic metaphor suggesting the tactile nature of an intangible abstraction. This literal *"handling"* of time is again expressed in Van's words "I delight sensually in time, in its stuff and spread, in the fall of its folds, in the very impalpability of its grayish gauze, in the coolness of its continuum" (537). Throughout the book, time is seen as "gray," as the neutral colorless medium in which colored events are taking place. One illustration is Van's recollection of a lecture series of which he writes: "I happen to remember in terms of color (grayish-blue, purple, reddish gray) my three farewell university lectures...on Bergson's Time...I recall less clearly, and indeed am able to suppress in my mind completely, the six day intervals between blue and purple, and purple and gray....The two intervals are seen by me as twin dimples each brimming with a kind of smooth grayish mist, and a faint suggestion of shredded confetti (which maybe, might leap into color if I allowed some casual memory to form in between the diagnostic limits)" (549). Van's meditation on memory and time concludes with the significant observation "Synesthetia, to which I am inordinately prone, proves to be a great help in this type of task" (549). The use of synesthesia in digging through the layers of the past is further illustrated in a process that might be called "mnemonic archeology." Van asserts that not only do events stored in memory have color but that they can be assigned to their proper chronological stratum by their relative degree of color saturation (546). *Speak, Memory* is an enactment of Nabokov's theory of synesthetic recall. It is perhaps not by chance that in those scenes where the mechanism of memory is foregrounded that the different sense modalities are given full rein as evidenced in the following passage:

I witness with pleasure the supreme achievement of memory, which is the masterly use it makes of innate harmonies when gathering to its fold the suspended and wandering tonalities of the past. I like to imagine, in consummation and resolution of those jangling chords, something as enduring in retrospect, as the long table that on summer birthdays and namedays used to be laid for afternoon chocolate out of doors, in an alley of birches, limes and maples at its debouchement on the smooth-sanded space of the garden proper that separated the park and the house. I see the tablecloth and the faces of seated people sharing in the animation of light and shade beneath a moving, a fabulous foliage, exaggerated, no doubt, by the same faculty of impassioned commemoration, of ceaseless return, that makes me always approach that banquet table from the outside, from the depth of the park—not from the house—as if the mind in order to go back thither, had to do so with the silent steps of a prodigal faint with excitement. Through a tremulous prism, I distinguish the features of relatives and familiars, mute lips serenely moving in forgotten speech. I see the stream of chocolate and the plates of blueberry tarts. I note the small helicopter of a revolving samara that gently descends upon the tablecloth, and, lying across the table, an adolescent girl's bare arm indolently extended as far as it will go, with its turquoise-veined underside turned up to the flaky sunlight, the palm open in lazy expectancy of something—perhaps the nutcracker...And then, suddenly, just when the colors and outlines settle at last to their various duties—smiling, frivolous duties—some knob is touched and a torrent of sounds comes to life: voices speaking all together, a walnut cracked...(170-71).

Mechanism
of memory

Sight
&
Angle of
vision

Colors
via a
prism

Sound

This long quotation has been given in full as an example and as a description of the mechanism and power of Nabokov's memory. The reader cannot but be amazed by the writer's almost magical power of conjuring up the minutia of the past. Nabokov believed that his "almost pathological keenness of the retrospective faculty is a hereditary trait" (75). It might also be supposed, though it is not suggested, that synesthesia is in some degree hereditary—given its presence in Nabokov's mother and son (SO 17).

Is there any basis for Nabokov's theory of the interrelation of synesthesia and memory, especially hypernormal memory? There is at least one precedent for Nabokov's claim.[27] The eminent Soviet neuropsychologist A.R. Luria worked with a subject who had well-nigh total recall. In the course of investigations over a period of nearly thirty years it was learned that the subject also displayed a very highly developed form of synesthesia. The data of all five of the sense modalities were cross-blended in his perceptions and recollections. Luria ultimately concluded that "the meaning of these synesthetic responses for the process of recall lay in the fact that the synesthetic components created, as it were, the background of each recollection by providing redundant information and thus assuring the exactness of the recollection" (19). If some part of a recollection was incorrect "the supplementary synesthetic cues failed to coincide with each other" thus letting the subject know that "something was not correct in his recollection. This forced him to correct the inaccuracy." The passage bears a remarkable resemblance to Nabokov's more poetic description of memory's use of "innate harmonies" in resolving the "jangling chords" of the mislaid past.

Although Nabokov mentions synesthesia almost *en passant* in his autobiography it proves to be a central facet of his existence and his memoir. For Nabokov it underlies the mechanism of memory, or rather the process of recollection, which in turn is the basis of the creative imagination. "The act of retention," Nabokov has said, "is the act of art, artistic selection, artistic blending, artistic recombination of actual events." "The Past," he continued, "is a constant accumulation of images . . . and the best we can do is to pick out and try to retain those patches of rainbow light flitting through memory" (SO 186). In this sense, synesthesia is part of the deep structure of *Speak, Memory.* It is instrumental in the creative act at the subconscious level. As manifested in colored hearing, and specifically in alphabetic chromesthesia, synesthesia plays a much more explicit, but still subtle role in the structure of Nabokov's memoir in that it affords an ideal emblem—first for the writer's creative process and then, even more elegantly, as a metaphor for the remarkable Russian and English literary careers which flow from his twin alphabetic rainbows. It is the alphabetic rainbows with their constituent spectral submotifs scattered throughout the memoir that give it its thematic center and integrate its parts. All of the rainbows blend back into the chromesthetic rainbow from which they sprang. It is appropriately Nabokovian that the meanings of Nabokov's synesthesia, so central to his autobiography, are to be inferred not from "reality" but from *The Gift* and *Ada,* his major works of Russian and English fiction.

## THE ALPHA AND OMEGA OF *INVITATION TO A BEHEADING*

Nabokov is a man of letters in the most literal (as well as the most general) sense of the term. We have seen how his alphabetic chromesthesia has been emblematized as a symbol of his creative life. Nabokov's interest in letters, the atoms of his art, is not limited to their color associations. For Nabokov the physical shape of the alphabetic symbols has visual meaning as well as color and sound value. The letters are alphabetic icons that mime as well as mean. Alphabetic icons are found in many of Nabokov's works where they serve as striking, if often incidental, adornment. Early in *Ada*, Marina together with her two children are awkwardly entertaining a monolingual Spanish dinner guest. The three wrack their brains in search of their few Spanish vocabulary items. Van's are poetic; Ada's are appropriately lepidopteral and ornithological; Marina's three words are: *aroma, hombre,* and "an anatomical term with a 'j' hanging in the middle'', i.e., *cojones* 'testicles' (46).

Nabokov employed this stylistic device from the very beginning of his long career. The 1925 story *Pis'mo v Rossiiu* presents a striking example of the intricacy and subtlety of Nabokov's manipulation of alphabetic icons. The story's Russian narrator is standing before a tall gravestone on which the deceased's widow has hanged herself during the night (47). In the soft dirt at the base of the monument he notices the sickle-shaped traces (*серповидные следы*/ 'serpovidnye sledy') left by the swinging heel of the hanging woman's shoe. Gazing at the C-shaped mark the narrator muses that even in death there is a childlike smile. The iconic letter play (which works only in the Cyrillic alphabet) stems from the fact that the sickle-shaped swinging heel print mimics the Russian letter 'C' which is the initial letter of the Russian word for 'death' (*смерть*/'smert''). The iconic play goes still farther, however, for the heel-print letter 'C', when turned on its side, indeed resembles the smiling mouth of a child's outline drawing of a moon face, e.g., ☺ .

The letter 'O' which is synesthetically described by Nabokov as evoking the image of an "ivory-backed hand mirror" in English and the color of almond milk in Russian lends itself to various iconic usages. An entire chapter in the autobiography is devoted to the young Nabokov's French governess, the obese Mademoiselle O. Here Nabokov imagines her nocturnal sleigh journey to the Nabokov estate: "All is still, spellbound, enthralled by that great heavenly O shining above the Russian wilderness of my past" (SM 61[1960]). In this passage the governess is recreated in a complex image combining her designation as Mademoiselle O, her rotund bodily image, and her whiteness, all subliminally compared to the moon which is evoked by the iconic letter 'O' with its synesthetic backdrop of the circular ivory-backed handmirror. The corresponding Russian text omits reference to the letter 'O' as such, but describes the moon as a luminous disk, and incorporates it into the Russian version of the above sentence which resounds with an improbable number of 'O's: *Vsyo tikho, vsyo okoldovano sveltym diskom pod russkoi pustynei moego proshlogo* (DB 88). Curiously, in the final version of the memoir, the 'O' icon is also omitted, but is replaced by a metaphor describing the moon as "fancy's rear-vision mirror" which makes tacit reference to Nabokov's synesthetic association of the letter 'O' with a circular mirror (SM 100).

In *The Gift*, the poet-protagonist Fyodor voices his complete indifference to political figures by remarking that their names in the press totally lack any association with real countenances, but become mere typographic marks on paper. The French statesman Herriot (in Russian *Эррио* 'Errio') is, for example, reduced in Fyodor's mind to an autonomous macrocephalic letter 'Э', a letter which is called a "backwards E" in Russian and which occurs primarily in exclamations and demonstrative pronouns— all having some obscure relevance to the character of the French political leader. The archaic Russian letter *izhitsa* (V) becomes an icon of perplexed concentration on a boy's forehead as he puzzles over an encyclopedia article on "Prostitution" in which the subject word is reduced to a space-saving abbreviation, the capital letter 'P' (DB 190). A somewhat similar example occurs in *Despair* when Hermann notes that a vein on his forehead stands out "like a capital M imperfectly drawn" (27). The English translation, while successfully evoking the desired physical shape, fails to capture another and more critical implication suggested by the Russian text where the 'M' is represented not by its typographical image but by its archaic proper name *mysl'* which, in addition to specifying the letter, has the primary meaning 'thought' (19). This is peculiarly appropriate to the narrative context since Hermann is formulating his mad scheme to switch identities with his presumed double and murder him.

A combined case of iconic representation and chromesthesia is to be observed in another early story, *"Groza"* (The Thunder Storm). Nabokov provides a clue in his introductory note to the English translation in which he writes "Thunder is *grom* in Russian, storm is *burya* and thunderstorm is *groza*, a grand little word with that blue zigzag in the middle." (DS 118). The 'Z' iconically depicts the jagged lightning bolt of the thunderstorm and in its Cyrillic form is, in terms of Nabokov's chromesthesia, "a lustrous lilac" (DB 27). The English letter is described as being of "thundercloud hue" (SM 34). A somewhat different sort of phenomenon that might be termed auditory iconicism is displayed in a description of a "greasy, clayey *zemskaya* (rural district) road". Nabokov parenthetically remarks "—what a bump in this designation—" referring to the indeed bumpy consonant cluster in the word *"zemskaya"* (G 89).

The preceding examples of alphabetic iconicism are incidental if amusing embellishments of their respective texts. In at least two of Nabokov's novels, however, alphabetic imagery plays a more substantial role. These are *The Real Life of Sebastian Knight* and *Invitation to a Beheading*. *The Real Life of Sebastian Knight*, Nabokov's first English-language novel, is the story of a biographer's search for the "real life" of his deceased half-brother, the Anglo-Russian author Sebastian Knight. Alphabetic iconicism figures in the novel's first paragraph. The nameless narrator, having weighed the matter, decides to divulge the identity of one of his sources of information—a woman to whom he had promised anonymity—apparently because he cannot resist the punning possibilities of the name: "Her name . . . is Olga Olegovna Orlova—an egg-like alliteration which it would have been a pity to withhold." Not only is a physical description of the old woman projected, but the visual image is reinforced by the repetition of the "ova" (eggs) in the patronymic and family names. Another blending of the orthography of a character's name and plot detail occurs when the narrator tries to recall the name of the village in which Sebastian lies dying. He has been summoned by a Doctor Starov. "Alexander Alexandrovich Starov. The train clattered over the points, repeating those x's" (163). The letter "x" links the doctor, the sound of the train on the tracks, and the unknown name of the village, the "x," that the narrator seeks. It also literally depicts the long sought intersection of the narrator and his half-brother Sebastian Knight. The letter (and sound) "x" figures in another passage in which the biographer refuses to speculate about Sebastian's sex life "because the very sound of the word 'sex' with its hissing vulgarity and the 'ks, ks' cat-call at the end, seems so inane . . ." (87). One suspects that the "x" is being viewed as a visual token of sexual union in conjunction with the "vulgar" sound represented by the spelling of the word: "ks, ks" is the Russian expression for calling a cat, as well as being the usual Russian transliteration of the English letter "x."

A farewell letter from Sebastian Knight to his mistress Clare Bishop provides a much more spectacular and explicit case of alphabetic iconicism. "Life with you was lovely—and when I say lovely, I mean doves and lilies, and velvet, and that soft pink "v" in the middle and the way your tongue curved up to the long lingering "l". Our life together was alliterative, and when I think of all the little things which will die, now that we cannot share them, I feel as if we were dead too . . . This is all poetry. I am lying to you. Lily-livered" (93). The use of the "v" and "l" letter shapes as vaginal and phallic graphic images requires no commentary. It might only be remarked that in Nabokov's synesthetic letter-color correspondences "v" is appropriately pink, rose quartz to be exact, while "l" is described as noodle-hued.

Nabokov's use of alphabetic imagery is not restricted to letters. Number shapes also project their outlines onto fictional and factual reality. "He died in the very beginning of 1936, and as I look at this figure I cannot help thinking that there is an occult resemblance between a man and the date of his death. Sebastian Knight d. 1936... This date to me seems the reflection of that name in a pool of rippling water. There is something about the curves of the last three numerals that recalls the sinuous outlines of Sebastian's personality" (154). The Russian letter for the "s" sound, i.e., "c", provides an even more perfect coincidence of number shape and initial letter for the Russian-born Sebastian ( Севастьян ). The fatidic 9, 3, and 6 all consist of combinations of the initial Russian letter.[28]

The theme of alphabetic imagery is set in a context of more general significance in the following passage.

> The answer to all questions of life and death, the 'absolute solution' was written all over the world he had known: it was like a traveller realizing that the wild country he surveys is not an accidental assembly of natural phenomena, but the page in a book where these mountains and forests, and fields, and rivers are disposed in such a way as to form a coherent sentence; the vowel of a lake fusing with the consonant of a sibilant slope; the winding of a road writing its message in a round hand... Thus the traveller spells the landscape and its sense is disclosed, and likewise, the intricate pattern of human life turns out to be monogrammatic, now quite clear to the inner eye disentangling the interwoven letters" (150).

The proper decipherment of the letters will give the adept the key, the answer to all questions, the ultimate reality which lies beyond the superficial appearances of this world. This, an expression of the theme of Sebastian Knight's last novel, is seen by his biographer as parallel to his own search for his half-brother's "real life." Despite this statement of the theme and the use of alphabetic images throughout the book, the latter do not seem to be integrated into the cryptogrammatic metaphor that lies at the center of the novel. In this sense, *The Real Life of Sebastian Knight* is but a retarded echo of an earlier treatment of this theme wherein the alphabetic tokens are integrated into the book's theme in a spectacularly intricate way. The use of letters as visual icons and their function as mediators of another truer reality finds its fullest expression in Nabokov's earlier Russian novel *Priglashenie na kazn'* (*Invitation to a Beheading*).[29]

*Invitation to a Beheading* is a dystopian novel set in a nameless, nightmarish state of the future. Apart from the initial courtroom sentencing scene and the final execution scene, the entire novel takes place in the prison-fortress where the protagonist, Cincinnatus, attended by his jailors and his executioner, awaits the unknown day of his beheading. Cincinnatus' crime is "gnostical turpitude," the perception and knowledge of forbidden things in a world where all things are already known and named. Overtly,

Cincinnatus' criminality takes the form of being opaque in a society whose citizens are all transparent, devoid of fresh perceptions, lacking dark corners in their minds or souls, people with no secrets from each other.

Cincinnatus, alone in this world, has intimations of another world, one "alive ... captivatingly majestic, free and ethereal" (E92/R97). The thematic structure of the novel is cast in terms of the opposition of these two worlds: the 'real' world of the prison and the society it represents, and the 'ideal' world of Cincinnatus' intuitions, a world which he feels to be far more real than that in which he awaits death. Much of the novel centers about Cincinnatus' mental probing of this ideal world and his vain efforts to find verbal means of expressing its reality both to himself and others. The novel as a whole is permeated by an alphabetic motif and the central theme of Cincinnatus' struggle to convey his insight is specifically associated with the device of alphabetic iconicism.

The very origin of Cincinnatus' awareness of his differentness from his fellows, of his inherent criminality, is linked with alphabetic symbols. Thinking back to his childhood, he recalls: "Well do I remember that day! I must have just learned how to make letters, since I remember wearing on my finger the little copper ring that was given to children who already know how to copy the model words from the flower beds in the school garden, where petunias, phlox and marigold spelled out lengthy adages" (E96/R101). The acquisition of letters marks the end of the protagonist's innocence.

The letter motif figures in a minor way on several occasions. While examining an old volume from the prison library Cincinnatus wonders " ... in what language is this written. The small, crowded, ornate type, with dots and squiggles within the sickle-shaped letters, seemed to be oriental—it was somehow reminiscent of the inscriptions on museum daggers" (E125/R127). Elsewhere we are told that "a drop of water had fallen on the page. Through the drop several letters turned from brevier to pica, having swollen as if a reading glass had been lying on them (E88/R94). The prison library also provides Cincinnatus with a copy of the novel *Quercus* where he finds "a paragraph a page and a half long in which all the words began with 'p'" (E123/R125).

The letter motif also finds expression in references to monograms and handwriting. Such is the mention of an "alligator album with its massive dark silver monogram" (E169-70/R168) and of Pierre, the executioner, whose handwriting is characterized as "fleecily curling script, elegant punctuation marks, [and a] signature like a seven veiled dance" (E118/R120). A more pointed occurrence of the letter motif is to designate the particular kindergarten division in which Cincinnatus teaches. In view of his doubtful reliability he is permitted to work only with physically defective children in division F (E30/R42). One of the old Russian letter names for 'F' was *fita* which has the secondary meaning of "one who is useless or superfluous." These and still other alphabetic references serve to keep the alphabet motif before the reader's eye.

A different dimension in the use of alphabetic devices is represented by a number of cases in which each usage is associated with the novel's theme at key points in the book's structure. Some pertain to points of character and plot; others to theme. Cincinnatus' death cell is adjacent to a cell occupied by one Pierre whose job it is first to befriend Cincinnatus and, having done so, behead him. Pierre is a paradigm of his totalitarian world whose denizens are banally trivial. He stands in opposition to Cincinnatus whose intimation of a different world and another mode of being convict him of a capital crime. The two coeval characters are contrastively paired in many senses. Cincinnatus is delicate, slender and neurasthenic, while Pierre is robust, plump and jolly; deep integrity/shallow vulgarity; artist/philistine; victim/executioner. This contrastive pairing comes to a head at a pre-execution gala dinner party at which Cincinnatus and Pierre are guests of honor. After the meal the guests go out into the night to view the execution-eve festive illumination.

> V techenie trekh minut gorel raznotsvetnym svetom dobryi million lampochek, iskusno rassazhennykh, v trave, na vetkakh, na skalakh, i v obshchem razmeshchennykh takim obrazom, chtoby sostavit' po vsemu nochnomu landshaftu rastianutyi grandioznyi venzel' iz П iЦ, ne sovsem odnako vyshedshii (187).

> For three minutes a good million light bulbs of diverse colours burned, artfully planted in the grass, in branches, on cliffs, and all arranged in such a way as to embrace the whole nocturnal landscape with a grandiose monogram of 'P' and 'C', which, however, had not quite come off (189).

The paired Russian initials '*П*' and '*Ц*' are, of course, those of Pierre (Пьер) and Cincinnatus (Цинцинат).Less obvious is that with the minor blemish of the "tail" on the "*Ц*" the two letters, not unlike the characters they nominate, are upside down mirror images of each other.[30] Nabokov provides a cue for the reader by alluding to the slight imperfection in the letter correspondence in his comment that the monogram "had not quite come off." It is also to be remarked that the "*П*" of Pierre, the headsman, is barred at the top while the "*Ц*" of Cincinatus is open—foreshadowing his ascension to a very different world. The letter shapes are used to mirror the opposition of the two characters. This effect is largely lost in the English translation where the physically dissimilar initials "P" and "C" can only pair the characters but cannot iconically oppose them.[31]

The above example uses the physical shape of the monogrammatic letters to emblematize the oppositional relationship between the two key characters and, through them, the two worlds of the novel. As we have said, this latter binary opposition which is manifested in a number of guises throughout the book serves as an organizing context for its central theme. Cincinnatus, awaiting the fall of the axe, feels a compulsion to communicate his sense of another world via his prison journal, to leave a record, a legacy against that day when someone may understand and benefit. Only Cincinnatus can convey the truth of that other dimly glimpsed world for, as he says, "I am the one among you who is alive. Not only are my eyes different, and my hearing and my sense of taste—not only is my sense of smell like a deer's, my sense of touch like a bat's—but most important, I have the capacity to conjoin all this in one point...." (E52/R62). The English translation fails to convey an important nuance here in that the word 'capacity' replaces the Russian *dar* in the sense of an innate talent. This is important for it is by this word that Cincinnatus identifies himself as an artist. He goes on to assert that, if granted time, he would write "about how part of my thoughts is always crowding around the invisible umbilical cord that joins this world to something—to what I shall not say yet..." (E53/R63).

In spite of Cincinnatus' initial assurance in his gnostic knowledge and in his 'capacity/gift' of expression, this task proves to be enormously difficult, and ultimately impossible. His struggle to convey his vision, to express the other world in the language of this world, is the thematic focal point of the novel. Cincinnatus' prison, as much else in the novel, is double. He awaits death in the prison-fortress of the totalitarian state and, more important thematically, in the prison-house of language.[32] The one is the usual place of repose for the political and intellectual dissident; the other, that of the verbal artist. Just as Cincinnatus' attempts to escape his physical prison are circuitously hopeless so are his efforts to break through the walls of the prison-house of language. The theme of the supreme difficulty of attempting to express the inexpressible is explicitly discussed in a number of passages in *Invitation to a Beheading*. It is precisely and exclusively in conjunction with these passages that a very special sort of alphabetic iconicism is cunningly interwoven into the text.

The prison-house of language theme has two interrelated aspects: the restricted capacity of the artist to convey his vision in the existing language, and the inability of his philistine audience to understand even that which can be expressed. We shall first examine a passage addressing the latter aspect. Cincinnatus is first denounced for opacity while still a child. Throughout his youth he tries to learn to mimic the transparency of his fellow citizens but cannot wholly succeed.

Okruzhaiushchie ponimali drug druga s poluslova—ibo ne bylo u nikh takikh slov, kotorye by konchalis' kak-nibud' neozhidanno, na izhitsu, chto-li, obrashchaias' v prashchu ili ptitsu, s udivitel'nymi posledstviiami (38).

Those around him understood each other at the first word, since they had no words that would end in an unexpected way, perhaps in some archaic letter, an upsilamda, becoming a bird or a catapult with wondrous consequences (26).[33]

The passage goes on to say that in the dusty town museum which Cincinnatus often visited there were many "rare marvellous objects, but all of the townsmen except Cincinnatus found them just as limited and transparent as they did each other. *That which does not have a name does not exist*.[34] Unfortunately everything had a name."

This is a succinct statement of the prison-house of language theme. The artist's potential audience cannot comprehend his message for their language is hermetic. All things are named and the nameless cannot even be conceived of, much less exist. On the other hand, the recognized universe, narrow and banal as it may be, is immediately and easily accessible to all. Speakers of the received tongue understand each other "at the first word." The only way in which new meanings, new insights, might be conveyed would be by the introduction of an additional letter. That Nabokov has chosen *izhitsa* for the unexpected letter is not by chance nor is his remark about its capacity to change "with wondrous consequences" an unmotivated figure of speech. *Izhitsa* is the final letter of the Old Church Slavonic alphabet, the thousand-year-old liturgical script of the Slavic peoples. Although the modern Russian alphabet is derived from that of the Church Slavonic, this particular character has long since been abandoned. The Church Slavonic *izhitsa*, in its turn derived from the Greek upsilon ($\gamma$), has the form $V$ and, as Nabokov suggests, physically resembles a slingshot ('catapult' in British English) or the head-on view of a bird in flight—both images visually suggestive of Cincinnatus' desire that his imprisoned words (as well as his person) take flight, that he might succeed in communicating with his fellow countrymen.

We noted above in the case of the mirror-image monograms of Pierre and Cincinnatus that the switch of alphabets from Russian to English resulted in the loss of an important detail serving to reinforce the basic dichotomy in the book. This is even more true in the case at hand. The *izhitsa* with its visual reference to slingshot and bird is useless for the English text since the English reader does not know the character's shape. Nabokov attempts to surmount this problem in the English version by drawing on the Greek alphabet and creating a new hybrid, a compound letter upsilamba, a blend of the letter upsilon ($\gamma$) which indeed visually mimics a flying bird, and lambda which in its lower case form ($\lambda$) resembles the inverted "Y"-fork of a slingshot. Nabokov has solved the *izhitsa* translation problem in an ingenious way. It should perhaps be noted, however, that just as the Russian reader, if he is to grasp the allusive imagery, must know the shape of the Church Slavonic *izhitsa*, the English reader must be familiar with the Greek alphabet.

The prison-house of language theme is resumed in Chapter VIII in which Cincinnatus meditates "on his knowledge of a realm forbidden and inaccessible to others . . . I know something. But the expression of it comes so hard" (77). In his prison-journal he records his fears that:

> . . . nichego ne poluchitsia iz togo, chto ia khochu rasskazat', a lish' ostanutsia chernye trupy udavlennykh slov, kak visel'niki . . . vechernie ocherki *glagolei*, voron'yo . . . [my italics—DBJ].

> . . . nothing will come of what I am trying to tell, its only vestiges being the corpses of strangled words, like hanged men . . . evening silhouettes of gammas and gerunds, gallow crows . . . (90).

The world *glagol'* is the proper name of the old Church Slavonic *"Г"* the silhouette of which does indeed mimic that of the gallows from which the corpses of Cincinnatus' strangled words will hang. The image is all the more effective in that it evokes Cincinnatus' imminent execution although it is to be by axe rather than rope. That the name for *"Г"* is *glagol'* is of particular thematic appropriateness in that its hard variant, *glagol*, is the Church Slavonic lexeme meaning "word," for words are the traducers of Cincinnatus' message.

The Englishing of this example of alphabetic iconicism is handled in the same way as in the preceding example, that is, by conversion of the Church Slavonic letter into its identically shaped Greek equivalent, the letter gamma (*Γ*). In an effort to convey a fuller sense of the Russian, Nabokov has added in the English the two alliterative words, "gerunds" and "gallow crows. The first of these is an ingenious but not wholly successful attempt to find a parallel to the second meaning of *glagol* since the Greek/English "gamma" refers only to the letter name and lacks the second, thematically relevant meaning "word." The inserted term "gerund" attempts to supply this latter meaning. "Gallow crows" is offered as a translation for the Russian *voron'yo* which is simply a collective noun for a group of ordinary crows. The use of "gallow crows" is obviously intended to call the reader's attention to the alphabetic imagery of the Greek letter gamma, i.e., its resemblance to a gallows. As an aside, it might be remarked that the shape of the Greek gamma is, strictly speaking, that of the single-armed gibbet rather than that of the gallows which has two uprights surmounted by a crossbar. (The latter finds its most apt alphabetic icon in the Cyrillic *"П"* or Greek "pi" which coincidentally, is the initial of *Пьер* (Pierre), Cincinnatus' executioner.

The principal way in which the "this world/ that world" thematic dichotomy is maintained throughout the novel is through the recurrent contrast of the Russian terms *tut* (here) and *tam* (there). This fundamental thematic contrast and the modes of its realization are the subject of a later essay. Here we touch on the *tut/tam* contrast only in so far as it bears on alphabetic iconicism. The *tut/tam* opposition is intensively and explicitly elaborated in Chapter VIII which is an extract from Cincinnatus' prison journal. It is here that Cincinnatus most directly confronts the problem of trying to convey his vision of a true reality *(tam)* in the context and language of the oppressive world of the prison *(tut)*.

In his journal Cincinnatus struggles to describe his "soul's native realm" and despite his difficulties he feels himself on the brink of success, saying "...I think I have caught my prey...but it is only a fleeting apparition of my prey!" (E94/R99).

Tam—nepodrazhaemoi razumnost'iu svetitsia chelovecheskii vzgliad; tam na vole guliaiut umuchennye tut chudaki; tam vremia skladyvaetsia po zhelaniiu, . . . Tam, tam—original tekh sadov, gde my tut brodili, skryvalis'; tam vse porazhaet svoeiu charuiushchei ochevidnost'iu, prostotoi sovershennogo blaga; tam vse poteshaet dushu, . . . tam siiaet to zerkalo ot kotorogo inoi raz siuda pereskochit zaichik . . ." (99-100).

There, *tam*, *là-bas*, the gaze of men glows with inimitable understanding; *there* the freaks that are tortured here walk unmolested; *there* time takes shape according to one's pleasure, . . . There, *there* are the originals of those gardens where we used to roam and hide in this world; *there* everything strikes one by its bewitching evidence, by the simplicity of perfect good; *there* everything pleases one's soul . . . ; *there* shines the mirror that now and then sends a chance reflection here . . ." (94).[35]

In spite of the intensity of his vision and his desire to express it, Cincinnatus cannot attain his goal for "Not knowing how to write, but sensing with my criminal intuition how words are combined, what one must do for a commonplace word to come alive and to share its neighbor's sheen, heat, shadow, while reflecting itself and its neighbor and renewing the neighboring word in the process, so that the whole line is live iridescence: while I sense the nature of this word propinquity, I am nevertheless unable to achieve it, yet that is what is indispensible to me for my task, a task of the not now and not here" (E93/R98). This last phrase leads Cincinnatus into a passage built around the Russian word *tut* (here) which is counterposed to the preceding *tam* (there) passage.

Ne tut! Tupoe "tut" podpertoe i zapertoe chetoiu "tverdo," temnaia tiur'ma, v kotoruiu zakliuchen neuemno voiushchii uzhas, derzhit menia i tesnit (98-99).

Not here! The obtuse *tut* (here) propped up and locked in by its pair of T's, the dark dungeon in which a relentlessly howling "UUU" of horror is entombed, confines me and constricts. (My translation-DBJ).

The cited passages afford the most obvious juxtaposition and explicit rendering of the oppositional pair *tut/tam* (here/there) in the book. It is not by chance that both passages are presented within the context of the prison-house of language theme. Cincinnatus cannot escape from the world of "here" into the world of "there" even though he doubts the reality of the former. He is incarcerated in the prison-house of language just as surely as he is in the prison-fortress. We have shown the use of the device of alphabetic iconicism to be closely associated with this theme and we shall show this is even more spectacularly so in the key passage at hand. Before doing so, however, I should like to comment on the phonetic symbolism of a part of the passage just quoted. If we reexamine the first part of the sentence, i.e., *Ne tut! Tupoe "tut" podpertoe i zapertoe chetoiu "tverdo"* ... , we see that the phrase is phonetically built on a series of "t" alliterations that take their origin from the key word *"tut."* Further, the latter half of the sentence, i.e., ... *temnaia tiur'ma, v kotoruiu zakliuchen neuemno voiushchii uzhas, derzhit menia i tesnit* is structured on the phonetic framework of the key word *tut*—specifically TTTUUUUUUTTT with six "U's" encapsulated by the twin "T" triplets. Note that the normal word order of the sentence has been modified in order to obtain this effect with its rather odd *derzhit menja i tesnit* 'confines me and constricts.' Returning to the key word, *tut*, we note that the two "T"s auditorily echo the twin "T"s of *temnaia tiur'ma*, Cincinnatus' 'dark dungeon.' Moreover, they enclose and confine the "UUU" sound which is the Russian expression of fright or terror as well as the initial vowel of *"uzhas"* ('terror') a word which is inserted in the midst of the alliterative "t's" of the above sentence and which, like *tut* itself, is purposefully scattered throughout the book.[36]

These phonetic features are merely the beginning of the intricacies surrounding *tut*. In addition to being used as a lexical and auditory symbol of the wretched world it bespeaks, *tut* also is being employed as a visual icon. Let us take a final look at the sentence in question: *Tupoe 'tut', podpertoe i zapertoe chetoiu 'tverdo', temnaia tiur'ma v kotoruiu zakliuchen neuemno voiushchii uzhas*... The *"tverdo"* here is not the Russian adverb 'firmly' (as many Russian readers believe it to be), but the homomorphic Old Church Slavonic name for the letter "T". Again using the device of alphabetic iconicism Nabokov is calling the Russian reader's attention to thematically relevant visual aspects of the word *tut*. Not only do the two "T"s of *tut* echo the twin T's of *temnaia tiur'ma* 'dark dungeon,' but they visually resemble two tall sentinels (*tiuremshchiki* 'jailors,' if you will) towering over and confining the "u" of Cincinnatus and his moan of terror.

This *tour de force* presents severe difficulties in translation from the point of view of both its phonetic and iconic properties. If the phonetic symbolism of the Russian is to be retained in the English, the latter must be a semantically equivalent sentence phonetically structured on a series of H's,

E's, R's & E's just as the Russian sentence incorporates its improbable sequence of T's, U's, & T's in order to obtain the thematic key word TTTUUUUUUTTT. Strict adherence to this pattern is, of course, impossible, but Nabokov and his son, Dimitri, who is credited as the translator, make a prodigious if not entirely successful attempt: "Not here! The *horrible* 'here,' the dark dungeon, in which a *relentlessly howling heart* is *incarcerated*, this 'here' *holds* and *constricts me*" (93). This manages to capture the necessary letters but not in the eloquent pattern of the Russian with its triplets of "T"'s symmetrically bracketing the prolonged exclamation of horror "UUUUUU." The *uzhas* 'horror' which phonetically and lexically embodies Cincinnatus' cry is replaced by "heart" which weakly echoes the key word "here," but loses the auditory mimicry of the exclamation of fear. The latter effect is, however, picked up in the English text by the "ow" of 'howling.'

The visual, iconic aspect of the sentence is completely lost in translation. Comparison of the English text with that of the Russian shows that Nabokov has simply omitted the phrase *podpertoe i zapertoe chetoiu 'tverdo'* (supported and locked in by its pair of "T"'s) which supplied the Church Slavonic letters underlying the sentinel imagery described above.

In sum, Nabokov has managed to preserve much of the ingenious phonetic symbolism of the original but has been forced to forego completely the alphabetic iconicism which, in the Russian original, is consistently associated with the prison-house of language theme. It is unfortunate that this particular bit of alphabetic imagery had to be sacrificed for, as we remarked above, the *"tut"* image, which is one of the poles of the major opposition underlying the theme of the book, has been cunningly elaborated into a multi-dimensional microcosm phonetically and visually (as well as lexically) expressive of the plight of Cincinnatus, the artist-prisoner.

As the day of Cincinnatus' beheading draws ever nearer his fear that he will not succeed in conveying his vision mounts: "... ah, I think I shall yet be able to express it all—the dreams, the coalescence, the disintegration—no, again I am off the track—all my best words are deserters and do not answer the trumpet call, and the remainder are cripples" (E205/R200).

Akh, znai ia, chto tak dolgo eshche ostanutsia tut, ia by nachal s *azov* i, postepenno, stolbovoi dorogoi sviaznykh poniatii, doshel by, dovershil by, dusha by obstroilas' slovami . . . (200). (My italics—DBJ)

Oh, if only I had known that I was yet to remain here for such a long time, I would have begun at the beginning and gradually, along a high road of logically connected ideas, would have attained, would have completed, my soul would have surrounded itself with a structure of words . . . (205).

A*z* is the proper name of "A," the first letter of the Old Church Slavonic alphabet. This usage of the Slavonic, although closely associated with the prison-house of language theme, is somewhat different from the preceding ones in that no visual iconicism is involved. There is a significant bit of wordplay, however. In Church Slavonic, *az*, as well as being a letter name, is the word for "I," "ego." Thus, Cincinnatus, in addition to using the cliché 'to start from the beginning, from the letter A' is also saying that, given the opportunity, he would have delivered a revelation from his innermost self for, as he observes, he is unique, the only person possessed of truth. In Russian usage, as in English, the initial and final alphabetic letter names are found together in stock expressions such as *ot aza do izhitsy* 'from alpha to omega', that is, 'from beginning to end'. The expression presumably goes back to Revelation 1:8. "I am Alpha and Omega, the beginning and the ending, saith the Lord, which is, and which was, and which is to come, the Almighty." Thus the utterance of Cincinnatus, the artist, about starting from *az*, 'from the beginning, from his innermost self' has a certain theological resonance for the Russian reader.[37]

The alphabetic wordplay based on *az* is of interest in still another way for while it is of itself less striking than the other examples, it occupies a position of marked symmetry in the use of the alphabetic device throughout the novel. The book is divided into twenty chapters, each of which (excepting the last two) covers one day of Cincinnatus' imprisonment. Cincinnatus is sentenced and arrives in his death cell in chapter I; the beheading occurs in chapter XX. The first occurrence of the prison-house of language theme and its associated device of alphabetic iconicism is in chapter II and involves the letter *izhitsa*. The last occurrence of the theme and its alphabetic token is in chapter XIX and involves the letter *az*. The formal parallelism of the symmetrically placed chapters is marked in still other ways. The first sentence of chapter II is: "The morning papers, brought to him with a cup of tepid chocolate by Rodion . . . teemed as always with color photographs" (E23/R35). The opening words from chapter XIX are: "Next morning they brought him the newspapers, and this reminded him of the first days of his confinement. He noticed at once the color photograph . . ." (E202/R197). Returning now to the alphabetic images we note that the *izhitsa* which occurs in chapter II is the omega of the Church Slavonic alphabet, while the *az* of chapter XIX is the alpha. Firstly, we may observe that the series of alphabetic symbols from *az* to *izhitsa*, from alpha to omega, is, like Cincinnatus' life span, now complete. Secondly, we may ponder what significance lies in the curious fact that it is the omega letter *izhitsa* that is introduced first and the alpha letter *az* last, each in their carefully and symmetrically counterpoised chapters. It may, of course, be by chance but chance plays a negligible role in Nabokov's work. As we have remarked, the novel is structured along an axis of superimposed oppositions of which the most basic is "this world/that world" (here/there). This world, the world of Cincinnatus' imprisonment, is an evil monolith, a society of people whose very awareness is imprisoned by their hermetic language. Cincinnatus visualizes a society, opposite in every way to his own, its reversed mirror image, an ideal world. Borrowing some terminology from another Nabokov work (*Ada*) we might call these worlds Terra and Anti-Terra, where Cincinnatus, as he says, finds himself "through the error" (E91/R96). There are a number of hints throughout the book that life on Anti-Terra is illusory, a dream state from which Cincinnatus will awake to find himself amidst beings of his own kind on Terra the Fair.[38] The moment of transition between these two worlds, the moment of awakening, is death. Taking this mirror image concept as an interpretive context, the placement of the omega before the alpha assumes a potential significance. The decreasing number of days of his life on Anti-Terra which are devoted to his unsuccessful attempt to grasp and explicate Terra the Fair is rapidly approaching zero, the moment of death: death from the point of view of Anti-Terra, but birth from the point of view of Terra, Cincinnatus' ideal world. Granted Cincinnatus' position on Anti-Terra (*tut*), it is understandable and apt that the liturgical letters which he uses in his vain struggle to penetrate and convey Terra (*tam*) are in reverse order. It is also apropos that he arrives at the beginning, *az* 'the I, the ego', on the day of his Anti-Terranian death.

It is instructive that the final appearance of the prison-house of language theme with its alphabetic symbol occurs in the last entry in Cincinnatus' prison journal. As he continues the passage cited above, Cincinnatus is interrupted (just as he has written and crossed out the word "death") by the unexpected arrival of Pierre who is to escort him to the place of the ceremony, the *coup de grace*. As a condemned man Cincinnatus is offered a choice of last wishes. Rejecting those proffered, he asks three minutes to "finish writing something . . . but then he frowned, straining his thoughts, and suddenly understood that everything had in fact been written already" (E209/R204). Cincinnatus, the artist, has come to understand the truth of this world: he cannot escape the prison-house of language. Only after the axe falls and the world of "here" disintegrates, can Cincinnatus make his way toward that other world in which "to judge by the voices, stood beings akin to him," (E223/R218) that is, beings who speak and understand his language.

*Invitation to a Beheading* is the most inhuman and abstract of Nabokov's novels. Action is minimal and the characters, apart from Cincinnatus, are deliberately fashioned as cardboard figures whose costumes and make-up can be and often are changed and interchanged. It is the complete anti-

Realistic novel. The book has been stripped of any human flesh (in character and event) in order to achieve maximal focus on a form and style that is of great technical brilliance and which, more importantly, seems peculiarly appropriate to its theme.

The novel, like other Nabokov works, is about language and art, literature and the *litterateur*. We have demonstrated at some length the theme of the prison-house of language—a theme that is a central concern of every serious writer. Cincinnatus is the paradigm of the writer; his plight, that of every artist. The spartan furnishing of the novel, its almost schematic structuring, throw the theme and the intricate subpatterns of its exposition into high relief. Given that the language of art is simultaneously the theme of the novel and the means of expressing that theme, it is difficult to conceive a more apt motif than that of the alphabetic letters which are themselves the building blocks of the prison. The iconic letters, a device of indisputable ingenuity but necesarily of limited application, represent a vain attempt to loosen the fetters of the prison-house of language for in their visual aspect they reach beyond the conventional lexical level of language toward a mystical ideal tongue in which words mime as well as mean, an artistic language of perfect clarity in which the correspondence between perception and percept and between percept and word is absolute.

The alphabetic motif is pervasive in the novel but, as we have noted, only one special manifestation of it is linked to the prison-house of language theme—the iconic use of the Old Church Slavonic letters.[39] Cincinnatus is striving to use language to break through the strictures of this world and describe an ideal world. What could be more appropriate than the mysterious alphabetic tokens of an archaic religious tongue—a language intended solely to intimate to the linguistic prisoners of this world the truth and beauty of the next, an ideal world where there is no gap between sound and sense?

In *Invitation to a Beheading* Nabokov has found still another, very different way of utilizing his alphabetic master motif of the verbal artist. In *Speak, Memory*, the very letter with its synesthetic associations draws language into the subverbal world of perception in an attempt to establish, even if minimally, a direct, unmediated tie between sensory data and language. *Invitation to a Beheading* draws upon the device of alphabetic iconicism in an attempt to transcend the limits of language in a more metaphysical sense. *Au fond* both works use their respective alphabetic motifs as emblems of the artist's striving to break through the barriers of language and express the inexpressible.

NOTES

Section One

1. Julian Connolly, "The Function of Literary Allusion in Nabokov's *Despair*," *Slavic and East European Journal*, 26, 3 (Fall 1982), 302-13.

2. Vladislav Khodasevich, "On Sirin," *TriQuarterly*, 17 (1970), 100. The full Russian text which initially appeared in the Paris émigré journal *Vozrozhdenie*, Feb., 1937, was reprinted as "O Sirine," in *Literaturnye stat'i i vospominaniia* (New York: 1954). A similar observation is offered by V. Weidle in his review of *Despair* where he remarks "The theme of Sirin's creative work is creativity itself." *Krug*, 1 (1936), 185. Professor Gleb Struve (1934) and the critic P.M. Bitsilli (1936) also recognized Nabokov's preoccupation with the theme of art. For their views, see *Nabokov: The Critical Heritage*, ed. Norman Page (London: 1982), pp. 48 & 58.

3. Andrew Field, *Nabokov: His Life in Art* (Boston, 1967), p. 102.

4. *The Random House Dictionary of the English Language*, ed. Jess Stein (New York, 1966).

5. First mentioned by John Locke in his *Essay on Human Understanding*, pt. 3, ch. 4, para. 11.

6. Roman Jakobson and Linda Waugh, *The Sound Shape of Language* (Bloomington, 1979), p. 197. This volume contains a survey of the interrelations between synesthesia and language structure, pp. 189-94. See also my "The Role of Synesthesia in Jakobson's Theory of Language" in *Essays to Honor Edward Stankiewicz*, ed. D.S. Worth and K. Naylor (Los Angeles, 1982).

7. For details on the musical chromesthesia of Scriabin and Rimsky-Korsakov, see Leonid Sabaneev, *Skriabin* (Moscow, 1923), pp. 169-83.

8. Roman Jakobson, "*Kindersprache, Aphasia und allgemeine Lautgesatze*," *Selected Writings*, I ('S-Gravenhage, 1962), pp. 387-88.

9. The earliest attested examination of synesthesia is the Latin medical dissertation by Dr. G.T. Sachs in Erlangen in 1812. *Historia Naturalis Duorum Leucaethopium Auctoris Ipsius et Sororis eius (The Natural History of Two Albinos: the Author Himself and His Sister)*, cited in Friedrich Mahling, "Das Problem der 'Audition Colorée'," *Archiv fur die gesamte Psychologie*, 57 (1926), pp. 165-301.

10. A.E. Engstrom, "Synesthesia," *Princeton Encyclopedia of Poetry and Poetics*, ed. Alex Preminger (Princeton, 1965).

11. Max Nordau, *Degeneration* (New York, 1895), p. 142.

12. *Words and Things* (Glencoe, 1958), p. 154. This point is also made by Stephen Ullmann, *The Principles of Semantics*, 2nd ed. (Oxford, 1957), p. 268. Ullmann is one of the few scholars who has devoted extensive study to literary synesthesia. See particularly the section "Panchronistic Tendencies in Synaesthesia," pp. 268-88. The only other major study of the topic is Glenn O'Malley, "Literary Synesthesia," *Journal of Aesthetics and Art Criticism*, 15 (1957), 391-411.

13. The history and interrelations of the three versions of Nabokov's highly stylized autobiography are complex. Most of the segments were initially written as vignettes for the *New Yorker* in the late forties and in early 1950. These and several other parts published elsewhere were reworked and published in book form as *Conclusive Evidence* (New York, 1951). An expanded and revised Russian version was published as *Drugie berega (Other Shores)* (New York, 1954). Finally, a considerably revised and augmented English version was published in 1966 as *Speak, Memory: An Autobiography Revisited*. Each subsequent variant has to some degree expanded its treatment of Nabokov's alphabetic chromesthesia. Quotes are from the 1966 *Speak, Memory* unless otherwise specified. Quotes from the Russian version are indicated thus: *DB*—).

14. Nabokov's wife and son also display alphabetic chromesthesia although their letter-color correspondences substantially differ from each other's and from Nabokov's. *Strong Opinions*, p. 17.

15. The English correspondences are on pages 34-35 of *Speak, Memory*; the Russian on page 27 of *Drugie berega*. In the following listing the approximate sound value of the Cyrillic letters is indicated by the English letter in parenthesis. If no parenthesized English letter follows, the sound value of the Russian letter is roughly that of the same letter in English.

16. *Poems and Problems*, pp. 158-59. The subsequently cited "*Voluptates Tactionum*" is on p. 166.

17. Our discussion is limited to the specialized variety of synesthesia known as alphabetic chromesthesia. In addition, Nabokov uses generalized synesthetic metaphors with some frequency. For examples, see Jürgen Bodenstein aus Königsberg, "*The Excitement of Verbal Adventure*": A Study of Vladimir Nabokov's English Prose (Heidelberg, 1977), pp. 226-29, and the corresponding appendix. The above quote on the origin of "Sirin" is from Andrew Field, *Nabokov: His Life in Part* (New York, 1977), p. 149.

18. Nabokov's discussion is accompanied by such comments as "I hasten to complete my list [of letter/color correspondences—DBJ] before I am interrupted," and "The confessions of a synesthete must sound tedious and pretentious..." (35).

19. A Russian spelling rule dictates that the vowel letter "ы" must never be used in initial position.

20. The phrase *Buchstaben von Feuer* is in German both in the original Russian text and in the English translation. It is apparently drawn from Heinrich Heine's early poem *Belshazar* and refers to the biblical "handwriting on the wall." Heine, like Nabokov, made much use of synesthetic metaphors in his writing. The author is indebted to Professor Harry Steinhauer for this information.

21. Colored pencils figure in a singular case of synesthesia related in *Ada*. Among the patients referred to Dr. Van Veen is one Spencer Muldoon who, born eyeless, chances to pick up a box of colored pencils "whose mere evocations...make one's memory speak in the language of rainbows...." Muldoon opens the box and fingers the pencils. A hospital researcher notes "the blind man's eyebrows went up slightly at red, higher at orange, still higher at the shrill scream of yellow and then stepped down through the rest of the prismatic spectrum..." (469). During subsequent tests the patient reports that in stroking the pencils he perceives varying degrees of "stingles" in his fingers, permitting him to establish the colors.

22. Nabokov uses the index in *Speak, Memory* as a device for revealing covert textual references and indicating thematic unities. As an example of the former, we mention the use of the autobiography's index to identify the presence of Nabokov's wife in the text although she is nowhere mentioned by name. Elaborate thematic chains are established by cross references such as that cited here in connection with the "rainbow motif." There is a similar thematic chain associated with the "butterfly motif." Nabokov points to the role of the index in his Foreword which ends with the quatrain: "Through the window of that index / Climbs a rose / And sometimes a gentle wind ex / Ponto blows." The *ex Ponto* allusion is one of great complexity and significance to Nabokov. The phrase is taken from the title of Ovid's *Epistulae ex Ponto* ("Letters from the Black Sea"). The poet Ovid spent the last years of his life on the shores of the Black Sea after his banishment by the Emperor Augustus. The poet-in-exile theme resounds again in the early XIXth century when Alexander Pushkin was exiled to the Black Sea area by Tsar Nicholas I. The nineteen-year-old poet Vladimir Nabokov departed from Russia via the Black Sea after the family's voluntary exile in that region following the revolution. The Pushkin theme pervades much of Nabokov's work just as Ovid was a frequent subject of allusion for Pushkin. See Clarence Brown's "Nabokov's Pushkin and Nabokov's Nabokov in *Nabokov: The Man and his Work*, ed. L.S. Dembo (Milwaukee, 1967).

23. Somewhat similarly Russian children utilize a mnemonic sentence: *Kazhdyi okhotnik zhelaet znat', gde spiat fazany.* (Every hunter wants to know where sleep the pheasants.) The

initial letter of each Russian word is that of one of the seven spectral colors: krasnyi, oranzhevyi, zholtyi, zelionyi, goluboi, sinii, fioletovyi.

24. The nonce rainbow word VIBGYOR (Roy G. Biv read backwards) is used in *Ada* where a hydrophonic telephone carries its message via *"vibrational vibgyors* (prismatic pulsations)," p. 83.

25. Both definitions are drawn from *Webster's Third New International Dictionary* (Springfield, 1961).

26. Nabokov's Russian language "Postscript to the Russian Edition of *Lolita*" is available in an English translation by Earl P. Samson in *Nabokov's Fifth Arc: Nabokov and Others on His Life's Work*, ed. J.E. Rivers and Charles Nicol (Austin, 1982), pp. 188-94.

27. A.R. Luria, *The Mind of a Mnemonist: A Little Book about a Vast Memory*, translated by Lynn Solotaroff with a foreword by Jerome S. Bruner (New York, 1968). The quotations here are my own from the Russian text, *Malen'kaia knizhka o bol'shoi pamiati: Um mnemonista* (Moscow, 1968). A somewhat similar case is reported in Gerald S. Blum, *A Model of the Mind* (New York, 1961), which reports the case of a synesthete who also possessed eidetic memory. A recent survey of the psychological literature on synesthesia may be found in Lawrence E. Marks, "On Colored Hearing Synesthesia: Cross-Modal Translations of Sensory Dimensions," *Psychological Bulletin*, 82, 3 (1975), 303-37.

28. *Speak, Memory* provides another example of numeric iconicism: "I was born in April 1899, and naturally, during the first third of, say, 1903, was roughly three years old; but in August of that year, the sharp "3" should refer to the century's age, not to mine, which was "4" and as square and resilient as a rubber pillow" (13).

29. *Invitation to a Beheading* was written in 1934 and first published in book form in Paris in 1938. Following the commercial success of *Lolita*, *Priglashenie na kazn'* was the first of Nabokov's hitherto untranslated novels to appear in English (New York, 1959).

30. This was first pointed out by Andrew Field in his pioneering study *Nabokov: His Life in Art* (Boston, 1967), p. 188.

31. Similar to the inverted mirror image of the initials *Π* and *И* is the paired opposition in Nabokov's *Ada* of the initials of the protagonists Van and Ada. Ada's stylized monogram, *V*, is a striking visual icon with its implication of Van in Ada (47).

32. I owe this expression to Frederick Jameson's *The Prison-House of Language: A Critical Account of Structuralism and Russian Formalism* (Princeton, 1972). Jameson, in turn, has borrowed the expression from Nietzsche whom he quotes in his epigraph: "We have to cease to think if we refuse to do it in the prison-house of language; for we cannot reach further than the doubt which asks whether the limit we see is really a limit." Nabokov's novel can be most fruitfully viewed as an exploration of this statement.

33. Nabokov's Englishing of *prashcha* as "catapult" is presumably a throwback to his Ango-Russian childhood. "Catapult" is the usual British term for the American "slingshot."

34. The English but not the Russian text italicizes this important sentence.

35. The English text differs from the Russian in that the initial solitary *tam* of the Russian is expanded into the trilingual triplet *There, tam, là bas* in the English text, while the numerous subsequent occurrences of "there" are italicized. As we have shown and shall show, the exigencies of translation have resulted in the loss of some of Nabokov's alphabetic icons and weakened, in still other ways, the force of the *tut/tam* opposition so central to the novel. Nabokov has apparently tried to offset these dilutions by the above-mentioned reduplications and underscoring in the English text.

36. Nabokov makes use of the sound symbolism of "u" in other of his works. A particular showy example is from the 1930 novella *Sogliadatai*: *"I togda ne sdobrovat' otdel'nomu individuumu s ego dvumia bednymi 'u' beznadezhno aukaiushchimisia v chashchobe ekonomicheskikh prichin"* p. 25 ("and then woe to the private individuum with his two poor u's hallooing hopelessly amid the dense undergrowth of economic causes"), p. 38. The Russian Symbolist

writer Andrei Bely uses the "u" sound as one of the motifs in his novel *Petersburg*. For a contrastive examination of iconic and phonetic symbolism in Bely and Nabokov, see my "Belyj & Nabokov: A Comparative Overview," *Russian Literature*, IX (1981), 388-93.

37. This resonance is reinforced by another pointed use of an Old Church Slavonicism elsewhere in the book. In his prison journal Cincinnatus speaks of his gradual reduction to an irreducible nucleus which says *"Ia esm'"* 'I am' (R95/E90). The use of *esm'* here is purely Church Slavonic.

38. See, for example, R97/E92 and R208/E213 as well as the concluding paragraph.

39. The use of the equivalent Greek letters to convey some of the alphabetic icons in the English translation fails to capture an important dimension of the original. The Old Church Slavonic letters are firmly and exclusively associated in the minds of all Russians (at least those of Nabokov's generation) with the ecclesiastic language with its implications of spiritual transcendence. Although the New Testament is in Greek, the Greek letters have no such implications for speakers of English.

# SECTION TWO

## NABOKOV AS ANAGRAMMIST

Alphabetic synesthesia and alphabetic iconicism are two ways in which the individual letters of a language (and the sounds they represent) can directly assume meaning. Through their inherent psychological associations (colors, textures, etc.) or visual aspect ($\gamma$—a bird in flight), the alphabetic symbols have direct meaning outside of the set of conventions that mediate between sound and sense. It is only within the conventions known as English and Russian that *dog* and *sobaka* refer to the same animal. In the language of semiotics the tie between signifier (letter, sound, word) and signified (meaning) is arbitrary. Synesthesia and iconicism are two modes of short-circuiting this disjuncture. To some degree, the medium becomes the message, although it must be stressed that the level of communication possible through such phenomena is doomed to remain quite primitive. Their role is ancillary, albeit aesthetically effective. Synesthetic and iconic meanings are attached to individual letter units and can not be "additive." As we might recall from Nabokov's English rainbow coinage KZPSYGV, such creations do not yield 'real' words. We enter the world of real language only where the tie between symbol and sense is a conventional one. In the previous chapter we dealt with the meanings of the letter in Nabokov's writing. We shall now move from the world of the letter to that of the word, where sound and sense converge.

The commonsense view is that word reflects world, that meaning or reality is primary, and word secondary. Reality (including fictional reality) changes and words are accordingly rearranged, recombined. In Nabokov's world, as in the Bible's, we may say "In the beginning was the word." To this we must append "—and the word was made of letters." For the verbal artist words and letters are a way of arranging and rearranging a fictional universe. In "realistic" fiction the traditional assumption that words reflect (fictive) events is maintained. Nabokov's writing ostentatiously undermines this assumption at every turn. Words reign; events are accordingly rearranged. The only 'reality' is the writer. This attitude is perhaps most clearly reflected in Nabokov's novelistic preoccupation with word games such as anagrams, and its derivatives, palindromes and Scrabble. Anagrams afford a parable of Nabokov's view and practice of art.[1] In many of the novels the anagram is paradigmatic. The letters of a word which apparently reflects a bit of fictional reality are suddenly transposed and "reality" is reordered. The signifier is reshuffled and the signified transmuted. A new fictive cosmology is created, altering the reader's perception of events in much the same way that the line drawing of a goblet suddenly becomes the profile of two human faces *en regard:* the artist as magus. Anagrams reveal (in the sense of Revelation) the master hand of the creator in many of Nabokov's works.

In the novel *Despair*, Hermann, one of the most despicable of Nabokov's heroes, fancies himself a writer. In his dual role as chief actor in and sole recorder of his demented scheme, he sees himself as a God-like figure manipulating the plot of his own life and the style of his meandering account. He is, of course, simply a pawn in one of Nabokov's chess game-like novels, but egotist that he is, he can not conceive that he is anything less than the sole master of his fate. So certain is he that he begins one of his chapters with the assertion "The nonexistence of God is simple to prove. Impossible to concede, for example, that a serious Jah, all wise and almighty, could employ his time in such inane fashion as playing with manikins . . . " (111). This is a rather heavy example of Nabokovian irony, for presiding over Hermann's world there certainly is an all wise Jah who may not be altogether serious, but is unquestionably almighty. Jah is, according to the *OED*, an English form of the Hebrew alphabetic symbol Yah, a shorthand version of Yawe(h) or Jehovah. The general meaning of 'Jah' is obvious from the context, but less apparent, at least to the Russianless reader, is that the Hebrew letter-symbol Jah is simultaneously a phonetic representation of the Russian letter *"Я"* which also serves as the first person pronoun "I", the "I" of the author. Thus Nabokov, unbeknowst to his character, asserts his divine authority by intruding into the world of his manikin at the very moment that Hermann is mocking the idea.

Another instance occurs in *Transparent Things* where the protagonist, Hugh Person, an editor working on the manuscript of an eminent writer known only as Mr. R., queries the spelling of the name of an incidental character, one Adam von Librikov, an anagrammatic Nabokov surrogate (75). Also unusual about Mr. R., a foreigner who writes in English, is that he appears to be the posthumous narrator of the novella—a fact ascertainable only from certain stylistic mannerisms peculiar to his speech pattern (*SO* 195). These facts suddenly fall into place when it is realized that the eminent author's designation, the capital letter "R" is a mirror-image reversal of the Russian letter *"Я"* again signifying the first person singular personal pronoun "I." Thus Mr. R., the writer-narrator who is creator of the people and events of *Transparent Things*, is an ego-alphabetic surrogate of Vladimir Nabokov who, moreover, anagrammatically incorporates Adam von Librikov into the novel of his author-persona.

Among the more anagram-riddled works of Nabokov is *Bend Sinister*. The events of the novel are set in a mythical country which has just undergone a revolution dedicated to the establishment of a dictatorship of the common man. The "common man" is personified in the dictator Paduk who believes that "all men consist of the same twenty five letters variously mixed" (60). Although the missing 26th letter is not named, it is obviously "I" referring to the novel's protagonist Adam Krug, an internationally famous philosopher who is the only great man his country has produced. Just as the revolutionary state of the average man has no need of the egoist letter/pronoun "I," it has no place for Krug, who, like the letter, is eliminated.

Anagrams are also central to an understanding of some of Nabokov's shorter pieces. The very early story *Uzhas* ("Terror") deals with the madness lurking on the edges of the narrator's mind and in token of this the word *uzhas* is repeatedly anagrammatized in the text, waiting its chance to break into the narrator's consciousness. In *The Vane Sisters* the narrator persistently derides the spiritualistic beliefs of the two sisters. After the death of the second sister, the still skeptical but wavering narrator unwittingly provides the conclusive evidence in the last paragraph of his story where the initial letters of each word form a message from the deceased sisters.

Nabokov is particularly fond of palindromes which are the most demanding form of anagram. Palindromes are of two types: reciprocal, such as 'deified' or 'mad Adam' which yield the same word or words forward or backward; and nonreciprocal, in which different words such as 'God' and 'dog' result. In the best palindromes of this latter sort the two words stand in a particularly congruous or incongruous relationship to each other such as 'evil/live' or 'T. Eliot/toilet'. As with his chromesthetic and iconic employment of letters, Nabokov sometimes incorporates palindromes into his narratives in such a way that they constitute a motif resonant with the theme of the narrative and, indeed, may express that theme more sharply and concisely than the plot itself.

One of Nabokov's earliest stories is built entirely on palindromic reversals that mirror the narrative palindrome that is the story's plot.[2] "A Guide to Berlin" (*Putevoditel' po Berlinu*) treats the favorite Nabokovian theme of future memories and asserts that the very sense of literary creation lies in the recreation of the minutia of the present as they will be seen "in the kindly mirrors of future times . . . when every trifle of our plain everyday life will become exquisite and festive in its own right" (94). These "kindly mirrors of future times" prove to be more than a felicitous phrase. The story contains five vignettes describing different aspects of Berlin life from this viewpoint. In the final scene set in a *Bierstube* the narrator watches the owner's small son sitting in the bar's backroom which serves as the living quarters of the publican's family. The narrator reflects that the scene in the barroom (including the narrator himself) being observed by the boy will be the lad's "future recollections." Unstated here is that the narrator is not merely imagining the scene from the boy's angle but is actually observing it from that point of view, for he is looking in a wall mirror hanging above and directly behind the boy's head. The role of the mirror is never made explicit nor is the fact that the mirror image reverses left and right. This last aspect of the theme is incorporated in the narrative in a variety of ways; most prominently in the form of palindromes which are the written language's equivalent to mirror-image reversal. The most pervasive palindromic figure is introduced near the beginning of the story when the narrator, a young Russian émigré writer, leaves his rooming house and notes a row of large utility pipes lying along the curb awaiting entrenchment. There has been an overnight snowfall and someone has written the word 'OTTO' on the fresh strip of snow atop one of the pipes (92). The narrator marvels at how the name, "with its two soft 'o's flanking the pair of gentle consonants, suited the silent layer of snow upon that pipe with its two orifices and its tacit tunnel." It is not only the snow that it suits, for the very shape of the word 'OTTO' with its 'O's at both ends mimes the shape of the pipe on which it is written. The word 'OTTO' is not, however, limited to its iconic function, for Nabokov, in both the English and the original Russian version, has anagramatically incorporated it into his description of the pipe with its twin Orifices and its Tacit Tunnel. But the fit between the two soft "O"s and the snow-covered pipe goes still further. For Nabokov, as we have previously observed, the letter "O" is white in color and is synesthetically linked with the image of an ivory-backed hand mirror. A close reading of the story shows that the 'OTTO' palindrome that occurs in anagrammatic form in each of the remaining story segments is another of the mirrors that gather up and reflect the narrator's theme of future memories.

Anagrams in their various forms are one of the devices by which the artist-creator penetrates the world of his creatures from his own world. The character who fails to perceive the playful handiwork of his creator is doomed to incomprehension of his world and the fate it prescribes for him. The situation is somewhat similar for Nabokov's readers. He who fails to decipher a key anagram may at best be consigned to a very partial understanding of the novel and denied the thrill of finding confirmation of his critical intuitions. The following essays which focus on anagrammatic aspects of *Ada* and *Pale Fire* are offered in evidence.

# THE SCRABBLE GAME IN *ADA*
## OR
## TAKING NABOKOV CLITORALLY

Games are integral to Nabokov's view of art and he has repeatedly stressed both the aesthetic pleasure of game composition and play and its kinship to the composition and enjoyment of the work of art—particularly his own.[3] His attainments as the creator of the *krestoslovitsa*, the Russian crossword puzzle, and as a composer of chess problems are well known.[4] Many of Nabokov's works, in addition to game-like strategies in their composition, overtly incorporate actual games. Although chess plays an important role in some of the novels, word games by their very nature are more central to Nabokov's art. Nabokov's "verbal circuses" range from iconic letter play through anagrams, spoonerisms, and puns, to more or less formal word games such as Word Golf and Scrabble. Although Nabokov often uses word games as ornament affording incidental amusement for the reader, they are also used to intimate character or theme, or to signal obscure but critical plot developments. In *Pale Fire*, for example, Kinbote's Word Golf triumph of transmuting LASS into MALE in four moves is a wry reference to his sexual preferences. More essential to theme and plot, however, is our realization that the anagrammatic names Kinbote and Botkin(c) signal the same person. *Ada* is the most riddled with word play of all of Nabokov's writings. The major themes of the book are captured in a recurrent bit of word play which might be reprised as "Ada is scient anent incest and the nicest insects." Although *Ada* is permeated with verbal pyrotechnics of the most diverse sorts, the most intensive and sustained sequence of thematic word play centers around the word game "Scrabble."

During the first idyllic Ardis summer, the Veen children, Ada, Van and Lucette, are presented with an ornate Russian *Flavita* set.[5] Ada proves to be a passionate and insatiable Scrabblist, while Van, a first-rate chess player, is an indifferent player.[6] Van, who as an adult becomes a professional parapsychologist, finds the game of interest only because words which appear in the course of play sometimes seem to have uncanny relevance to the lives of the players. The game affords an opportunity of "catching sight of the lining of time" which, as Van later writes, "is the best informal definition of portents and prophecies" (227). This is seen both on the level of factual trivialities as when Ada's letter blocks spell out (in scrambled form) the Russian word KEROSIN while a kerosine lamp is being mentioned and, much more importantly, on the thematic level. It should be noted that, as is traditionally the case with portents, the oracle is in enigmatic form—an anagram.

Sex is a paramount theme in *Ada* and the primary arena for its realization is the relationship between Van and Ada. Their affair constitutes the major plot line of the novel. There is, however, a strong secondary plot line equally expressive of the theme: Lucette's sexual obsession with Van. Although Van is strongly attracted to his half-sister, he does not reciprocate her love and strives to avoid further incestuous entanglement. All of the encounters between Lucette and Van are marked by strong erotic undercurrents, and the continuing Scrabble game becomes the context for an anagrammatic motif echoing the theme of Lucette's sexual obsession with her half-brother and also her sexual relationship with her sister Ada.

The Scrabble motif is most prominently displayed in two chapters (I-36 & II-5) which are separated by 130-odd pages and eight years of the characters' lives. The chapters are also thematically linked by their focus on Lucette's hopeless role in the siblings' sexual triangle. The earlier chapter describes the Scrabble set itself, Ada's record coup for a single play, and ends with loser Lucette in tears as Ada and Van force her off to an early bedtime so that they may turn to other pastimes. Even at eight, little Lucette understands all too well why the lovers are eager to be alone. The later Scrabble chapter describes an interview between Van and Lucette (now sixteen) in Van's rooms at Chose University where he is, as he says, an "assistant lecher." Enraged by Ada's infidelities, Van has seen neither of the girls in four years, during which time they have been, *inter alia*, engaged in a lesbian relationship with each other. Now, via Lucette, Ada is sending a note pleading Van's forgiveness. Lucette, who has declared her own love for Van in an earlier letter, attempts to seduce him under the pretext of delivering Ada's letter. This she essays largely through mimicry of Ada's speech and manner, although she also plays on Van's jealousy through her account of Ada's lovers and her own affair with her. Van, although erotically aroused by his visitor's tactic, is too distracted by the possibility of a reunion with Ada to respond to Lucette's wiles. In both chapters the Scrabble games serve as a playing field for the expression of Lucette's sexual obsession with Van and all the anagrammatic portents that arise during the games are in the course of Lucette's plays.

The first thematic portent occurs during a game which takes place on a crucial day in July of 1884. "... in the bay of the library, on a thundery evening (a few hours before the barn burned), a succession of Lucette's blocks formed the amusing VANIADA, and from this she extracted the very piece of furniture she was in the act of referring to in a peevish little voice: 'But I, too, would like to sit on the divan'" (226). Lucette's suggestive sequence VANIADA ("*i*" is the Russian word for "and") additionally refers to the black, yellow-cushioned divan on which Van and Ada are sitting, and on which the two children first couple later that same night while the barn burns (I-19). From Lucette's point of view the divan from which she is excluded signals the theme of her unrequited love for Van. The divan becomes a leitmotif in several of Van and Lucette's subsequent conversations. The first of these takes place during the interview in Van's rooms eight years later and the last in Lute (Paris) shortly before the sea voyage that ends in the suicide of Lucette, whom Van has brutally rejected. She pleads "Oh, try me, Van! My divan is black with yellow cushions" (464). It is not by chance that DIVAN contains intermingled the letters of the names Van and Ada but not those of Lucette.[7]

In a later Scrabble game, the one in which Ada scores her record coup, Lucette examines her hopeless jumble of letter blocks, wailing *"je ne peux rien faire, . . . mas rien*—with my idiotic *Buchstaben* REMLINK, LINKREM . . ." (227). The proposed KREMLIN is properly rejected as not being a Russian word, and, at Van's prompting, Lucette settles for KREMLI 'Yukon prisons' which is to intersect Ada's ORHIDEYA 'orchid.' Orchids are a constant motif associated with Ada and, as several critics have pointed out, have obvious sexual connotation.[8] Etymologically the word is derived from the Greek word for "testicle" (a fact alluded to in the novel—245) and, more relevantly, is used in the context of the book as a metaphor for "vagina." Recreating his first congress with Ada on the famous divan, octagenarian memoirist Van recalls that "his impatient young passion . . . did not survive the first few blind thrusts; it burst at the lip of the orchid" (121).[9] Not realized by any of the participants in the Scrabble game is that Lucette's letter blocks also form the arcane word MERKIN (with a leftover "L" for Lucette) meaning "pudendum."[10] It would doubtless seem far-fetched to regard this anagrammatic conjunction of Lucette's MERKIN and Ada's ORHIDEYA as a portent of their subsequent sexual liaison were it not part of a developing pattern. Also to be considered is that the reader has been alerted that Van's interest in Scrabble focuses precisely on such coincidences.

A further childhood Scrabble game is recounted by Lucette several years later during her visit with Van.[11] Lucette is younger and far less brilliant than her *Wunderkind* siblings and in order to expedite their games Van often prompts her play. Of one such occasion Lucette recalls "You examined and fingered my groove and quickly distributed the haphazard sequence which made, say LIKROT or ROTIKL and . . . when you had completed the arrangement, you and she came simultaneously *si je puis le mettre comme ça* (Canady French), came falling back on the black carpet in a paroxysm of incomprehensible merriment; so finally I quietly composed ROTIK ('little mouth') and was left with my own cheap little initial" (379). The innuendoes in the passage are, like Ada's caterpillars, rampant, although some are more apparent than others. Apart from the introductory fingered groove, Lucette's ROTIK "little mouth" might appear innocent were it not for the Russian KLITOR "clitoris" that lurks in the bilingual vulgarism LI(C)KROT and its diminutive companion ROTIK—L. Doubt is dispelled by Van's response that "a medically minded *English* Scrabbler, having two more letters to cope with, could make, for example, STIRCOIL, a well-known sweat-gland stimulant, or CITROILS, which grooms use for rubbing fillies" (379). The clues are abundant both in the double meanings of "grooms" and "fillies" and, more subtly, in the phrase "sweat-gland stimulant". The glands (from the Latin *glans, glandis* "acorn" or "glans") being stimulated are the glans clitoridis and the glans penis which become the topic of a running series of multilingual word plays, anagrammatic and otherwise, that pervade the interview between Van and Lucette.

Van both anticipates and dreads Lucette's visit for he feels that it will set off, as he says, "internal fires."[12] Lucette, in so far as she resembles Ada, is an object of intense sexual desire for Van. Lucette enters the apartment, her red mouth disclosing her tongue and teeth in readiness for a welcoming embrace which will signal, she hopes, the beginning of a new life for both of them. Wary Van deflects her oncoming kiss with the warning "Cheekbone." In reply, Lucette, somewhat confusingly, murmurs "You prefer *skeletki* (little skeletons)" as Van applies light lips "to his half-sister's hot, hard pommette" (367-68). Why should Van prefer "little skeletons"?[13] On one level *skeletki* is prompted by the 'bone' of cheekbone, but given the scene's sexual motif there can be little doubt that *skeletki* is a Scrabble anagram for SEKEL', the Russian vulgarism for the glans clitoridis. "Pommette," in addition to being the French word for "cheekbone," also means "a small knob such as that found on the end of a sword hilt of a cross pommée." The latter allusion prefigures an entire *krestik* (crosslet)-kissing motif in the ensuing dialogue.

The word game continues. When nervous Lucette uses an unlikely number of sibilants Van harshly reproves her stylistic lapse by declaring "We don't want any baby serpents around" (369). Lucette replies, "This baby serpent does not quite know what tone to take with Dr. V.V. Sector. You have not changed one bit my pale darling, except that you look like a ghost in need of a shave without your summer *Glanz*." To this speech Van mentally appends "And summer *Mädel*," referring to Ada. The iconic V-sector requires no commentary but the *Glanz* reference is not so apparent. The Veen family rather casually switches back and forth among English, Russian and French, but not German. *Glanz*, the German word for "luster," refers not to Van's winter pallor, but to the medical term 'glans' which is how a Germanless English reader might pronounce the word.[14]

Lucette's campaign to displace Ada in Van's bed entails a detailed account of her own seduction by Ada. She launches her attack by asking

Van whether Ada had written him about "Pressing the Spring." Lucette begins her explanation in a roundabout fashion by recalling to Van a scrutoir or secretaire which stood at the foot of the VANIADA divan in the Ardis library. The sisters had challenged Van to find and "release the [scrutoir's] orgasm or whatever it is called" (374). When Van eventually finds the "yielding roundlet," he presses it and a secret drawer shoots out. In it there is "a miniscule red pawn" (374) which Lucette still keeps as a souvenir. The incident, she says, "preemblematized" her affair with Ada in which we "were Mongolian tumblers, monograms, anagrams, adalucindas. She kissed my *krestik* while I kissed hers" (377). Van interrupts to maliciously query the meaning of the word. Is it, he wonders, something like the little red stud or pawn in the secret drawer of the scrutoir: perhaps an ornament, "a small acorn of coral, the *glandulella* of vestals in ancient Rome" (378)? Accounts of the accouterments of the vestals do not mention such an ornament, but the word itself is the Latin dimunitive of the omnipresent *glans, glandis* "acorn" which by virtue of physical resemblance also specifies the corresponding sexual organs.

With the introduction of the *krest/krestik* "cross" motif, we move from sly permutations of real sexual terms to a set of sexual symbols largely of Nabokov's own devising.[15] As Van reluctantly returns Lucette's welcoming embrace he inhales her "paphish" Degrasse perfume (*eau de grace*) and through it "the flame of her Little Larousse." Stroking her russet head Van finds he cannot touch the "upper copper" without imagining at once the "lower fox cub and the paired embers." "The cross (*krest*) of the best-groomed redhead (*rousse*). Its four burning ends" (368). This vision of "the four embers of a vixen's cross" (377) torments Van throughout their conversation and permeates its language in many ways. The sexual cross submotif edges into blasphemy when Van viciously harries Lucette about the meaning of her (and Ada's) secret word *krestik* (378). "Of course, I remember now" says Van. "A foul taint in the singular can be a sacred mark in the plural. You are referring . . . to the stigmata between the eyes of pure sickly young nuns whom priests had over-annointed there and elsewhere with cross-like strokes of the myrrherabol brush." The *krestik* (crosslet-clitoris) theme is also echoed anagrammatically in the description of the Scrabble games. In one of the earliest games Lucette sorts out her opening seven letter blocks "in her *spektrik*" (the little trough of japanned wood each player had before him)" (226). This is well before the introduction of the *krestik* motif but the subsequent Scrabble description (cited above) in which Van fingers Lucette's groove while helpfully redistributing her letters leaves no doubt that Lucette's *spektrik* is but a sly scramble of her *krestik. Krests* also anagrammatically flourish in Lucette's reference to an erotic art album called *Forbidden Masterpieces* which she finds, appropriately enough, in a box of "*korsetov i khrestomatiy* (corsets and chrestomathies)" (376). The *krest* motif enters still another linguistic dimension in its English incarnation of a later chapter. As Van arrives in a Swiss town in 1905 in anticipation of a final reunion with Ada, the place name, Mont Roux, prompts his thought "our little rousse is dead" (509). Looking around, he sees in the landscape the colors associated with Lucette (russet and green) and with Ada (black and white). "Mount Russet, the forested hill behind the town, lived up to its name and autumnal reputation, with the warm glow of curly chestnut tress; and on the opposite side of Leman, Leman meaning lover, loomed the crest of Sex Noir, Black Rock." The blackness of Ada's nether crest has already been established by Lucette in her account of their lesbian frolics. She describes her sister as a "dream of white and black beauty, *pour cogner une fraise,* touched with fraise in four places, a symmetrical queen of hearts" (375).[16] Thus the russet-embered Russian *krest* "cross" is transformed into the fraised English "crest" of Ada's Sex Noir.

The four burning embers of the cross/*krest* serve as one of Lucette's leitmotifs throughout the chapter and much of the book. Van's persistent image of Lucette in these terms dates from his first Ardis summer when he and Ada, seeking a few minutes of privacy, imprison the eight-year-old Lucette in her bath. Van notices that her "armpits showed a slight stipple of bright floss and her chubb was dusted with copper" (144). The scene is Van's unconscious *point de repère* on seeing the now sexually mature Lucette. Aroused, he realizes that he had hardly known her before except as an "embered embryo" (367). This embered image informs the interview in yet another way, for it is curiously permeated with words containing the sequence EMB: ember, embryo, emblazed, embrasure, embrace, preemblematize, November, etc. Nor is the association of this sequence with Lucette restricted to the one scene.[17] After Van and Ada are temporarily reunited through Lucette's miscalculated intermediary role, the brother and sister suborn the unwilling Lucette into a three-way sexual *ébat.* After the distraught Lucette flees, Van pens her a note apologizing for inveigling "our Esmeralda and mermaid in a naughty prank" and remarks that "remembrance, embers and membranes of beauty make artists and morons lose all self-control" (421).

Still other words assume sexual significance in the context of the chapter. Double entendres flourish around the innocuous French word *cas* "case." After Lucette correctly identifies an allusion to Bergson, "assistant lecher" Van Veen offers to reward her with "a B minus *dan ton petit cas,*" or, alternatively, "a kiss on your *krestik*" (377). Lucette's account of Ada's infidelities evokes Van's response "It's a gripping and palpitating little case history" (381). The final case occurs during the final shipboard dinner just before Van's ultimate rebuff and Lucette's suicide. Sensing that Van is on the brink of yielding to her entreaties, Lucette continues her imitation of Ada. Trying to keep his mind off Lucette's charms, Dr. Veen speaks of the case history of one of his patients, His attempt is in vain, however, for "another case (with a quibble on *cas*) engaged in his attention subverbally" (484). A male counterpart to Lucette's "quibbled on *cas*" occurs when she vainly tries to lure Van ever deeper into an embrace. Van brushes away her probing fingers and reiterates his disinclination to complicate his already incestuous love life. Lucette accusingly says ". . . you've gone far enough with me on several occasions, even when I was a little kid; your refusing to go further is a mere quibble on your part" (467). Van's parts are the object of further attention as he warms to the mental image of Lucette's *"petit cas."* His "condition" leads him to the stray reflection that "One of the synonyms of 'condition' is 'state' and the adjective 'human' may be construed as 'manly' which is how Lowden recently translated the title of the *malheureux* Pompier's cheap novel *La Condition Humaine*" (377).[18]

Van's conversation contains at least two other highly suspect, if inconclusive, bilingual allusions to the chapter's thematic motif. Lucette has just referred to the divan in the library. She recalls that at its heel end there was a closet in which Van and Ada had locked her while engaged in their *ébats* on the divan.[19] Van remarks that the closet had "a keyless hole as big as Kant's eye" and adds, parenthetically, that "Kant was famous for his cucumicolor iris" (373). This rather odd statement refers to Lucette's green eye peering through the closet keyhole. Lurking in the phonetic background, however, is the vagrant thought that the French pronunciation of Kant /kã/ is a near homophone of *con* /kõ/ and that the peculiar locution "cucumicolor iris" has, with the exception of the "t" supplied by the earlier "Kant," all of the letters of the omnipresent "clitoris." Similar associations surround one Coniglietto. Van, momentarily overcome with remorse at his harrying of Lucette, pleads her pardon saying "I'm a sick man. I've been suffering for these last four years from consanguine-ocanceroformia—a mysterious disease described by Coniglietto. Don't put your little cold hand on my paw" (379). Coniglietto is one of the six doctors in *Ada* who are united by their leporine cognomens: the French-Swiss Lapiner (Alpiner), the Russian Krolik, the German Seitz (= Russian *zaiats* "hare"), the French Lagosse, and a Russian Dr. Nikulinov (= Latin *cuniculus*). Dr. Coniglietto's name is of particular interest in the context of the chapter motif because of its partial phonetic resemblance to the older English word for rabbit—"cony" or "cunny" (from Latin *cuniculus*) which also meant a "pudendum maliebre," apparently by reason of its similarity to derivatives of the Latin *cunnus* "vulva."[20] Van and Lucette's verbal intercourse displays at least one further and much less problematic multilingual pun on this same root. During their shipboard flirtation Van's attentions to Lucette are momentarily distracted by a statuesque blonde in a skimpy gold lamé bathing suit. The jealous Lucette promptly nicknames her "Miss Condor" (nasalizing the first syllable)" [con d'or], a sobriquet that Van calls the best Franco-English pun he has heard (481).

The words "lips" and "slit" also lend their secondary sexual meanings to the erotically charged subtext of Van and Lucette's meeting. Van is enraged at Lucette's detailing of Ada's sexual adventures and repeatedly vents his wrath on "the redhaired scapegoatling . . . whose only crime was to be suffused with the phantasmata of the other's innumerable lips" (378).[21] Lucette prefaces the account of her lesbian relationship with Ada with the comment that perhaps she should simply have pressed the doorbell button and slipped her note "into the burning slit" and left (370). This and an earlier line of allusion surface again anagrammatically in the title of Van's favorite novel, *Slat Sign*, which is twice mentioned in the conversation and which unscrambles into SLIT and GLANS (with a reuse of the L). The interview ends no less erotically than it began as Van, now knowing he will be reunited with Ada, gives the spurned paranymph Lucette a farewell embrace in which he thrusts his hands into the "vulvas" of the mole-soft sleeves of her fur coat and permits her to gauge the tangibility of his feeling for her with the knuckles of her "*gloved h*and" (387).[My underscoring]

The events of *Ada* take place on a planet called Demonia or Anti-Terra. Van devotes his professional life to research in the field of Terrapy—the study of a possibly unreal counterworld named Terra which seems to correspond in topography and chronology to our world, the world of the reader. For the inhabitants of Demonia, however, the existence of Terra is problematic. The evidence for Terra, Demonia's distorted twin, is in the ravings of the mad, in dreams, and in portents. These are thought to be "leaks" in the space-time barrier that separates the two worlds. As a scholar Van attempts to study Terra by collating such ravings, dreams and portents. His investigations suggest that events on Terra are warped versions (both chronologically and ontologically) of events on Demonia. From the viewpoint of Terra (and the reader) the reverse is true. A grasp of *Ada*'s cosmology is important in understanding what follows, for Van sees (or fails to see) the portents of the Scrabble game as intimations from Terra.

The crucial Scrabble set has an interesting history. It is presented to the children by one Baron Klim Avidov "an old friend of the family (as Marina's former lovers were known)" (223). Baron Avidov, who makes no appearance in the novel, is then the source of the thematic portents introduced into the narrative through the Scrabble board. In the world of Demonia, Anti-Terra, the Baron, an ex-lover of Marina, is the word father of the children just as Demon, another lover of Marina, is the biological father of Van and Ada. The name Baron Klim Avidov is a perfect anagram of

Vladimir Nabokov, who is of course the ultimate, or Terranian father of the events in *Ada*.[22] The portentous Scrabble games do indeed manifest glimmers of another world but not in the way assumed by Van.

The chapter that introduces the Scrabble motif is prefaced by a discussion of the use of dictionaries for purposes other than "those of expression—be it instruction or art" (222). Ada, the ardent Scrabblist, likens such usage of the lexicon to "the ornamental assortment of flowers (which could be, she conceded, mildly romantic in maidenly headcocking way)" (222). In the coy phrase "maiden(ly) headcocking way" *Grossmeister* Nabokov sets the theme of the Scrabble sections and leads off the riot of erotic word play that permeates those chapters.[23]

The Scrabble game motif (in addition to its non-utilitarian delights) fulfills a traditional literary function in the book—that of ornamenting the theme of Van and Lucette's relationship through an erotically charged subtext. In doing so, it illustrates a larger principle of Nabokov's aesthetic canon. He has written that "pure art is never simple, being always an elaborate, magical deception." Nabokov sees his art as a form of play, a game, and has argued that in works of art, as in chess problems, the contest is not between the characters but between the author and the world. Nabokov's writings demand from the reader close attention and active participation. Many require "solving" if they are to be fully appreciated by the reader. The involvement of the reader in the Nabokovian game of art is, however, a secondary activity. From Nabokov's point of view, the art of a work resides in the elegance and subtle intricacy of its composition, in the construction of the puzzle. This is attested by Ada's comment prefacing the Scrabble chapters that "verbal circuses...might be redeemable by the quality of brainwork required for the creation of a great logogriph..." (222). This view of art is admittedly a tendentious one, but whatever standards we choose to apply, *Ada* is Nabokov's most elaborate "verbal circus."

## THE INDEX OF REFRACTION IN *PALE FIRE*

*Pale Fire* is among most the fiendishly complex of Nabokov's novels. The narrative comprises several levels of reality/unreality and it is for the reader—or should we say the solver—to determine which is the "correct" one. In part this depends upon determining the identity of the narrator and the extent to which he is trustworthy. The answer, we shall argue, lies in an anagram and the clues are to be found in the novel's artful index.

*Pale Fire* displays a structure perhaps unique in a work of fiction. Its form is obviously inspired by and modeled on Nabokov's monumental edition of Pushkin's *Eugene Onegin*.[24] Like Nabokov's *Onegin*, *Pale Fire* consists of an editor's introduction, a long poem, a much longer set of commentaries by the editor and, finally, an index. Among other things, the novel is a parody of academic editions of literary masterpieces and of the academic world in general. More important, however, is that the mimicry of this form has provided Nabokov with a new contextual playground for the games so central to his art.

The plot is susceptible of two basic interpretations—each with a number of variants. The first of the more or less plausible levels of interpretation coincides with that of the narrator, Charles Kinbote, "actually" the incognito Charles the Beloved, last king of Zembla, who is an instructor at Wordsmith College. A fellow faculty member, the eminent aging poet John Shade, is Kinbote's next-door neighbor. Living in fear of assassination by the revolutionaries who have taken over his country, Kinbote forces his friendship on Shade and, while never openly admitting his "true" identity, primes the poet for an epic poem glorifying the events of his reign. Shade is indeed working on a long poem, but it is about his own life, his speculations on death, and the meaning of art. Kinbote optimistically and mistakenly assumes that the unseen poem is based on his own regal reminiscences. On the day of the poem's completion, Shade is fatally shot by a stranger named Jack Grey (alias Jacques d'Argus) as the poet and Kinbote walk across the lawn toward the latter's house. Kinbote believes the bullet was meant for him. Still under the misapprehension that the unread poem is a retelling of his Zemblan reign, Kinbote takes the manuscript and leaves town planning to prepare the poem for publication. On reading the poem, Kinbote finds it is unrelated to his Zemblan theme. Seeing his chance for immortality fading, Kinbote persuades himself that "enemies" (most specifically Shade's wife) have forced the poet to suppress his true theme. On rereading the work, however, Kinbote discovers that it contains covert allusions to his own royal story. That the truth be known, he writes a set of commentaries in which he explicates the "real" meaning of the poem incorporating his own regal autobiography and some 250 years of Zemblan history.

A second, closer reading affords quite a different interpretation of events. Kinbote's rented house belongs to one Judge Goldsworth—who happens to resemble his neighbor John Shade (267). It is unobtrusively made known that the judge once passed sentence on a homicidal maniac who (as Kinbote admits) "somewhat resembles Jacques d'Argus" (83), an escapee from an institution for the criminally insane, who has returned to seek vengeance on the sentencing judge. He kills the poet Shade whom he mistakes for Judge Goldsworth. In the light of this reading, it is clear that Kinbote is mad and that his identity as Charles the Beloved is part of his delusion, as is his obsession that he is the object of an anti-royalist assassination plot.[25] The commentaries to the purloined poem are thus simply an account of Kinbote's delusional world, past and present.

This level of interpretation seems to account for many of the events of the narrative and is based chiefly on a very close reading of Kinbote's Introduction and Commentary. In fact, however, a number of mysteries, one major and a number of minor ones, remain to be resolved. What of the somewhat peculiar Index? Why is it there? There is, of course, a formal basis for it since the novel is in the form of a scholarly work.[26] But since the book is in fact a novel, on finishing the commentaries the reader is inclined to skim the index and set the volume aside. Even if an assiduous reader does attempt to use the index he will quickly discover that it is of limited utility. Fairly important characters are listed only cursorily, e.g., Sybil Shade ("S wife, *passim.*") or not at all, e.g., Gerald Emerald who, in the course of another entry, is noted as being "not in Index." Very minor characters and place names (including at least one not in the text at all) are given extensive entries. All this plus the quirky nature of some of the more routine entries lead the reader to suspect that the Index is far more than an ordinary reference aid, and that it plays some role in the book, i.e., it is an integral part of, rather than an ancillary appendage to, the novel.

*Pale Fire*'s Index proves to be a document no less bizarre than the deranged Kinbote's commentaries. Like them, it has almost no relevance to the poem, but only to that portion of the Commentary which adduces the Zemblan theme and, to a lesser extent, to Kinbote's life at Wordsmith College and his relationship to John Shade. The major portion of the index is a "Who's Who" of Zemblan history, particularly the reign and flight of Charles the Beloved, and a gazeteer to the royal kingdom. Of the eighty-eight entries, forty-four refer to persons connected with the Zemblan theme and another twenty-one are Zemblan place names.

The Commentary's ineptly maintained "official" viewpoint that Kinbote and the king are separate people is largely dispensed with in the Index. The prefatory note to the Index explains that the three main characters are referred to by the capital letters G, S, and K. Consultation of the appropriate index entries shows that G stands for the killer (Grey/Gradus/D'Argus) and S for Shade. The entry under K, however, refers the reader to the entries for Charles II and (Charles) Kinbote. The index listings under Charles II conclude with "See also Kinbote." In his commentary to line 131, Kinbote cites an omitted variant line "Poor old man Swift, poor _____, poor Baudelaire", and launches into a complex discussion of the missing name, darkly implying that the trochee "Kinbote" has been suppressed. The index reference to this same line eliminates all doubt of the correctness of the editor's surmise with its coy reference entry "poor who?" under Kinbote's name. The megalomania of the editor/commentator is also reflected in the fact that under Kinbote we find sixty-seven entries plus another twenty-one under Charles II. Against this total of eighty-eight, Shade, the author of the poem being annotated, rates only forty-six entries, almost all of which in fact feature Kinbote rather than the poet. Typical is one of the earliest index entries under Shade's name: "his [Shade's—DBJ] first brush with death as visualized by K, and his beginning the poem while K plays chess at the Student Club." All roads lead back to Kinbote who has compiled the index to support his claims.

Many of the index entries are amusing but essentially gratuitous asides having no bearing on the events of the narrative. Some, however, far from performing the referential function usual for index listings, serve as springboards for new information heavily stamped by the personality of the narrator. Boscobel, for example, a Zemblan toponym fleetingly mentioned in the Commentary, evokes an ecstatic index entry as the "site of the Royal Summerhouse, a beautiful, piny and duny spot..., soft hollows imbued with the writer's most amorous recollections; now (1959) a 'nudist colony'—whatever that is, ...." A town described in the text as "rowdy but colorful Kalixhaven where the sailors are" is identified in the Index as a seaport of "many happy memories." The Commentary's "little blue-jeaned fisherman" who stands in the river near K's mountain cabin rhapsodically evolves in the Index into "the little angler, a honey-skinned lad, naked except for a pair of torn dungarees, one trouser leg rolled up, frequently fed with nougats and nuts, but then school started or the weather changed, 609" (309). Another such indexual oddity may be found under *Garh*, a farmer's daughter who appears briefly in the text but to whose index citation is appended "Also a rosy-cheeked gooseboy found in a country lane, north of Troth, in 1936, only now distinctly recalled by the writer." Such samples of the idiosyncratic nature of the Index could easily be multiplied.

Cross references afford Nabokov the opportunity for a different kind of entertainment. Before Charles the Beloved is spirited away from Zembla, the crown jewels are hidden away. The revolutionaries import two Soviet specialists to ferret out their hiding place. Although the pair dismantles much of the palace in their search, they are unsuccessful, and Kinbote repeatedly mocks their vain efforts. This mockery is carried over into the Index. One of the early entries is that for *Andronnikov and Niagarin* who are identified as "two Soviet experts in quest of buried treasure . . . ; see Crown Jewels." Consulting *Crown Jewels*, one is launched on a seemingly pointless paper chase through a series of cross references: under *Crown Jewels* we find "see Hiding Place"; *Hiding Place* in turn directs us to *Potaynik* (an archaic Russian word for cache) which refers the reader to the entry "*Taynik*, Russ., secret place; see Crown Jewels" thus bringing us full circle. A further fillip is added in one of the entries under *Charles II* which reads "his Russian blood, and Crown Jewels (*q.v.* by all means)." Still further examination of the Index turns up the following curious entry: "*Kobaltana*, a once fashionable mountain resort near the ruins of some old barracks now a cold and desolate spot of difficult access and no importance but still remembered in military families and forest castles, not in the text." Why such an elaborate entry for a place not mentioned in the text? Nabokov gives the game away in an interview with Alfred Appel. Kobaltana is the *taynik* (SO 92).

The Index serves as a playing field for still another game involving cross references. Shade is much given to Word Golf which he plays with Kinbote. In his Commentary, Kinbote gives a few examples of his own (but not Shade's) Word Golf creations including "lass" to "male" in four stages. In the unlikely event that the reader thinks to consult the Index he will find the solution via a series of cross references: the entry *Lass* says "see *Mass*"; the *Mass* entry reads "*Mars, Mare*, see *Male*". The *Male* entry refers the reader to *Word Golf* which sends us back to *Lass*. The anagrammatic game Word Golf will prove to have an important role in our decipherment of *Pale Fire*.

Editor Kinbote significantly remarks in his Foreword that most of the poem's allusions to Zembla actually occur in the draft variants which Shade deleted from the fair copy but which the editor has incorporated in the commentary notes. The reader is well advised to regard some of the variant readings with caution. In the commentary to line 12 of the poem, a variant couplet is introduced: "Ah, I must not forget to say something / That my friend told me of a certain king" (74). The editor confesses that he is not at all sure he has properly deciphered "the disjointed, half-obliterated draft." The reader's suspicions are confirmed in the commentary note to line 550 in which Kinbote is moved to admit that the two earlier lines are "distorted and tainted by wistful thinking," but then assures us that this "is the *only* time . . . that I have tarried . . . on the brink of falsification" (227-28). Can Kinbote be believed? Here again it is the Index that supplies the answer and it is, not surprisingly, "no." In the Index we find a heading "Variants" which catalogues seventeen discarded variant readings. Although the admittedly forged couplet attached to line 12 is not included, the editor has apparently had a belated attack of conscience for three of the variant references are followed by the parenthesized admission "(K's contribution . . . )." Internal evidence suggests these, together with the previously conceded "contribution" constitute a complete list. Two of the seventeen entries are apparently on the margins of the fair copy (and hence, presumably, in Shade's handwriting) and three are Kinbote's "contributions." This leaves twelve variants—a figure which is given twice in the text as the number of index note cards containing variants (15 & 300). Thus only by close examination of the Index can the reader sort out the commentator's falsifications from Shade's own text. Since Kinbote's argument that the poem alludes to his own autobiography rests almost entirely on certain of the variants, the admission that these are fabricated utterly damns his case.

Nabokov has found yet another unusual usage for his Index. There are a small number of characters in the book who are very pointedly *not* listed in the Index. Among these are Professors H. and C., Kinbote's colleagues at Wordsmith, who, much against his will, have been belatedly designated co-editors of Shade's poem. Rather than simply omitting them from the Index, the editor makes his wrath more explicit. Among the index references under *Kinbote* we find "his contempt for Professor H. (not in Index)." Professor C. meets a similar reproof in the same listing with "he [Kinbote-DBJ] and S shaking with mirth over tidbits in a college textbook by Professor C. (not in the Index)."

A much more important use of the "not in the Index" ploy is in connection with a young English instructor at Wordsmith to whom Kinbote assigns the euphonious name Gerald Emerald (24). Emerald is, appropriately enough, given to wearing green, a fact alluded to in three of his five scenes in the book: "a young instructor in a green velvet jacket" (24); ". . . pup in a cheap green jacket" (268); and "the man in green" (283). Emerald has earned Kinbote's animosity by rejecting his amorous advances and then subjecting his senior colleague to public ridicule. Following a party at which Kinbote demonstrates a few amusing Zemblan wrestling holds to the guests, he finds in his pocket an anonymous note saying "You have hal . . . . . s real bad, chum" (98). Kinbote attributes the note to "a certain youthful instructor of English" obviously meaning Emerald who is later accused (inaccurately, it seems) of having given the regicidal Gradus/Grey a ride to Kinbote's house (283-84). Emerald also figures in a key scene which takes place in the Common Room of the Faculty Club. A visitor has remarked the resemblance of Kinbote to Charles the Beloved. Emerald produces an old encyclopedia volume containing a picture of the ornately uniformed monarch and observes "Quite the fancy pansy. . . ." Kinbote rises to this bit of *lèse majesté* replying that Emerald is "a foul-minded pup in a cheap green jacket" (267-69). The sole overt reference to Emerald in the Index is under *Kinbote* where we find the entry "his participation in a Common Room discussion of his resemblance to the king, and his final rupture with E. (not in the Index)." There is, however, an earlier entry also under *Kinbote* (in reference to line 741 of the poem) that certainly appears to refer to Emerald: "his [Kinbote's-DBJ] loathing for a person who makes advances, and thus betrays a noble and naive heart, telling foul stories about his victim and pursuing him with brutal practical jokes." If the reader consults the commentary note to line 741 he will discover nothing ostensibly about Gerald Emerald, but rather an imagined account of a meeting between Gradus, the assassin, and his superior, one Izumrudov, a merry fellow "in a green velvet jacket" (255). Editor Kinbote, who is the author of a book on surnames, meticulously (and inaccurately) explains that Izumrudov's name is derived from that of "an Eskimo tribe sometimes seen paddling their umyaks on the *emerald* waters of our northern shore." Later in the same paragraph Kinbote refers to Izumrudov as "the *herald* of success."[27] Kinbote concludes his account of the meeting with the remark "the gay green vision withdrew—to resume his whoring no doubt. How one hates such men" (256). Thus the observant English reader is supplied with the name Gerald Emerald as well as the clue that both men wear green. It is only the Index, however, that allows the Russianless reader to confirm his suspicions that Emerald and Izumrudov are identical—at least in Kinbote's deranged mind. This confirmation comes in the above-cited index entry for line 741. The index entry ("his loathing for a young person... brutal practical jokes") clearly refers to the young English instructor Gerald Emerald, while the commentary passage to which it refers concerns only Izumrudov (255-56).

This interpenetration of the real Emerald and the imaginary Izumrudov can be properly understood and motivated only if we accept an interpretation of the novel based on the assumption that Kinbote is mad. Those who have slighted him in the "real" world of Wordsmith are reincarnated as villains in his fantasy world. Another example may be seen in the case of the Shadows, the regicidal revolutionary group who have their real counterpart (and probable basis) in the group of scholars who are attempting to retrieve Shade's manuscript from Kinbote for proper editing. Headed by Wordsmith Professors H. and C., this group is referred to by Kinbote as the Shadeans (14 & 18) i.e., Shadeans = Shadows. The Shadeans are after Kinbote just as the Shadows are after King Charles. These transubstantiations, while by far the most critical, are perhaps not the only such cases in the novel. There is at least a parallel between one Gordon Krummholz, a fourteen-year-old musical prodigy with whom the deposed king dallies in Geneva, and Assistant Professor of Music Misha Gordon, who turns up in some of the Wordsmith scenes. The foregoing are quite apart from several other typically Nabokovian doublets in the book. These include the Zemblan actor and royalist hero, Odon, and his traitorous half-brother Nodo, and the similarly paired and opposed Barons Mandevil, Radomir and Mirador, respectively. Sudarg of Bokay, "a mirror maker of genius" reflects Jakob Gradus. When the young king's tutor Mr. Campbell plays chess with his transposed French counterpart Monsieur Beauchamp, their game appropriately ends in a draw (127-27).

One of the major controversies surrounding *Pale Fire* centers on whether Kinbote and Shade (and Gradus) are separate, independent identities within the framework of the novel. On the surface of the matter the poem is written by Shade and all else by Kinbote. A number of critics, however, have confidently asserted that there is but one fictive narrative voice within the novel.[28] This implies that Shade and Kinbote are not separate characters but that one is the fictional creation of the other. Andrew Field says flatly that "the primary author . . . must be John Shade" (302). His argument is based on the assertion that the poem and the Commentary (which have very little patent connection with each other) share a common theme—death. Further, it is argued that the artist Shade can create an insane character but that the insane Kinbote, while no less an artist, cannot create a Shade, given his particular type of insanity (317). Page Stegner, who argues that Shade and Grey/Gradus are creator and character, tentatively concludes that "the entire story including the poem is a fabrication of the artist-madman Kinbote . . ." (130). Although not made explicit, it appears that Stegner's opting for Kinbote's primacy derives from the assumption that Shade and Grey/Gradus integrade, while Kinbote alone retains his fictional integrity. Ergo, Kinbote is the author. Field rejects Stegner's reasoning, remarking that "positing Kinbote as prime author (in addition to the fact that it contradicts all the many secret notes left throughout the novel) is . . . just as confusing as the apparently obvious idea that Kinbote and Shade are quite separate" (318). Unfortunately Field does not indicate "the many secret notes" that prove Shade's primacy. Both interpretations yield interesting insights and, if nothing else, testify to the ingenuity of Nabokov's most elaborate Chinese box puzzle. Notwithstanding their diversity, these views concur in one respect. Much of their speculation about the separateness and/or identity of the three protagonists and the closely related issue of narrative voice is based on psychological assessments of character, and other such extra-textual information.

Nabokov has often linked his creative process to games and game-like activities such as the composition of chess problems. At their most abstract level games are artificial constructs whose play is governed by rules which are internal to the game (and indeed are the game) and which have no necessary connection with the external world. They are hermetic worlds. An examination of Nabokov's fiction shows that his novelistic games and puzzles are rule-governed. In a conversation with Robbe-Grillet, Nabokov described the composition of *Lolita* as "being akin to the composition of a chess problem in which certain rules must be followed.[29] Corollary to this is that the information necessary to solve such problems be found in the text. The above-mentioned identification of Izumrudov with Gerald Emerald through the semi-anagrammatic encoding of the latter's name in the text serves as one example. *Ada* provides a particularly good example in the scene where Demon confronts Van and orders the incestuous couple to part. As the stunned Van descends the stairs, a riddle floats through his mind: "My first is a vehicle that twists dead daisies around its spokes; my second is Oldmanhattan slang for 'money'; and my whole makes a hole" (444). Van returns to his apartment, takes his pistol out and "introduces one cartridge into the magazine." "Cart" is the answer to the first part and "ridge" to the second. But the reader cannot be expected to know that "ridge" actually is an old Manhattan (Dutch) word for money. If we reread the preceding page, however, *before* the riddle is posed, we find Demon saying, "I cannot disinherit you: Aqua left you enough 'ridge' and real estate to annul the conventional punishment." Again the solution is in the text.[30] *Ada* also provides a much more crucial example: the information necessary for determining Van and Ada's common parentage is likewise encoded in the text. All this suggests that the answer to our question about the identity of *Pale Fire*'s narrator should be sought within the text and that evidence based on "character" and/or external sources should be regarded with extreme caution.

Both the poem and the Commentary provide evidence suggesting (contrary to the critical views expressed above) that Shade and Kinbote are distinct characters. Each possesses knowledge and abilities not available to the other. Kinbote, but not Shade, knows Russian (268) and uses it as the basis of a number of bilingual puns in his Commentary. Kinbote decides the optimal form of suicide is a jump from a plane with "your packed parachute shuffled off, cast off, shrugged off—farewell, *shootka* (little chute)!" (221). *Shootka* in addition to being a mock-Russian diminutive of "chute" (fall) is, quite coincidentally, the Russian word for "joke". A similar sort of pun is found in the account of Charles the Beloved's escape from Zembla in which he mentions the village shops where one "could buy worms, gingerbread and *zhiletka* blades" (99). The play here is based on the English "Gillette" versus the Russian meaning of "vest." Neither of these puns is particularly funny (as might be expected from the humorless Kinbote) but both demonstrate his knowledge of Russian. A more effective Russian-based pun occurs in Kinbote's rendition of the New Wye landscape with its three conjoined lakes: Omega, Ozero, and Zero. The names are supposedly speciously derived by the early settlers from native Indian words. This is plausible only if the Indians or the settlers were Russian since *ozero* is the

Russian word for "lake" (92). The *korona-vorona-korova* / crown-crow-cow correlation (260) adduced by Kinbote is also relevant here as are the many Zemblan words and phrases with their mixed Slavic-Germanic base. Shade, on the other hand, is credited with knowing Latin, German, and French, but in neither Commentary nor poem is there anything that leads us to believe that he knows Russian.

A further bit of evidence of the same sort, but less trustworthy because more easily faked, is Shade's knowledge of natural history contrasted with Kinbote's blunders in this area. Kinbote's inept exegesis on Shade's reference to the "Toothwort White," is a case in point (183-84). Also germane is Kinbote's limited prowess as a poet. As we noted above, Kinbote grudgingly concedes that certain variant verses are his own creations. Examination of Kinbote's contributions amply bears out his assertion that notwithstanding his own remarkable gift of literary mimicry he cannot write poetry. As he ruefully remarks, one of his contributed couplets does "not even scan properly" (228).

There is also negative evidence. The Index which resolves a considerable number of problems and which, we shall subsequently see, holds the answer to one of the major puzzles of the novel, contains nothing to support the assumption that Shade, Kinbote, and Gradus are less than separate identities. In spite of the widespread view that only one of the three protagonists is "real," there is no solid evidence to support this idea and much to refute it.[31]

There is at least one area of agreement among all critics of the novel: Kinbote certainly is mad and certainly is not Charles II of Zembla. It is not by chance that he is Charles the Second since he is a projection of Charles the First, i.e., Charles Kinbote. Note that the rather extensive genealogy of the Zemblan royal family does not contain any Charles I. If we accept the fact the narrator is not (as he thinks) Charles II, why should we believe his assertion that he is Charles Kinbote? We probably assume this because the Wordsmith College setting is (within the context of the novel) apparently real (as is the poem) and people in that community address the narrator as Kinbote. In other words, there appears to be third party evidence. Reflection shows, however, that this evidence is no more reliable than that pertaining to the scenes set in Zembla, for in both cases Kinbote is the sole source of information. Given this, we have as much reason to be suspicious of Kinbote's identity as Kinbote as we do of Kinbote as Charles the Beloved. If Kinbote is not Kinbote, who is he? Here once again it is the Index, used as a key to the Commentary, that provides the answer. Among the odder entries, we find:

Botkin, V., American scholar of Russian descent, 894; kingbot, maggot of extinct fly that once bred in mammoths and is thought to have hastened their phylogenetic end, 247;

bottekin-maker, 71; *bot*, plop, and *botelïy*, big-bellied (Russ.); botkin or bodkin, a Danish stiletto.

The entry is peculiar on a number of grounds. For one, Botkin has no role in the narrative and is mentioned only once, that *en passant*. For another, V. Botkin does not figure in any of the commentary notes cited in the index entry under his own name. Consulting the commentary to line 894, we find an account of the following discussion in the Wordsmith Faculty Club lounge (264-69).

> Professor Pardon now spoke to me: "I was under the impression that you were born in Russia, and that your name was a kind of anagram of Botkin or Botkine?" Kinbote: "you are confusing me with some refugee from Nova Zembla" [sarcastically stressing the "Nova"]. "Didn't you tell me, Charles, that *kinbote* means regicide in your language?" asked my dear Shade. "Yes, a king's destroyer," I said (longing to explain that a king who sinks his identity in the mirror of exile is in a sense just that). Shade [addressing the German visitor]: "Professor Kinbote is the author of a remarkable book on surnames" (267).

Thus the initial reference under *Botkin* in the Index directs the reader not to a passage about Botkin, but to Kinbote whose name is asserted to be an anagram of Botkin(e), a suggestion that Kinbote, an expert on names, rejects quite firmly. The reader, however, may well remember a number of similar anagrammatically transposed names in Kinbote's Zemblan commentaries: Campbell/Beauchamp, Radomir/Mirador, Odon/Nodo, etc. Kinbote also bristles at the suggestion that he is Russian, that is, a *Nova* Zemblan refugee, whereas he is actually from Zembla, a distinct country with its own tongue.

The second index entry under V. *Botkin*, "king-bot, maggot of extinct fly...," refers to a commentary note recounting a public outburst by Sybil Shade in which she alludes to Kinbote as an "elephantine tick; a king-sized botfly; a macaco worm; the parasite of a genius" (171-72).[32] Here again, the cited passage concerns not Botkin (under whose name the reference is listed) but Kinbote. It is worth noting that of the various terms of abuse he suffers, Kinbote seizes upon "king-bot" (rather than "tick" or "macaco worm") as the head word for his informative index entry. Equally instructive is that Sybil's "*king*-sized *bot*fly" can anagrammatically refer equally well to either Kinbote or Botkin. Thus both of the two initial index entries under V. *Botkin* refer the reader to passages not about Botkin but about Kinbote, and both specifically point out the anagrammatic relationship of the two names.

The remaining items under V. *Botkin* seem to have even less connection with the American scholar of Russian descent. Two of them concern possible etymologies of the name. In a discussion of family names (arising from that of Shade's mother's maiden name), Kinbote remarks *à propos de rien* that some names "derive from professions such as Rymer, Scrivener, Limner (one who illuminates parchments), Botkin (one who makes bottekins, fancy footwear) and thousands of others" (100). Significantly, the name Botkin, which is drawn from a very different lexical layer, is casually dropped in among those of a literary nature, and the etymology given is wrong. There is no connection between the name Botkin and bottekins, nor does Botkin seem to be attested as an English name— although (with a different etymology) it is common in Russian. The Danish "stiletto" reference is equally otiose since it lacks any page reference to the Commentary where, however, we find Kinbote noting the insistence of some purists that in suicides "a gentleman should use a brace of pistols, . . . or a bare botkin (note the correct spelling)" (220). Finally, Kinbote gratuitously offers the reader the two Russian words *bot* "plop" and *botelïy* "big bellied" presumably as etymological cognates to Botkin's name.[33] These lack page references to the Commentary because they never occur there.

Except for Sybil's abusive outburst, all of the text passages relating to the *"bot"* theme have parenthetic comments. Nabokov is very fond of inserting important information in his novels in the form of parenthetical asides.[34] One might reasonably assume that the parentheses together with the index listing of all of the above, seemingly irrelevant, items are intended to direct the reader's attention to the *"bot"* theme, and presumably to V. Botkin himself even though none of the pages cited under his index listing involve his presence.

Still more curious is that the only actual reference to Professor Botkin in the narrative is not cited in his own index entry. Kinbote keeps a pocket notebook in which he, Boswell-like, has jotted down some of Shade's random remarks. One of these notebook entries which Kinbote incorporates in his Commentary reads, "Speaking of the Head of the bloated Russian Department, Professor Pnin, a regular martinet in regard to his underlings (happily, Prof. Botkin, who taught in another department, was not subordinated to that grotesque 'perfectionist'): How odd that Russian intellectuals should lack all sense of humor when they have such marvelous humorists as Gogol, Dostoevski, . . ." (155). The reader's attention is directed to the parenthesis.

This mysteriously unindexed passage suggests that there is indeed a real Professor Botkin on campus. Inasmuch as the V. Botkin index references actually concern Kinbote and two of them point out the Kinbote/Botkin(e) anagram, it seems certain that Kinbote is Botkin. If this assumption is true (and the evidence is quite persuasive), it raises still another question. Who is the shadowy V. Botkin? Is Botkin perhaps a Wordsmith faculty member who is writing a novel about the entirely fictional characters Kinbote, Shade, and Gradus? The idea would be attractive were it not that Botkin and

Kinbote are almost certainly the same person. More plausible is that Shade, his poem, and his killer are all real, as is V. Botkin, a drab Wordsmith faculty member, who creates a new identity for himself as the exotic Zemblan exile, King Charles the Beloved, who is passing himself off as Charles Kinbote. Botkin's complex delusion is humored by Shade and tolerated by others. We recall here the party at Professor H.'s where Botkin/Kinbote accidentally overhears Shade's response to an unheard comment: "That is the wrong word," he said. "One should not apply it to a person who deliberately peels off a drab and unhappy past and replaces it with a brilliant invention" (238). Botkin/Kinbote obtusely fails to realize that he is the topic of conversation. The reader naturally assumes that Shade's comment refers to Kinbote's royal delusion, but it is equally probably that it refers to Botkin's delusion that he is Kinbote. Botkin has completely submerged his own personality (and name) in his gaudy guise as Kinbote, the exiled incognito king. He acts and writes from within his delusional persona. The pattern is not an uncommon one in Nabokov's work and is found in both *The Eye* and *Look at the Harlequins!*.

Our assumption that mad Botkin, the "American scholar of Russian descent," is the narrator finds support in an otherwise troubling passage at the end of his commentary. "Kinbote," alone in his mountain cabin, harks back to his fanciful Zemblan childhood and quotes for the reader an adage from his old nurse "God makes hungry, the Devil thirsty." He then continues, "Well, folks, I guess many in this fine hall are as hungry and thirsty as me, and I'd better stop, folks, right here" (300). This abrupt and unique change of stylistic register is puzzling especially in that "Kinbote" immediately lapses back into his arch, slightly Baroque, "imperial" speech style. It is difficult to believe that the Zemblan "Kinbote" (ostensibly a newcomer to our shores) has this sort of substandard colloquial American English at his disposal. His mask has slipped and the face of the American scholar Botkin appears momentarily.

It is symptomatic of Botkin's schizophrenia that his three identities are anagrammatically related, albeit imperfectly so: King Charles the Beloved contains the name Kinbote which in turn includes Botkin(e). In a sense, the three faces of the novel's narrator grow out of the anagram game of Word Golf. Word Golf may make yet another contribution to *Pale Fire*.[35] Could it not be that Botkin's three personalities, their roles, and their interrelations are parallel to "Kinbote's prize Word Golf offering: the bilingual twin series CROWN-CROW-COW and their Russian equivalents KORONA-VORONA-KOROVA—an "artistic correlation" flaunting astronomic odds (260). The association of CROWN (KORONA) and King Charles immediately presents itself. But what of CROW (VORONA) and COW (KOROVA) with Kinbote and Botkin? Here we are on less firm ground but not without resource. Kinbote, like Shade, is much interested in birds as attested by his remarks in the opening lines of his Commentary and by the bird motif that runs throughout the book. Of further note is that the Russian word VORONA "crow" enters into a number of set phrases such as *belaia vorona* "white crow," i.e., *rara avis*, and *vorona v pavlinnykh per'iakh* "crow in peacock's feathers." Such phrases seem peculiarly apt in describing the garrulous and gaudy Kinbote. It is the drab Botkin(e) who evokes, more ambiguously, the COW (KOROVA). Here we can only point to the bovine echoes of his name: kine, the historic plural of "cow," and the *bot*fly that infests cattle. Each of the three faces of Botkin is echoed in the Word Golf series just as his three names are anagrammatic echoes of each other. The bilingualism of the anagrammatic series mimicks the dual ethnic identity of the "American scholar of Russian descent."

Within the world of *Pale Fire*, V. Botkin is the source from which all else flows. It is he who creates his two anagrammatic personae and their worlds and who, in his guise as Kinbote, is the protagonist, the editor, and the narrator. We are not yet, however, at the end of our paper chase. Nabokov has a penchant for incorporating himself into his novels, sometimes by description, sometimes by initials, and often by anagrams such as Vivian Darkbloom, Baron Klim Avidov, Blavdak Vinomori, or Adam von Librikov. The name Botkin contains the N, B, O, K of Nabokov. Also note that Botkin is the sole person in the Index to be listed with an initial—an initial that could be either the V of Vladimir or the final V of Nabokov. In the world of anagrams, V. Botkin, the narrator, stands closer to Nabokov than do his creations Charles Kinbote or Charles the Beloved. This alphabetic affinity is appropriate to Nabokov's author persona, the character to whom [in his guise as Kinbote] he entrusts his cherished KORONA-VORONA-KOROVA / CROWN-CROW/-COW anagram. This bilingual sequence occurs not in a Word Golf game where one might expect it but in a discussion of fatidic misprints. In his poem Shade recounts his search for evidence of immortality. The poet has earlier experienced a momentary death during which he saw "a tall white fountain" (59). Shade later reads an account of a woman brought back from death who reports the identical vision (61). Hope of Life Eternal soars, but the corroborating evidence proves to be based on a misprint: mountain not fountain. It is this experience that leads the poet to his well-known lines: "Yes! It sufficed that I in life should find / Some kind of link and bobolink, some kind / Of correlated pattern in the game, / Plexed artistry, and something of the same / Pleasure in it as they who played it found" (63). Shade has been denied an answer to his question but in compensation has been given the raw material of his art. It is in the context of Shade's misprint that Kinbote adduces his KORONA-VORONA-KOROVA / CROWN-CROW-COW correlation.[36] Botkin, like Shade, has been given the stuff of art from which he creates his fantasy: The drab, bovine Botkin imagines himself the flamboyant "white crow" Kinbote, who believes himself the dethroned King Charles of Zembla. But who gives him the letters to play with? It is the name of author Nabokov that supplies most of the letters of V. Botkin's name and flickers in and out of the KORONA-VORONA-KOROVA sequence.[37] Here we may be verging into the madness of Baconian acrostics that Nabokov mocks in *Bend Sinister*, but Nabokov's writings (including *Bend Sinister*) testify to his frequent use of such devices.

The Nabokovian KORONA-VORONA-KOROVA with its English counterpart CROWN-CROW-COW, described by Kinbote in his own index listing as "a lexical and linguistic miracle" (309), is Nabokov's gift to Botkin to arrange as he will. There is some reason to think that Botkin is vaguely aware of his status as author-persona. In response to a self-posed question about his future plans, Botkin, again setting aside his mask as "Kinbote" says: "I may assume other disguises, other forms, but I shall try to exist. I may turn up yet, on another campus as an old, happy, healthy, heterosexual Russian, a writer in exile, sans fame, sans audience, sans anything but his art" (301). Although Kinbote (and with him, Charles II) is to die by his own hand (SO 74), Nabokov's anagrammatic persona may undertake new roles. V. Botkin awaits new lexical playing fields and new words to play with.

Anagrams play a vital role in our understanding of the labyrinth of *Pale Fire* and show once again that such word games are one of the ways in which Nabokov's fictional worlds relate to each other. The failure of the characters to recognize their literal kinship with each other is but a dimension of their failure to find the name of their creator who orchestrates the letter play that makes up their worlds. Each anagrammatic letter transposition effects a reordering of the novel's fictional cosmos and betrays the presence of the master anagrammatist. *Ada* uses its anagrams largely within the limited context of the Scrabble game but it is no accident that the names of Van (and Ada) are contained within that of Baron Klim Avidov, the anagrammatic presenter of the Scrabble set. *Pale Fire* employs anagrams in a much more far-reaching way to spell out and link the multiple inner worlds of the novel to each other and to join them to that of spelling master Nabokov.

## NOTES

### Section Two

1. A typological survey of Nabokov's uses of alphabetic symbols may be found in my "Nabokov as a Man-of-Letters: The Alphabetic Motif in his Work," *Modern Fiction Studies*, 25, 3, pp. 397-412.

2. For a detailed treatment, see my "A Guide to Vladimir Nabokov's *Putevoditel' po Berlinu*," *Slavic and East European Journal*, 23, 3, pp. 353-61.

3. See, for example, the September 1965 film interview conducted by Robert Hughes for the Television 13 Educational Program in New York. It is available under the title "Interview: The Novel (Vladimir Nabokov)." The comments on games do not appear in the printed version in *Strong Opinions*, pp. 51-61.

4. A section of *Speak, Memory* is devoted to his pastime as a composer of chess problems (288-93) and some of his published problems have been collected in *Poems and Problems*. Nabokov also records that among various sources of income in Berlin, his favorite was the composition of the first Russian crossword puzzles for the émigré newspaper *Rul'* (283). *Krestoslovitsy*, the name proposed by Nabokov for his creations, did not become the standard term, although *krossvordy* continue to be enjoyed by émigrés and Soviets alike.

5. "*Flavita*" (an anagram of the Russian word *alfavit* "alphabet") is, according to memoirist Van Veen, an old Russian game once again popular under the name "Scrabble." Nabokov's *Flavita* differs from the modern Russian edition of "Scrabble" only in minor details. There are slightly more letters, and the colors of the playing board squares differ. Scoring, however, is identical, and Ada's record coup of 383 points for the Russian word TORFYaNUYu (top left of board) works out perfectly (227).

6. Van records that "in a match at Chose he defeated Minsk-born Pat Rishin (champion of Underhill and Wilson, N.C.)" (224). The allusion is evidently to "patrician" Edmund Wilson whose Russian competence is obliquely referred to on the following page where in a discussion of Russian dictionaries reference is made of "a small but chippy Edmundson." Nabokov's notes to the Penguin edition of *Ada* explicate a part of the allusion but do not identify Nabokov's old friend and adversary. A similar allusion to Wilson is found in *Speak, Memory* in a scene describing the agonized expression on the face of "the world famous grandmaster Wilhelm Edmundson when, during a simultaneous display in a Minsk cafe, he lost his rook, by an absurd oversight, to the local amateur and *pediatrician* [my italics-DBJ] Dr. Schach, who eventually won" (132). The repeated "Minsk," which appears to be alphabetically drawn from Edmund K. Wilson, is another allusion to Wilson's command of Russian. Minsk is the capital of an area where Byelorussian, a language similar to but different from standard Russian, is spoken. Many Russians consider Byelorussian to be simply a debased form of Russian. The Penguin *Ada* identifies "Underhill" as a back translation of the name "Podgoretz" (*pod* 'under' and *goretz* 'hill'). This is presumably a reference to the literary critic Norman Podhoretz.

7. For other occurrences of the "divan motif", see pp. 41, 115-22, 209, 225, and 373.

8. For a survey of the role of orchids in *Ada*, see chapter V, "Ada or Orchids," in Bobbie Ann Mason, *Nabokov's Garden: A Guide to Ada* (Ann Arbor, 1974), pp. 72-92.

9. A similar flower trope is used by mad Aqua who tells her doctor "I know you want to examine my pudendron, the Hairy Alpine rose in *her* album . . ." (25).

10. Nabokov also found occasion to use this word (current in XVIIth - XVIIIth century-English) in *Lolita*. Speaking of his first wife, Humbert says, "Although I told myself I was looking merely for a soothing presence, a glorified *pot-au-feu*, an animated merkin, what really attracted me to Valeria was the imitation she gave of a little girl" (27).

11. Although the description is treated by memoirist Van Veen as a part of their conversation, it is suggested by the fictitious editor Ronald Oranger that it may have an "epistolary source"—specifically in Lucette's earlier love letter to Van. See pp. 366 and 374.

12. The "infernal fires" is a bilingual allusion to Ada since the Russian adjectival derivative of her name means 'infernal.' Another such bilingual pun is found in Ada's favorite expletive 'Pah!' (pp. 38, 196, 247, and 526) which is mimicked by Lucette during her meeting with Van. *Pah* is a Nabokovian transliteration of the Russian word for "groin."

13. Much of the dialogue is in Russian although Van reproduces it in English (380). In Russian "cheekbone" is *skula* from which the transition to *skeletki* "little skeletons" is more apparent.

14. Van's glans comes in for further attention at the end of the scene. See p. 387.

15. Both *krest* "cross" and its diminutive *krestik* are used throughout the scene. The former designates, as Van says, "the four embers of a vixen's cross." The diminutive form seems to refer only to the lower ember. *Lolita* affords another imperfect anagrammatic permutation on the KRESTIK theme via the German *Kitzler* "clitoris." Humbert tracks Quilty and Lo through motel registers via their encrypted clues. Humbert scoffs at their transparency saying ". . . any good Freudian, with a German name and some interest in religious prostitution, should recognize at a glance [!-DBJ], the implication of Dr. Kitzler, Eryx, Miss" (252). As Carl Proffer notes in his *Keys to Lolita* (Bloomington, 1968) not only does Kitzler mean "clitoris," but Mt. Eryx in Sicily was the site of a temple to Venus in which the priestesses were prostitutes (14).

16. *Pour cogner une fraise* (pseudo-French for "to coin a phrase") is, as the notes to the Penguin *Ada* inform us, another bilingual pun. The French meaning would be "to thump a strawberry—specifically, redhaired Lucette. The English "fraise" is in reference to Ada's nether ruff.

17. Although the association of the EMB sequence with Lucette is clear, its meaning is not. It may be relevant that in Nabokov's alphabetic chromesthesia, M and B are both shades of red, one of Lucette's motif colors (SM 35). See, however, Nabokov's response to an interviewer's question about incest as a moral theme in *Ada*: "Actually, I don't give a damn for incest one way or another. I merely like the 'bl' sound in siblings, bloom, blue, bliss, sable." *Strong Opinions*, pp. 122-23.

18. Lowden is a blend of Robert Lowell and W.H. Auden whose paraphrases of Russian poets were a source of irritation to Nabokov. The *malheureux* ('unfortunate') author is André Malraux while the name Pompier is drawn from the French word for 'fireman' which here, however, has the meaning 'conventional' or 'hack.' Malraux's *La Condition Humaine* is one of Nabokov's *bêtes noires*. For a detailed critique, see *The Nabokov-Wilson Letters*, ed. Simon Karlinsky (New York, 1979), pp. 175-78.

19. In a later conversation with Van, Ada says of Lucette ". . . we shan't be afraid of her witnessing our *ébats* (pronouncing on purpose, with triumphant hooliganism, for which my prose, too, is praised, the first vowel *à la Russe*" (395). The recommended pronunciation yields the fundamental Russian obscenity *yebat'*.

20. Eric Partridge, *A Dictionary of Slang and Unconventional English* (New York, 1967).

21. The "lip motif" is developed more fully in I-17 which is devoted to Van and Ada's "kissing phase." This chapter also marks the beginning of a dictionary motif that is reintroduced at the start of the Scrabble chapter (I-36).

22. Nabokov used this same anagrammatic device to insert his name in a similar sexual word-game scene, albeit on a much more modest scale, in *Transparent Things*. Editor Hugh Person is correcting the galley proofs of Mr. R's new novel. The scene being checked involves a mother and daughter caressing their lover on a perilous mountain ledge. Proofreader Hugh is puzzled by certain things in the text: "—what did 'rimiform' suggest and how did a 'balanic plum' look." The *OED* informs us that the former means "Having a longitudinal furrow, slitted," while the latter is defined by *Webster's III* as "of or relating to the glans of the penis or

of the clitoris." It derives from the Greek *balanites* 'acorn-shaped.' One Adam von Librikov (Vladimir Nabokov) also graces the scene in question (74-75).

23. My discussion of the word games in the two chapters (I-36 & II-5) is largely restricted to the lexical sexual motif introduced through the Scrabble game. There are numerous other areas of allusion and word play that I have touched upon lightly or not at all. In my analysis of Nabokov's logograph of sexual anatomical terms, I have treated the various word plays as individual items linked only by their sexual meaning. I should like to suggest one further possibility. It may be that many of the key terms are related to each other in a formal as well as a semantic sense. Compare the stunning logograph in *Pale Fire* where the Russian Word Golf series KORONA "crown," KOROVA "cow" and VORONA "crow" is formally parallel to the English series CROWN, CROW, COW whose members, however, are interrelated by single letter deletion rather than single letter substitution as in the Russian (260). There appears to be something remotely similar in the relationship of certain key terms in *Ada's* Scrabble logograph: KREST(IK) — SEKEL' — KLITOR, and CROSS(LET) — CREST— CLITORIS. The parallel is tantalizing but imperfect in that the members of each series are not related to each other in elegantly specifiable ways as in the *Pale Fire* example. Could there be missing links in the text?

24. *Eugene Onegin: A Novel in Verse by Alexander Pushkin*, translated from the Russian with a commentary by Vladimir Nabokov (New York, 1964). Although Nabokov's *Onegin* was published two years after the appearance of *Pale Fire*, it was substantially complete in 1957 (I, xii-xiii). Pushkin's masterpiece and Nabokov's translation-interpretation of it figure in other Nabokov novels. For a discussion of the role of *Onegin* in *Ada*, see Section Four below.

25. This reading was first advanced by Mary McCarthy in her essay "Vladimir Nabokov's Pale Fire," *Encounter*, 19 (October 1962), pp. 71-89. An equally astute reading is provided by Nina Berberova, "The Mechanics of *Pale Fire*," in *TriQuarterly*, 17 (1970), pp. 147-159.

26. Quite apart from the index itself, there is a minor index motif within the poem. In the poetic description of the room of Shade's late aunt Maud, we read of a "... verse book open at the Index (Moon, Moonrise, Moor, Moral), ..." (36).

27. My underscoring of "herald" and "emerald." The "herald/Gerald" homophony involves Russian-English word play. Due to certain peculiarities of various systems of transliterating Russian and English letters, it is possible to transliterate the name Gerald into Cyrillic and then, using a different set of correspondences, to convert it back to English spelling as Herald. The reader who knows Russian is spared the bit of detective work outlined in the text above by his awareness that the name Izumrudov is derived from *izumrud*, the Russian word meaning emerald.

28. Among the critics who have debated this question, we mention the following: Page Stegner, *Escape into Aesthetics: The Art of Vladimir Nabokov* (New York, 1966); Andrew Field, *Nabokov: His Life in Art* (Boston, 1967); Julia Bader, *Crystal Land: Artifice in Nabokov's English Novels* (Berkeley, 1972); and Carol T. Williams, " 'Web of Sense': *Pale Fire* in the Nabokov Canon," *Critique*, 6, 3 (Winter 1963), 28-45.

29. J.-F. Bergery, "Tandis que *Lolita* Fait le Tour du Monde l'Entomologiste Nabokov, l'Agronome Robbe-Grillet Échangent Leurs Pions sur l'Echiquier Littéraire," *Art: Lettres, Spectacles*, 746 (October 28 - November 3, 1959), p. 4. Also cited by Andrew Field in *Nabokov: His Life in Art*, p. 324.

30. Nabokov also repeats his second clue in a much simpler form: "My second is also the meeting place of two steep slopes." This further attests the author's punctiliousness in adhering to the rules of the game.

31. Mary McCarthy, certainly one of the most astute readers of the novel, finds no reason to doubt the equal fictional reality of Shade and Kinbote. Her analysis of the novel in the above-cited *Commentary* essay was the first to argue the now generally accepted view that "Kinbote" is acutally V. Botkin. Neither Miss McCarthy nor her successors have, however, provided any systematic demonstration of the accuracy of this surmise.

32. The index note's description of the king-bot as having bred in mammoths and having hastened their phylogenetic end is, of course, equally apt as an account of the relationship between the parasite Kinbote and the poet Shade who dies as a result of the infestation.

33. Both of these rare words are dialect terms not found in dictionaries of standard Russian, but only in Nabokov's beloved *Dal'*, a Russian dictionary noted for its inclusion of folk terms and adages.

34. Two examples will suffice. In *The Defense*, the covertly unfolding pattern of duplicated "moves" in Luzhin's life, is revealed in the parenthetical insert (country house...town... school...aunt), p. 214. In *Ada*, the secrets of Van's birth and Ada's conception are both signaled by the casually inserted phrase *c'est bien le cas de la dire* in conjunction with the key words "Special Delivery" (8) and "conceived...the brilliant idea..." (26).

35. Both Mary McCarthy in her *Encounter* essay and R.H.W. Dillard (*The Hollins Critic*, 3, 3, [June 1966]), 1-12) have drawn upon Word Golf in their explication of the novel, albeit in a much less specific sense than we shall propose. For commentary on their views as well as those of Andrew Field, see his *Nabokov: His Life in Art*, pp. 312-15.

36. Although Botkin is our conjectured (fictive) source for the anagram, it is especially appropriate that Kinbote, the deposed King, be the ostensible source since the anagrammatic series stems from a case of *lèse-majesté*. A newspaper story of the coronation of a Russian tsar reported that a VORONA (crow) rather than a KORONA (crown) had been set on the ruler's head. The misprint was "corrected" on the next day to KOROVA (cow) (260).

37. The "b" of Nabokov is missing from the Russian series while "r" (a transliteration of the Russian letter "р") is absent from NABOKOV. If, however, the Russian "р" is turned upside down, it becomes the Engish "b" of Nabokov. Another even more far-fetched possibility (but one found in *Transparent Things*) is to read the medial English "R" in reverse, i.e., yielding the Russian letter "Я" meaning "I", the "I" of author Nabokov.

# SECTION THREE

# NABOKOV AS LITERARY CHESS PROBLEMIST

*Speak, Memory* is perhaps the only *literary* autobiography to include a chess problem composed by the author. Nabokov published his first chess problem three years before his first novel[1] and was still active in problem composition during the last decade of his life when the London publication of two of his problems reportedly gave him more pleasure than the appearance of his first poems in St. Petersburg over fifty years earlier (*SO* 110). Nabokov emphasizes the autobiographic importance of this elegant, but ideally sterile, art form in a curious way. The twenty years of European exile during which all of the Russian novels were written are covered in one chapter of the autobiography, the next to the last. In substance, the chapter has but two topics: a curiously impersonal discussion of the émigré literary scene and an intensely personal discussion of chess problem composition. The organizing motif of the chapter is the famous figure of the tripartite spiral with its initial "thetic" arc, the opposing "antithetic" arc, and the "synthetic" arc that partially embraces its origins and forms a new "thetic" segment. The "thetic" part of Nabokov's life corresponds to the twenty Russian years, and the "antithetic" to the twenty-one years in European exile which appropriately concludes with Nabokov's departure for America, the beginning of the third, the "synthetic" arc. This elaborate metaphor is again caught up in Nabokov's description of the chess problem that ends the chapter. (293)

The problem, one that Nabokov feels to be his best, is designed for the ultrasophisticated solver. The solution is, according to its composer, rather simple and might be found quickly by a novice. This is the "thetic" solution. The more sophisticated solver, beguiled by the presence of a tempting and fashionable theme, will work his way through several entertaining but fruitless lines of play: the "antithetic" arc. The by now ultrasophisticated solver will finally arrive at the simple key move which should afford him "a synthesis of poignant artistic delight" (291-2). Nabokov completes the composition of this problem (after two or three months of effort) on the day that he finally secures (by bribery) the family's French exit visa. Hitler was already in the Low Countries. Nabokov has completed the "antithetic" phase of his existence and is ready to embark on the synthetic phase with his arrival in America. The chess problem with its triadic mode of resolution precisely emblematizes the composer's career at the time of its composition.

Chess is also used as one of the patterning devices that reaches across chapter boundaries and unites the disparate details of a single theme: the death of Nabokov's father. As a boy of eleven or twelve, one of the many pleasures Nabokov shared with his father was the solving of chess problems (191). This is first mentioned in the context of the son's sudden concern when he learns that his father has challenged a right-wing newspaper editor to a duel. The duel is averted at the last minute and the autobiographer remarks that "several lines of play in a difficult chess composition were not blended yet on the board" (193). When the Crimea, the Nabokovs' first place of exile, is taken by the Bolsheviks, Nabokov's father, a former minister in the local (anti-Communist) government, eludes Bolshevik death squads by adopting the mimetic disguise of a doctor, although keeping his own name ("'simple and elegant,' as a chess annotator would have said of a corresponding move on the board") (245). As the Nabokovs leave the Crimea, their ship is under fire. As it zigzags out of the harbor, father and son sit playing chess with a set containing a headless knight and a poker chip for a rook (251). The lines of play in this chess composition attain their final blending only three years later when the father is shot while shielding a friend from a monarchist assassin in a Berlin auditorium. The king is dead. Checkmate.

The analogy of the chess problem was not far from the author's mind during the writing of *Speak, Memory*. Shortly after its publication in 1951, Nabokov told an interviewer: "What interested me is the thematic lines of my life that resemble fiction. The memoir became the meeting point of an impersonal art form and a very personal life story.... It is a literary approach to my own past.... With me, it is a kind of composition. I am a composer of chess problems."[2] This attitude is also reflected in one of the autobiography's few references to Nabokov's novels. Nabokov compares the difficulties of speaking of his late brother to "that twisted quest for *Sebastian Knight* (1940) with its gloriettes and self-mate combinations..." (257). *Sebastian Knight*, the story of a man's search for his half-brother, is shot through with chess allusions, so much so that Edmund Wilson thought (wrongly, according to the author) it might be a literary chess game.[3]

Almost all of Nabokov's novels make use of chess imagery. In the early *King, Queen, Knave*, Martha and her husband's nephew Franz conspire to kill the huband. At a Christmas party the adulterous couple moves about the parquet-square floor of the parlor: Franz crosses the room diagonally while Martha's movement combines the oblique and the straight. The movements are those of the Knight and the Queen, and the description of the scene quickly evolves into an elaborate chess analogy prefiguring their coordinated attack on the King. Nor is it by chance that Franz, the knave of the title, is the knight errant.[4] Real chess games also regularly occur in the novels. *Lolita*'s Humbert Humbert, who plays chess with his colleague Gaston, sees "the board as a square pool of limpid water with rare shells and strategems rosily visible upon the smooth tesselated bottom, which to my confused adversary was all ooze and squid-cloud" (235). Humbert's self-congratulations are premature for just after a mid-game telephone call telling him that Lo has again missed her music lesson, he loses his Queen to the pervert Gaston just as he will soon lose Lo to Quilty.[5]

A chess figure of great appeal to Nabokov is the *Solus Rex*. The name refers to a specialized class of chess problems in which the black King, the sole black piece on the board, is under attack. As in all ordinary chess problems, he is doomed to be checkmated in a few moves. The question is not "whether" but "how long" and even this is preordained by the problem composer. The *Solus Rex* chess image has obvious relevance to the figure of the doomed Grandmaster Luzhin in *The Defense* and was actually used as the title of Nabokov's unfinished novel about an artist who believes himself to be the doomed ruler of a mythical country. In *Pale Fire*, Kinbote refers to the plight of King Charles prior to his escape from Zembla as "what a composer of chess problems might term a king-in-the-corner waiter of the *solus rex* type" (118-19). Further, the final index entry under *Charles II* (who signs his royal proclamations with a small black crown) is *"Solus Rex, 1000"*—a most peculiar reference since the poem has only 999 lines. It will also be recalled that Kinbote unsuccessfully urges "Solus Rex" upon Shade as the title of his poem (296). The figure occurs once again in *Pnin* where the flight of *Pale Fire*'s King Charles is faintly foreshadowed in a twin dream shared by Pnin and his ex-wife's son Victor Wind. Each dreams of a royal Pnin, a *Solus Rex*, in flight from revolutionaries awaiting a rescue vessel (86 & 109-110). Gerald Adamson, the John Shade-like figure in *Look at the Harlequins!* is also referred to, *en passant*, as *Solus Rex* (160).

The preceding examples of chess imagery in Nabokov's fiction are restricted to particular incidents or characters. Such examples, although effective, do not represent the main thrust of chess in Nabokov's writing. Nabokov groups literature and chess problem composition in a single chapter of his autobiography and he is quite explicit about the connection between the two themes. Following a discussion of the ecstatic agony of problem composition, he remarks that the real struggle in chess problems, as in novels, is not between Black and White (the characters) but between the composer and the solver (writer & reader) (290). The parallel is again emphasized in a comparison of chess problem composition to "the writing of one of those incredible novels where the author, in a fit of lucid madness, has set himself certain unique rules that he observes, certain nightmare obstacles that he surmounts, with the zest of a deity building a live world from the most unlikely ingredients . . ." (291). That the "incredible novels" include his own is affirmed in the author's previously cited response to a French interviewer's question about the genesis of *Lolita: Je sais que c'etait un certain problème que je voulais résoudre, je voulais trouver une solution économe et élégante, comme dans les problèmes d'échec ou il y a certaines règles qu'il faut suivre.* Following a discussion of *The Defense* he goes on to say that he is a composer of chess problems, something quite different from chess games, and affirms that he more or less consciously sees each of the novels as a literary chess game.[6]

Like many writers, Nabokov has drawn on the "life as a chess game" metaphor with its image of people as witless pawns being moved about in accord with the unfathomable schemes of divine players. Nabokov's most memorable use of this metaphor is in the poem "Pale Fire." In a scene we have previously discussed Shade has just learned that his presumed evidence of immortality is a misprint but that seeking the "correlated pattern" in life's game is the compensation of the artist—man's nearest approach to the gods: "It did not matter who they were. No sound, / No furtive light came from their involute / Abode, but there they were, aloof and mute, / Playing a game of worlds, promoting pawns / To ivory unicorns and ebon fauns;" (63). *The Defense,* Nabokov's major chess novel, is an account of a Grandmaster's unsuccessful attempt to decipher the intent of the chess gods and understand the pattern of his own existence. Strangely, it is not Grandmaster Luzhin who proves most attuned to patterns emanating from the involute abode of the gods, but Fyodor Godunov-Cherdyntsev, the young writer and chess problemist who is the hero of Nabokov's novel *The Gift.* Fyodor, the happiest of Nabokov's heroes, is successful both in divining the chess-like pattern of his life and in transmuting it into his art. This sense of the artist as an active intermediary between two worlds is a central feature of Nabokov's aesthetic cosmology, and chess is another of the playing fields used by the author to probe the nature of consciousness and the role of art and the artist.

## TEXT AND PRE-TEXT IN *THE DEFENSE*

*The Defense* (*Zashchita Luzhina*, 1930) is widely regarded as Nabokov's first mature novel and was well received in the émigré community even by those who had been repelled by the deliberate artificiality of his earlier *King, Queen, Knave.*[7] The novel seems to display a certain human warmth that is lacking in many of Nabokov's works but, upon closer inspection, this sense of humanity is somewhat illusory. None of the characters, apart from the inarticulate Luzhin and his wife, have any depth of personality, nor do most even have names. It is perhaps the helplessness of Grandmaster Luzhin both in everyday life and in his living chess game with insanity that makes him among the more sympathetic of Nabokov's heroes. Notwithstanding Luzhin's ineffectual charm, *The Defense* is one of Nabokov's most mechanistic works and its overt patterning is schematic. As we shall see, the patterning is at a deeper level than the novel's plot.

The story line of *The Defense* is a simple one. At its opening, Luzhin is a morose, solitary boy of ten spending his summer at the family country house near Petersburg. Summer is over and Luzhin's father, a writer of popular children's books, has just nervously informed his son that he will begin attending school upon their return to town. The next morning Luzhin flees from the village railroad station and runs through the woods back to the summer house where he hides until retrieved by a black-bearded peasant accompanying his father. Luzhin is predictably miserable in school. The only person with whom the boy feels any affinity is his pretty young aunt who turns out to be his father's mistress. She introduces Luzhin to chess on the very day that the boy's mother learns of the affair. Young Luzhin begins to skip school in order to play chess at his aunt's house with one of her aged suitors. On one such occasion his geography teacher narrowly misses seeing him on the street when the wary truant ducks aside to stare into a hairdresser's shopwindow where he finds "the frizzled heads of three waxen ladies with pink nostrils ... staring directly at him (E50/R37). Luzhin makes phenomenal progress but keeps his knowledge of chess secret from his parents and schoolmates. During the following summer his father accidentally learns of his son's gift, and the prodigy makes his public debut. Luzhin soon succumbs to a long illness and in its aftermath makes his first trip abroad. At a German health resort he by chance encounters a tournament where he establishes his European reputation at age fourteen.

In mid-chapter between two paragraphs, time suddenly telescopes and it is sixteen years later at the same health resort. Grandmaster Luzhin is talking to a young Russian woman who will become his wife. We subsequently learn that during the earlier part of the intervening years his career had been managed by a Svengali-like chess promoter, Valentinov, who had eventually dropped his aging prodigy. Socially, Luzhin has progressed little beyond the morose, taciturn boy of his childhood despite his international stature as a chess player. His father has recently died in Berlin. Luzhin, in Paris at the time of the death, had belatedly gone to visit the grave, but failing to find it, had begun to feel unwell. A doctor advises him to go to a spa. He has now, animal-like, returned to this familiar resort to recuperate and to prepare for a forthcoming tournament in Berlin. Here he is befriended by his future bride. Following a bizarre courtship he returns to Berlin for his tournament.

He plays brilliantly, winning or drawing match after match, progressing toward a final game with Turati against whose novel opening attack Luzhin has devised a new defense. (He had lost an earlier tournament to Turati.) During the days Luzhin plays his tournament matches, while in the evenings he visits the kitsch Russian home of his fiancée's affluent parents. As the days pass, the patterns of chess increasingly interfere with Luzhin's always faint grasp on the real world. The presence of his fiancée among the spectators at a match vaguely disturbs him and he sends her home. The final game of the tournament arrives and Luzhin, playing black, sits down against Turati who does not commence with the opening attack for which Luzhin has especially readied his defense. The game proceeds with neither man gaining substantial advantage until it is adjourned to the following day. Just prior to the adjournment Luzhin feels a searing pain in his hand from a forgotten cigarette match. The Master is now so deeply sunk into the pure world of chess he cannot regain the world of reality. He wanders about the chess café seeing the patrons as chess pieces: "... Luzhin realizing that he had got stuck, that he had lost his way in one of the combinations he had so recently pondered, made a desperate attempt to free himself, to break out somewhere—even if only into nonexistence" (E140/R123-4). A voice says "go home" and Luzhin murmurs "Home... So that's the key to the combination" (E141/R124-5). He stumbles out of the Berlin cafe and begins to run through a wooded park. As he runs he feels a pain "pressing down from above on his skull, and it was as if he were becoming flatter and flatter, and then he soundlessly dissipated" (E143/R126). Luzhin in his madness has moved from the three-dimensional world of reality into the two-dimensional world of the chess board.

Luzhin awakes in a sanatorium tended by a black-bearded psychiatrist who, along with Luzhin's fiancée, assures him that he must totally forswear chess if he is to save his sanity. Outside the country hospital window Luzhin sees a scene reminiscent of the Russian countryside and concludes "Evidently, I got home" (E160/R141). Luzhin's memories gradually return but "he returned to life from a direction other than the one he had left it in." (E161/R143). Guided by his fiancée and the doctor, he suppresses his chess memories and recreates his past starting from his pre-chess childhood. He is soon released and returns to town where he marries his fiancée. Luzhin's chess-free life proceeds smoothly for a time until the night of an émigré charity ball where he encounters a former schoolmate who reminisces of their youth. Luzhin denies knowing the man and is unaccountably distressed. During sleepless nights he ponders the secret meaning of the encounter. He senses it is merely a continuation of a developing combination and resolves to "replay all of the moves of his life from his illness until the ball" (E201/R186). The pattern eludes him, however. The attentions of Luzhin's wife are now distracted for several weeks by the appearance of a guest, a childhood acquaintance who has arrived from the Soviet Union with her morose eight-year-old son for a visit to Berlin. This woman knows the aunt who had taught Luzhin to play chess. By chance Luzhin (who is protected by his wife from all things that might evoke his old chess life) overhears a passing allusion to his aunt and suddenly the pattern he has been seeking falls into place: "With vague admiration and vague horror he observed how awesomely, how elegantly and how flexibly, move by move, the images of his childhood had been repeated (country house ... town ... school ... aunt) but still he did not quite understand why this combinational repetition inspired his soul with such dread" (E214/R193). The parallels are in fact much more intricate than Luzhin realizes. His flight "home" from the Turati match parallels his childhood flight from the railroad station; the black-bearded psychiatrist—the black-bearded peasant who retrieves him; Berlin—Petersburg; the populous charity ball with his former schoolmate—the school; and the Soviet visitor with her small, morose son—his aunt and little Luzhin himself. Once again an abstracted Luzhin burns his hand (E233/R211). These and a myriad of other details from his new post-chess life are all combinatorial repetitions of his pre-chess existence. Although he is now aware of the unfolding pattern, Luzhin is strangely unable to foresee the aim of the attack and formulate a reasoned defense. Terror-stricken, Luzhin attempts an "absurd, unexpected act that would be outside the systematic order of life" to confuse the sequence of moves planned by his opponent (E242/R221). He wanders at random into a shop which, alas, turns out to be a hairdresser's with a wax dummy of a woman with pink nostrils (E242-244/R221-2). A trap. Returning home, he encounters his former chess-father Valentinov (now a movie producer) who has been seeking Luzhin for a bit part in a chess film in which Turati will also appear. Mrs. Luzhin has hitherto succeeded in keeping Valentinov away from her husband, but now the producer whisks the dazed Luzhin off to his studio. As he sits in Valentinov's office, Luzhin is once again submerged in the world of chess: "The key was found. The aim of the attack was plain. By an implacable repetition of moves it was leading once more to that same passion which would destroy the dream of life. Devastation, horror, madness" (E246/R255). On a round table Luzhin sees a picture of "a white-faced man with lifeless features and big American glasses, hanging by his hands from the ledge of the skyscraper" (E247/R225).[8] Luzhin flees Valentinov's office and stumbles home in a fog. His wife, frantic at his state, tries to calm him with talk of a long-postponed visit to his father's grave before their planned departure on holiday, but Aleksandr Ivanovich, murmuring that he must drop out of the game, locks himself in the bathroom and drops to his death into the black square of the courtyard.

The structure of Nabokov's chess novel seems remarkably straightforward—especially considering the intricacies afforded by the model of chess and the subtleties of some of the later novels. The key idea is, prototypically, repeated twice in the book. During Luzhin's final tournament, his two worlds interblend. The Berlin apartment of his fiancée's parents is filled with Russian guests and kitschy Russian gimcracks. Luzhin, in a chess-saturated haze, thinks he is back in Russia: "It diverted him especially as the witty repetition of a particular combination, which occurs, for example, when a strictly problem idea, long since discovered in theory, is repeated in a striking guise on the board in live play" (E133/R117). The idea occurs once again just after Luzhin has recognized the pattern being reenacted by the appearance of the aunt-surrogate: "Just as some combination, known from chess problems can be indistinctly repeated on the board in actual play—so now the consecutive repetition of a familiar pattern was becoming noticeable in his present life" (E213/R193). These statements precisely describe the "chess mechanism" of the novel.

This raises a curious point about the book. Chess is, of course, thematically central to the novel—its guiding metaphor. Its hero is a grandmaster whose entire world is chess, and the novel is appropriately saturated with chess imagery. The oddity is that repetition, the central mechanism of the novel's structure, is not a significant factor in either chess play or problem-solving. Nabokov's Foreword to the 1964 English translation offers the information that planted "chess effects are distinguishable not only in ... separate scenes" but that "their concatenation can be found in the basic structure of this attractive novel" (9). Among the "structural" effects cited are Luzhin's sui-mate and a literary version of "retrograde analysis." It is worth noting that both of these terms are from the world of the chess problem—*not* the chess game. Chess problems are a highly specialized aspect of chess whose composition and solution entail skills quite distinct from those of the chess game-player. Problems are chess solitaire and are by definition (in most types of problems) "rigged." Black always loses. The most common type of problem requires White to move first and to mate in a specified number of moves—usually two or three. In a general sense this is analogous to the situation in Nabokov's novel. Luzhin, who plays black, is doomed to be mated upon the completion of a certain number of forced moves.

The two types of problems that Nabokov mentions in his preface are special varieties of problems with goals quite at variance with those just described. Neither of the problem types specifically discussed by Nabokov seems to fit the events of the novel. This is most obvious of sui-mate. Sui-mate problems are an inversion of the more usual types of chess problems. The aim is for White, who in problems (as in games) always has the first move, to force Black to mate White's own King in a fixed number of moves. White "wins" by committing suicide. On casual consideration there would appear to be an obvious parallel between sui-mate and Luzhin's suicide. The difficulty with this seemingly attractive analogy is that Luzhin plays Black in his crucial games and normally wears black. Even after his recovery he attempts to buy a suit with "a dark gray square" pattern, although he is forestalled by his watchful fiancée. (E169/R151)

The second type of chess problem that Nabokov adduces as part of the novel's basic structure is one involving retrograde analysis. "Retrograde analysis" pertains to a type of problem in which the object is not merely to mate but, for example, "to prove from a back-cast study of the diagram position that Black's last move *could not* have been castling or *must* have been the capture of a white pawn *en passant*" (10). Put more simply, retrograde analysis involves the reconstruction of some part of a hypothetical game that has resulted in the present board position. The analysis is requisite to answering such possible problem questions as "Whose turn is it to move?" or "Is castling legal?", etc.[9] Nabokov implies that the procedure for solving retrograde analysis problems resembles his treatment of the events in Chapters Four, Five, and Six. It is in Chapter Four that sixteen years unaccountedly elapse between fourteen-year-old Luzhin's entry into a tournament at the German health resort and Luzhin sitting at a table in the same resort talking to the unidentified owner of a purse lying on the table. In Chapter Five the focus shifts (for the only time in the novel) to Luzhin's father, who has died two months before. Through his musings we learn of his son's life in the intervening years. Then at the beginning of Chapter Six the owner of the handbag, Luzhin's future fiancée, materializes and the earlier conversation is resumed *in medias res*. The analogy between this literary device and retrograde analysis is so loose as to be virtually nonexistent. It is true that the reader is seemingly presented with the problem of reconstructing the missing years leading up to the present "board position," i.e. Luzhin's conversation with his fiancée-to-be, but the information is supplied in the following chapter. There is no analysis at all—

at least for the reader-solver. Nor is there a problem from Luzhin's point of view since he knows the moves of his autobiography. The missing "moves" are revealed (through the father) and there is no "problem" in the sense the word is used in retrograde analysis.[10]

Nabokov's introduction of the chess problem concepts of sui-mate and retrograde analysis in his Foreword is puzzling. They seem either misleading (sui-mate) or irrelevant (retrograde analysis). Neither has any patent connection with the unfolding pattern of repetition central to the novel. Given this, one is tempted to assume that the fault lies with the uncomprehending reader—and it well may. There is, however, some reason to suspect that Nabokov is setting a trap for the reader just as the wax dummy with the pink nostrils has been laid as a trap for Luzhin.

In his Foreword to *The Defense*, as in prefaces to other of his translated works, Nabokov virulently attacks the efforts of "hack reviewers—and, generally persons who move their lips when reading. . . ." Noting that such readers "can not be expected to tackle a dialogueless novel when so much can be gleaned from its Foreword," he specifically directs their attention to "the pathetic way my morose grandmaster remembers his professional journeys . . . in terms of the tiles in different hotel bathrooms and corridor toilets—that floor with the blue and white squares where he found and scanned from his throne imaginary continuations of the match game in progress. . . ." Nabokov then describes three hotel toilet scenes in which Luzhin, the black king, sits on his porcelain throne and surveys various chessboard-like tile floor patterns. It has been pointed out by Fred Moody that *none* of these scenes are, in point of fact, to be found in the novel.[11] They are deliberate traps for the inattentive reader-reviewer. Our examination of the questionable parallels between the chess problem concepts of sui-mate and retrograde analysis and various turns of the novel's narrative suggests that these references may be no less bogus than the missing bathroom-tile chessboard scenes. Nabokov says, "I think a good combination should always contain a certain element of deception" (SO 12).

Is there anything in the booby-trapped Foreword that is to be trusted? Aside from a ritualistic attack on Freudian critics who are warned against seeing chess pieces as Oedipal incarnations of the author's family life,[12] there is only one remaining chess reference: "Rereading this novel today, replaying the moves of its plot, I feel rather like Anderssen fondly recalling his sacrifice of both Rooks to the unfortunate and noble Kieseritsky—who is doomed to accept it over and over again throughout an infinity of textbooks, with a question mark for a monument" (8). Nabokov does not identify this game but it is one of the most famous in the history of chess. So renowned is the game that it has its own name, "The Immortal" and is included in virtually every chess anthology. It was played in London in 1851 between the German Adolf Anderssen, World Champion 1851-1858, and Lionel Adalbert Bagration Felix Kieseritsky, a grandmaster of Livonian origin who settled in Paris.[13] We shall see that this game, its players, and the type of moves involved are all central to Nabokov's novel.

Anderssen's sacrificial play in this game is stunning in that by game end he has taken only three of Black's pawns (and no pieces), while sacrificing a Bishop, both Rooks, and his Queen, as well as two pawns. The heart of this game is Anderssen's double Rook sacrifice—a play which is among the most spectacular in chess and one that occurs very rarely. Kieseritsky has lost, although he has overwhelming material strength. So elated was Kieseritsky by the genius of his opponent that he immediately sent a copy of the game to Paris for publication.[14] Nonetheless the spectacular defeat may have not been without its psychic toll. Kieseritsky returned to Paris, and within two years he was in a mental home, the Hotel de Dieu, where he died on May 18, 1853 and was buried in a pauper's grave.[15] The parallel with mad Luzhin is interesting but not overly impressive in itself. What Nabokov does *not* tell the reader of his preface is that this game was not the first but the *second* in which Kieseritsky had fallen prey to the proffered temptation of the rare double Rook sacrifice. Nine years before in a game against Schwartz (Paris, 1842), Kieseritsky had yielded to the same fatal lure.[16] The real Kieseritsky, like the fictional Luzhin, played Black in both of his games and, one might surmise, must have experienced the same horror at seeing the same set of moves once again unfolding before him.

Luzhin's nemesis is the Italian player Turati against whom he elaborates his defense. Turati is described as "a representative of the latest fashions in chess, [who] opened the game by moving up on the flanks, leaving the middle of the board unoccupied by pawns but exercising a most dangerous influence on the center from the sides. Scorning the cozy safety of castling he strove to create the most unexpected and whimsical interrelations between his men" (E96/R82). The "latest fashion" in chess that Nabokov is describing in his 1930 novel is the Hypermodern school which was headed by Hungarian Richard Réti, a brilliant player-theoretician (and problemist) who won many important tournaments in the decade before his death in June 1929 at age forty.[17] One suspects that it is not by chance that the last syllable of the name of Nabokov's Turati echoes the name of the Hungarian player.[18] The name may also be intended to evoke the Russian word for Rook, *tura*, reflecting Turati/Réti's preference for lateral rather than frontal control of the center.

The reason, I would propose, that Nabokov invokes the shadow of Réti behind his Turati, Luzhin's arch-opponent, has to do with the central facet of the Anderssen-Kieseritsky game, to wit, the rare and spectacular double-Rook sacrifice. Just as Kieseritsky won notoriety in chess history as being twice the victim of this elegant sacrificial maneuver, Richard Réti, in a single year (1920), twice inflicted the double-Rook sacrifice upon the same opponent, Machgielis Euwe.[19] All four of these games, the two lost by Kieseritsky and the two won by Réti, are sufficiently noteworthy in chess lore to be included in one of the standard handbooks, Vladimir Vukovic's *The Chess Sacrifice*. Of the seven games that Vukovic uses to illustrate his discussion of the double-Rook sacrifice, Kieseritsky and Réti figure in four!

The pattern of repetition is central to Luzhin's fate as it was to Kieseritsky's. My conclusion seems plausible but doubt remains. The key allusion to the Anderssen-Kieseritsky game is made in a preface written thirty-five years after the novel itself, and the novel's text does not itself appear to contain any reference to Anderssen's "Immortal." My argument would be strengthened if it could be shown that there is some more specific parallel between game and novel plot. There are such literary works and Nabokov was aware of at least one: Lewis Carroll's *Through the Looking Glass* in which the characters are equivalent to specific chess pieces and in which a chess problem underlies the moves of the book's plot.[20] Although Nabokov has asserted that none of his novels are plotted chess *games*,[21] his careful statement does not exclude chess *problems*, nor does it exclude individual chess-like plot moves.

The center of the Anderssen's *Immortal* is the double-Rook sacrifice which led to Kieseritsky's doom, but Nabokov's novel does not seem to contain characters who might reasonably be identified with the sacrificial Rooks. It must be noted, however, that Rooks are not what double-Rook sacrifices are about. Rooks can be sacrificed in various ways, but when chess players speak of double-Rook sacrifices they have in mind the particular case when the opposing Queen is permitted to capture both Rooks stationed in their own back rank. The immediate purpose of the Rook sacrifice is the diversion of the opposing Queen far from the real scene of the action.[22] The Rooks are simply irresistible decoys *to trap and neutralize the opposing Queen thus depriving the King of its strongest defender.* This situation finds an exact parallel in Nabokov's novel—not once but twice. It will be remembered that Luzhin sends his fiancée away from the tournament before the game with Turati—a move that completely severs him from reality, represented in the novel by his fiancée/wife (E124/R108-9). This unobtrusive fact is repeated in a more ostentatious way when the prolonged visit of the Soviet lady (the aunt-surrogate with her Luzhin-like son) takes Mrs. Luzhin's attention away from her husband at precisely the time when he is locked in losing battle with his chess demon (E209-221/R189-200). Just as in a double-Rook sacrifice the Queen is sent off on a seductive wild-goose chase (a Rook hunt) that ends in the checkmate of her King, Mrs. Luzhin is decoyed away from the scene of the main action where her husband fights for his sanity and his life. Nabokov duplicates this feat (in a minor key) is his 1964 Foreword. Through the use of deceptive allusions, he sends the reader off on a wild-goose chase looking for castles in the air.

Chess has often been seen as a metaphor for life. Nabokov uses it as a metaphor for art in both a general sense (Art with a capital A) and in a more specific sense—as a structuring device for parts, if not wholes, of some of his novels. Each of these usages, general and specific, corresponds to a particular aspect of chess and involves a critical distinction perhaps not familiar to the reader with a casual knowledge of chess: the chess game versus the chess problem. A game by definition is a competition between two (or more) persons who play in accord with a given set of rules. Luzhin perceives himself to be engaged in such a contest. The moves, however, are autobiographical rather than within the confines of a chessboard. His shadowy opponent is fate, and losing the match means losing his sanity. He has lost the first match and now is engaged in a terrifying rematch. Recognizing the emerging pattern of repetition, the combinational attack, he mistakenly believes in the possibility of victory. When his defense fails, he resigns the game via suicide. Luzhin fails to recognize that he is not involved in a game but in a fiendishly designed chess problem. In other words, he is not a player in a chess game, but a pawn in a chess problem. In problems, all pieces are in a sense pawns, for all moves are foreordained by the composer.

Nabokov himself has drawn the analogy between art and the chess problem, remarking that the latter requires from the composer "the same virtues that characterize all worthwhile art: originality, invention, conciseness, harmony, complexity, and splendid insincerity" (*PP* 15). Deceit is no less fundamental to Nabokov's art than to his chess problem compositions. In Nabokov's *Defense*, even deceit is used deceptively. It plays a minor if diverting role when Luzhin is lured into his absurdist defense of visiting the hairdresser's wax figures only to realize he has been duped. The major role of deceit in *The Defense* is not within the chess-game-like text (where character plays against character) but in the chess problem-like relationship of author and reader. In this latter relationship, the playing board is not so much the novel's text but its pre-text, the authorial "Foreword." Nabokov's pre-text, as we have shown, contains a series of miscues, of feints, to throw the reader-solver off the track and obscure the mechanism if not the theme of the novel. In addition to these false tries, the Foreword does in fact contain a clue to the correct theme which proves to be quite a simple one—repetition. The clue, however, is perhaps even more devious than the answer. The famous Anderssen-Kieseritsky game which Nabokov cites contains little or nothing that informs poor Luzhin's losing battle with fate. The reader must know the key fact of the history of this match—to wit, that it was the second time that Kieseritsky (who shortly thereafter went mad) had been deceived by the double-Rook sacrifice with its ploy of decoying away Black's Queen. In his Foreword composer Nabokov has laid a trap for his reader-solver just as Luzhin's opponent has trapped him. Nabokov has described his notion of strategy in chess problem composition as "Deceit, to the point of diabolism, and originality, verging upon the grotesque" (SM 289). This concept of strategy has been enacted in the tactics of Nabokov's twice-born chess novel.

## THE CHESS KEY TO *THE GIFT*

Nabokov's *Dar (The Gift)* is reckoned by its author and by many of his readers as his finest Russian novel.[23] It is by far the longest and most complex of his Russian works and, at least on the surface, his nearest approach to the tradition of the classical XIXth century Russian novel.[24] It is, as its protagonist Fyodor says of the book he himself plans to write, a "novel with 'types', love, fate, conversations... and with descriptions of nature" (E361/R392). *The Gift* is all this and more for it is a study of the creative process enveloped in a brilliant display of Nabokovian structural and stylistic pyrotechnics. The novel's theme is elaborated in the unfolding of two major plot lines. The more obvious is the gradual coming together of Fyodor and his beloved, Zina Mertz, in a protracted pattern of approaches and withdrawals ending in their final union. The second and more fundamental line of development is the ripening of Fyodor's artistic talent which leads to the creation of *The Gift*. Both of the plot lines are structured in terms of a chess problem.

The "gift" of the title has several meanings in the context of the novel, but the most central is Fyodor's artistic talent. As the story opens, the young writer is basking in the aura of an imaginary review of his first book of poems which has just appeared. A few months later, responding to stirrings of "something new, something still unknown, genuine, corresponding fully to the gift which he felt like a burden inside himself," he undertakes, but fails to complete, a biography of his late father, a noted explorer and lepidopterist (E106/R108). Still later, prompted by an unlikely set of circumstances, Fyodor writes a biography of Nikolai Chernyshevski, the utilitarian literary and social critic whom the young writer sees as the bad seed in Russia's aesthetic (and political) development. As the novel draws to a close and all of its themes are resolved or nearing resolution, Fyodor senses the "maturing of his gift, a premonition of new labors" (E339/R367). The new labor is, of course, *The Gift*.

The theme of Fyodor's gift must be understood to encompass more than his writing alone: it also includes his perceptiveness and sensibility. In his day-to-day life Fyodor is almost subliminally storing precious visual details which will enter into his art. He reflects, "Where shall I put all these gifts with which the summer morning rewards me—and only me? Save them up for future books?... one wants to offer thanks but there is no one to thank. The list of donations already made: 10,000 days—from Person Unknown" (E340/R368). The figure of 10,000 gifts is not chosen randomly for it is the approximate duration of Fyodor's conscious existence—twenty-seven years. A further aspect of Fyodor's gift is his *audition colorée* which we have shown to be one of Nabokov's metaphors for the creative process. Even Fyodor's name, the Russian form of "Theodore," means "gift of God."

The gift theme refers to Russian literature as a whole, as well as to Fyodor's talent and sensibilities. Russian literature is as much a hero of *The Gift* as is Fyodor himself, for the novel is Nabokov's homage to his native literary heritage. Fyodor sees himself as heir to that tradition, and two of his own works are in some measure inspired by Pushkin and Gogol, the seminal figures of modern Russian literature. Fyodor's abortive biography of his explorer father is in part suggested to him by his reading of Pushkin's *Journey to Arzrum* (E106-108/R108-110), and Pushkin is a pervasive presence behind that portion of the narrative. The composition of the Gogolian Chernyshevski biography is similarly preceded by a period in which Fyodor is immersed in *Dead Souls* (E192/R175).[25] It is significant that, alone among Fyodor's writings, his projected novel, *The Gift*, the book that marks the end of his apprenticeship, is not prefaced by allusion to particular godheads in the Russian literary pantheon. *The Gift* itself does not stand in the shadow of any single Russian literary voice but rather is a compendium deliberately echoing the voices of Russian writers from Pushkin to Pilnyak all set within a stylistic context that is purely that of Nabokov. Many authors are invoked and stylistically paraphrased—Blok and Bely prominent among them. The theme of literature is also implicit in the book's wry survey of the émigré literary scene and in its lampoon of émigré literary criticism.

*The Gift* is fundamentally a *Künstlerroman*, albeit scarcely a traditional one from the structural point of view. The basic chronological framework of the novel is seemingly linear, although there are a number of flashbacks and inserted set pieces of which the longest is Fyodor's Chernyshevski biography. In terms of the overall patterning of the novel this episode (omitted in the novel's first publication) is the centerpiece. His biography, Fyodor says, is composed "in the shape of a ring ... (so that the result would be not the form of a book, which by its finiteness is opposed to the circular nature of everything in existence, but a continuously curving, and thus infinite, sentence)..." (E216/R230). Within the clasp of its ring Chernyshevski's life unfolds in a series of spiraling "themes," the most pervasive of which is the hero's myopia ("the spectacles theme") which becomes the guiding metaphor for Chernyshevski's aesthetic and social *Weltanschauung*. Other themes include "angelic clarity," "writing exercises," "the perpetual motion machine," "traveling," and so on. These, very loosely imposed on a chronological line, are the organizational nodes of the biography which at its end close the circle with Chernyshevski's death scene and birth announcement. The biography as a whole is enclosed within a sonnet of which a double tercet prefaces the work and an octave forms the epitaph.

This same ring structure with self-contained spiralling thematic nodes characterizes the framework of *The Gift* as a whole. Like the Chernyshevski biography, *The Gift* displays the form of the legendary snake swallowing its own tail. The novel relates a period from the life of the young writer-protagonist and ends with him outlining a novel based on the same events. Contained within this all-encompassing master circle are a number of episodes, some of which have their own circular shape. Most prominent among these is, of course, the Chernyshevski biography. A lesser example is Fyodor's book of poems about his childhood which opens with a poem about a lost ball and concludes with a poem in which the ball is found. The story of Yasha, a young Russian émigré poetaster and student who becomes involved in a psychologically twisted *menage à trois* and kills himself, is aptly referred to as "a triangle inscribed in a circle" (E54/R50).[26] The tale of Fyodor's explorer-father, lost and presumed dead, is also ultimately circular in shape. Another self-reflexive aspect of *The Gift* is to be found in its inclusion of Fyodor's reviews of his own work and, to a lesser extent, by his alter ego Koncheyev. In some sense all of the novel's episodes are encompassed within its circular framework.

*The Gift*, like other Nabokov novels, has a leitmotif that echoes and augments the book's theme of art and the artist. The dominant motif of *The Gift* is Fyodor's keys (in Russian *klyuchi*). Just as the gift theme is multi-faceted, its accompanying motif is also complex in its reverberations. Like the theme itself, the motif functions on several levels. Keys not only play a pivotal role in the novel's plot but serve as the basis of an extended set of thematic allusions echoing different aspects of the novel's theme. We shall first examine the plot role of the keys and then turn to their three thematic dimensions.

The novel opens as Fyodor stands on the street watching a couple named Lorentz moving into a new lodging into which the young poet has himself moved earlier that day. The landlady lets him in mentioning that she has left the house keys in his room (E19/R13). As Fyodor goes out in the evening to visit his friends, the Chernyshevskis, he wonders "Did I take the keys?" Checking his raincoat pocket he finds the "clinking handful, weighty and reassuring" (E41/R36). It is only when he returns home late in the evening that he discovers that the keys in his pocket are those to his previous residence. Pacing the street Fyodor composes a poem while waiting for someone to open the door. At length Mrs. Lorentz lets out a visitor and Fyodor gets in. As it happens Fyodor is acquainted with the visitor, an artist named Romanov, who subsequently invites the poet to the regular soirées given by the Lorentzes which are attended by one Zina Mertz. Not caring for Romanov, Fyodor declines and misses meeting Zina, the girl with whom he will later fall in love. When Fyodor finally enters his room, he sees "the glistening keys and the white book" on the table (E67/R65). The book is Fyodor's newly published collection of poems. The young poet remains at the rooming house for two years during which time he supports himself by giving lessons and doing translations, but through apathy he misses one job that would have brought him together with Zina. As he leaves for the last time, he returns the keys to his landlady and reflects that the distance to his new residence is "about the same as, somewhere in Russia, that from Pushkin Avenue to Gogol Street" (E157/R169). Fyodor's new room is in the apartment of the Shchyogolevs whose daughter, Zina Mertz, is an admirer of Fyodor's verse. Their initial involvement is precipitated by a key. A few days after Fyodor moves in, Zina is sent downstairs with the outside door key to await the arrival of a guest. As she stands waiting in the darkened hallway absently jingling the keys on her finger, Fyodor, who has followed her down, approaches her. She agrees to meet him the next evening. Since Zina refuses to see Fyodor in the apartment, the two, unable to be alone together, meet nightly in the steets. Eventually fate breaks through this impasse when Zina's stepfather obtains a job in Denmark leaving the empty apartment to the lovers for a time. The key motif enters again. The day before the Shchyogolevs depart, Fyodor's keys are stolen as he sunbathes in a park. Fyodor consoles himself for their loss thinking that he will use the set left behind by the departing Shchyogolevs. In the confusion, however, the Shchyogolevs leave not only their own keys but those of Zina (which they had borrowed) inside the locked apartment. As the train leaves they tell Zina Fyodor will let her in with his keys. The parents depart, the lovers spend their last money on dinner in a cafe and slowly walk arm in arm back to the vacant apartment unaware that neither has a key. Thus the novel's first day and last day, some three years and three months apart, end indentically.

Fyodor's missing keys evoke the dominant feature of his existence— exile. Exile has become a metaphor (as well as a reality) bespeaking the condition of the artist in the XXth century. Generally the writer, and especially the young, unknown writer, is perhaps the most severely handicapped kind of exile for his work is uniquely dependent on language and culture. In exile he is deprived not only of the cultural milieu from which his writing derives but also of much of his potential audience. Although Fyodor is physically denied his native land he retains access to something far more important—its language and literary heritage. As Fyodor remarks in a letter to his mother, he finds exile from Russia easier to bear than many others, "because I know for certain that I shall return—first because I took away the keys to her, and secondly because, no matter when, in a hundred, two hundred years—I shall live there in my books—or at least in some researcher's footnote" (E362/R393). Fyodor has given up the keys to Russia itself but not to its literary tradition.

There is perhaps an echo of this theme in one of Fyodor's early poems which describes an old and much loved childhood toy. The toy is a brilliantly plumaged, mechanical Malayan nightingale perched on an artificial tropical plant. When the boy wheedles the key from the housekeeper and winds the toy's decrepit mechanism, no sound emerges, but days later a chance passing footstep sets off a belated outburst of birdsong (E23/R18). Given Nabokov's view of art as artifice, this seems to strike a certain resonance with Fyodor's situation.

Although exile, especially penurious exile, may be an unpleasant state for an artist, it is not without advantage. Fyodor detests philistine Germany (*Karmaniia* "Pocket-land," as he calls it) and its obsessive concern with locks and keys—a fact alluded to by his mother after her removal to relatively lock-free Paris (E362/R393). Fyodor is nonetheless aware of the positive effect of the alien environment on his artistic creativity. In the above mentioned letter he gives among his reasons for remaining in Germany "my wonderful solitude in this country, the wonderful beneficient contrast between my inner habitus and the terribly cold world around me; you know, in cold countries houses are warmer than in the south, better insulated and heated" (E362/R393). Not only does exile provide Fyodor a hothouse environment for his own creative efforts, but it affords him an external basis for that radical reevaluation of Russian literary history which forms one of the subthemes of *The Gift*.[27] Fyodor's forcible alienation from his native land has not deprived him of the only key that really matters—the key to his art.[28]

The *klyuch*-key motif is sounded yet again in a second thematic dimension of *The Gift*. The book has two heroines: Russian literature and Zina Mertz. The Russian literature theme is present from the first, but Zina appears only around the midpoint in the long novel. She is subtly evoked, however, several times before being formally introduced.[29] On the first night of the narrative Fyodor (with the wrong keys) is walking back to his new abode. As he approaches the house he comes to "the square where we dined" (E65/R62). This alludes to the book's closing scene in that same square where Fyodor and Zina have dinner and he first tells her his conception of *The Gift*. This and other references to Zina become clear only on a second reading. The role of Zina remains obscure even after Fyodor has moved into the Shchyogolev apartment some two years after the opening of the narrative. As the young man lies abed smoking his first cigarette of the day, he is mentally composing a long poem which is woven into the text over some twenty pages. The poem is untitled but contains the recurrent injunction to an unknown girl to "be true to fantasy alone" (E168 & 169/R175 & 199). The opening stanza enjoins the girl to love only that which is rare and fleeting. The following two stanzas evoke the nocturnal setting of the lovers' meeting in the Berlin streets. The poet then invokes his Muse:

> Kak zvat' tebia? Ty polu-Mnemozina,
> Polu-mertzan'e v imeni tvoem,
> —I stranno mne po sumraku Berlina
> S poluviden'em stranstvovat' vdoem (176)

> What shall I call you? Half-Mnemosyne?
> There's a half-shimmer in your surname too.
> In dark Berlin, it is so strange to me,
> To roam, Oh, my half-fantasy with you (169).

Fyodor, echoing the tradition of Baroque verse, has incorporated the name of his newly beloved, Zina Mertz, (until now scarcely mentioned in the narrative) into his poem. Zina is indeed half Mnemozina "Mnemosyne" and half mertzan'e "shimmer." This brilliant phonetic play is not, however, the only intricacy associated with Zina's name. In Greek mythology the Muses are the daughters of Zeus and Mnemosyne, the goddess of memory. The name Zina (or Zinaida in its full form) is derived from the name Zeus.[30] Zina is in the most literal sense half Zeus, her father after whom she is named, and half Mnemozina, whose daughter she is and half of whose name she bears. Zina is Fyodor's Muse in a very real as well as in a metaphoric sense. Not only does Fyodor conceive his biography of Chernyshevski at the start of their romance, but Zina quite literally fills the role of Muse during its composition. Each evening the lovers meet in a dingy cafe where Fyodor reads his day's work to Zina whose perfect pitch invariably causes Fyodor to yield to her judgment in stylistic matters (E216/R230). Even more explicit is Fyodor's remark that there "was an extraordinary grace in her responsiveness which imperceptibly served him as a regulator, if not as a guide" (E217/R231). Fyodor continues his love poem to Zina:

> Est' u menia sravnen'e na primete
> dlia gub tvoikh, kogda tseluesh' ty
> Nagornyi sneg mertzaiushchii v Tibete,
> Goriachii klyuch i v inee tsvety (176).

> In honor of your lips when they kiss mine
> I might devise a metaphor sometime:
> Tibetan mountain snows, their glancing shine,
> And a hot spring near flowers touched with rime (169).

It is in these lines that we find the second incarnation of the "key" motif. The allusion is present only in Russian and is lost in the English translation because it is based on a non-translatable bit of wordplay. In the poem

Fyodor is, via his metaphor, comparing the touch of Zina's lips to "a hot spring near flowers touched with rime." In Russian the word for "spring" is *klyuch*, a homophone of *klyuch* meaning "key."[31] Moreover, the metonymic association of Zina's lips with a mountain spring is not an idle one. Zina is, as we have noted, Fyodor's Muse, and the Muses are traditionally associated with mountain springs.[32] The nine Muses of Greek mythology who dwelt on Mount Parnassus were guardians of the Castalian Spring which was the font of artistic inspiration.

The Castalian Spring aspect of *The Gift*'s *klyuch*-key motif is not developed as extensively as its literary heritage or chess plotting counterparts. There would seem to be only two echoes of this variant of the motif and both are somewhat indistinct. As Fyodor ponders the origins of the fatal flaw in Russia's cultural and historical development, he wonders where XIXth century Russia's "urge toward the light" had gone wrong. When had this "strange dependence between the sharpening of thirst and the muddying of the source" arisen (E187/R197)? Here again the English text loses an important nuance of the original for the muddied "source" is in Russian *istochnik* whose primary meaning is "spring"—in this case the well-fount of the Russian cultural heritage.[33]

The second echo of the *klyuch* "spring" motif is also muted but is critically positioned in the narrative framework. At the final café dinner after Fyodor has outlined his plan for writing *The Gift* he tells Zina that before undertaking the novel he first wishes to do a translation in his own manner "from an old French sage" (E377/R409). The sage is unnamed but is almost certainly Pierre Delalande who is referred to earlier as the author of *Discours sur les ombres* (E321-2/R346-7).[34] Fyodor quotes a passage from memory:

> "there was once a man . . . he lived as a true Christian; he did much good, sometimes by word, sometimes by deed, and sometimes by silence; he observed the fasts; he drank the water of mountain valleys (that's good, isn't it?); he nurtured the spirit of contemplation and vigilance; he lived a pure, difficult, wise life; but when he sensed the approach of death, instead of thinking about it, instead of tears of repentance and sorrowful partings, instead of monks and a notary in black, he invited guests to a feast, acrobats, actors, poets, a crowd of dancing girls, three magicians, jolly Tollenburg students, a traveler from Taprobana, and in the midst of melodious verses, masks and music he drained a goblet of wine and died, with a carefree smile on his face . . ." Magnificent, isn't it? If I have to die one day that's exactly how I'd like it to be" (E377/R409-10).

Is it too much to see the "water of mountain valleys" as part of thematic "key-spring" motif system? Perhaps, but something may be said in its favor. Throughout his work Nabokov is much given to emphasizing critical "throw-away" clues by inserting parenthetical comments, e.g., "(that's good, isn't it?)." The other argument is contextual. If we choose to see the mountain waters as the legendary fount of inspiration, the nameless man of the parable becomes perforce an artist, one inspired by the Muses. His chosen death also suggests this, for his funeral feast is a celebration of the arts which will transcend his own death.

Zina, although she is Fyodor's Muse and guardian of the wellspring of inspiration, is not alone in this role. We earlier noted that *The Gift* has two heroines: Zina and Russian literature. Russian literature has its own fountainhead: the writings of Alexander Pushkin. His work informs all of Nabokov's writings but especially the Russian ones.[35] Pushkin's early literary education was in the tradition of XVIIIth century French classicism, and much of his poetry draws heavily on this model with its rhetorical use of figures from the Greek pantheon. The gods, goddesses, and other creatures of Greek mythology are often invoked.[36] Prominent among them are Mnemosyne and her daughters, the Muses, together with their sacred spring. One Pushkin poem of this sort seems to have a special relationship with *The Gift* in general and with the *klyuch* motif in particular. It is entitled *"Tri klyucha"* (The Three Springs).[37]

> V stepi mirskoi, pechal'noi i bezbrezhnoi,
> Tainstvenno probilis' tri klyucha:
> Klyuch Iunosti, klyuch bystryi i miatezhnyi,
> Kipit, bezhit, sverkaia i zhurcha.
> Kastal'skoi klyuch volnoiu vzdoxnoven'ia
> V stepi mirskoj izgnannikov poit.
> Poslednii klyuch—kholodnyi klyuch Zabven'ia,
> On slashche vsekh zhar serdtsa utolit.

> In the worldly steppe, sad and boundless,
> Mysteriously burst forth three springs:
> The Spring of Youth is a spring rapid and rebellious,
> It boils, it runs, sparkling and rippling.
> The Castalian Spring with its surge of inspiration
> Gives drink to exiles in the worldly steppe.
> The final spring is the cold Spring of Oblivion.
> It most sweetly quenches the ardor of the heart.

Pushkin's *"Tri klyucha"* would seem to inform *The Gift* in several ways. The *klyuch* figure is central to both: most specifically the Castalian Spring of inspiration. Perhaps the most significant aspect of the poem's Castalian Spring is its role as a source of inspiration for the exiles of the world. This is precisely the plight of Fyodor in *The Gift*. The poem's Spring of Youth also seems to have some relevance for Fyodor the young poet. The last, the Spring of Oblivion, is less obviously in accord with the theme of *The Gift*, but it might be suggested that the old French sage's parable on the death of the artist is a faint echo of the third fountain, the Spring of Oblivion. Even if we restrict our attention to the Castalian Spring that nourishes the exile, there would seem to be grounds for suggesting Pushkin's poem as one subtext for the *klyuch* "key-spring" motif pattern in *The Gift*.

The proposal is merely an extension of a proposition that is patently true even without reference to Pushkin's *"Tri klyucha"*—to wit, *The Gift* has a major Pushkin subtext, and Pushkin is clearly the godfather of Fyodor's, writing (as he is of Nabokov's). Nor is it by chance that *The Gift* ends with a valedictory sonnet that mimics the form and style of a Pushkin *Onegin* stanza.[38]

Like Pushkin's poem, Nabokov's novel has three *klyuchi*. We have shown the relevance of the key motif to one of the themes of *The Gift*—the gift of the Russian language and literary heritage. A second aspect of the gift theme is the Castalian spring *(klyuch)* of inspiration that enables Fyodor to create his poetry and biography of Chernyshevski and which will culminate in his composition of *The Gift*, a transmutation of the events of (fictional) biography into art. The structure of *The Gift* is intricate, and its very patterning is a third dimension of Fyodor's creative gift. Fyodor consciously formulates his plan to write his book only at the very end of *The Gift*. A careful rereading, however, reveals a series of allusions which, in retrospect, form a complex thematic pattern that underlies the unfolding story line and forecasts the eventual coming together of the lovers and demarcates the evolutionary stages of Fyodor's talent. We shall see that the plot moves of *The Gift* are explicitly modeled on those of a chess problem (not a chess *game*) and it is in this context that the novel's "key" motif assumes its third guise.

Chess plays a dual role in *The Gift*, for in addition to ultimately providing a schematic model for the plot development of the novel itself, it also prompts Fyodor to undertake his first completed major prose work, the biography of Chernyshevski. The writing of the Chernyshevski biography comes about by chance. Passing time in a Russian bookstore between lessons Fyodor idly leafs through the Soviet chess magazine "8x8." Although he is distressed by the mechanical clumsiness of the chess problems by young Soviet composers, he buys the magazine (E186-7/R195-7). Fyodor also finds in the journal an article "Chernyshevski and Chess" containing excerpts from Chernyshevski's diary which display such logical and stylistic ineptitude that Fyodor is perversely enchanted by them. Returning to the arid chess problems, Fyodor begins to ponder Russia's cultural and political decline, and he suddenly comes to see Chernyshevski, the patron saint of the liberal and radical intelligentsia, as the witless villain. So bemused by the idea is Fyodor that on the following day he checks out the complete works of Chernyshevski from the state library and undertakes his controversial biographical study.

The Chernyshevski biography is not, however, the primary focal point of the chess theme. Further examination of his newly acquired copy of "8 x 8" leads Fyodor to a disquisition on the nature of chess problems. The young writer is an indifferent and reluctant player of chess but is, like Nabokov himself, a gifted composer of chess problems. In their composition he finds certain mysterious lessons and feels that as a writer he derives something from the very sterility of the exercise (E182-3/R191). For Fyodor the process may center on the bizarre combination of two themes or perhaps the elaboration of a completely new theme.[39] Fyodor's meditation on the creative psychology and strategy of chess problem composition gradually shifts into the actual elaboration of a problem in which we follow Fyodor's exhausting and maddening effort to embody his original intuitive conceptualization on the chess board. Many hours later Fyodor notes that "Everything had acquired sense and at the same time everything was concealed. Every creator is a plotter;..." (E184/E193). Surveying his completed problem, Fyodor admires its elegance and intricacies "but perhaps the most fascinating of all was the fine fabric of deceit, the abundance of insidious tries (the refutation of which had its own accessory beauty), and of the false trails carefully prepared for the reader." Note well that Fyodor ends his description of his problem with a reference to the reader rather than the solver, for the statements that every creator is a plotter and its corollary on the role of deceit are programmatic declarations introducing chess as the model for the plotting of Fyodor's novel-to-be. This discourse on chess problem strategy also provides the context for the reassertion of the "key" motif.

In a properly designed chess problem the solver's initial effort is directed toward finding the uniquely possible opening move for White that will force mate on Black in a specified number of moves.[40] This critical opening play, ascertainable by the determination of the *theme* of the problem, is called the "key" move or, more often, simply the "key." This is what Fyodor alludes to in his description of his completed problem: "The key to it, White's first move, was masked by its apparent absurdity—but it was precisely the distance between this and the dazzling denouement that one of the problem's chief merits was measured..." (E184/R193). We shall see that this statement applies equally to the novel's plot.

The first structurally important chess allusion comes at a juncture in the plot arising from Fyodor and Zina's growing impatience to be alone. At length, fate affords a solution when Zina's stepfather obtains a job in Copenhagen, leaving the apartment to the lovers until new tenants move in. Fyodor marvels at the simplicity of the solution to a problem that had seemed so complex "that one could not help wondering if there was not a mistake in its construction" (E338/R356). Noteworthy is that Fyodor's response to fate's elegantly simple resolution of this impasse is cast in the language of the chess problem. As they sit at the café table before going home together for the first time, it suddenly strikes Fyodor that apart from habitual mental thralldom there had been no reason why they could not have left the Shchyogolev apartment and gotten their own place in the preceding months:

> "but at the same time he knew subrationally that this external obstacle was merely a pretext, merely an ostentatious device on the part of fate, which had hastily put up the first barrier to come to hand in order to engage meantime in the important, complicated business that secretly required the very delay in development which had seemed to depend on a natural obstruction" (E374/R406-7).

Fyodor's mind now turns to his projected novel and the chess analogy becomes still more explicit: "Pondering now fate's methods..., he finally found a certain thread, a hidden spirit, a chess idea for his as yet hardly planned 'novel'..." (E374-5/R407). Fyodor, speaking to Zina, foresees the story line of his novel as "Something similar to destiny's work in regard to us. Think how fate started it three and a half odd years ago...." He then details the three attempts made by fate to bring them together. The first attempted key move occurs when the Lorentz' move into the building in which he had just rented a room. Mrs. Lorentz is the former drawing teacher of Zina who often attends the evenings given at the Lorentz studio. The painter Romanov who shares the Lorentz' studio invites Fyodor to their soirées but the young poet, disliking the artist, does not accept the invitation. Continuing his chess problem analogy, Fyodor surveys this first try, dismisses it as crude, remarking "this cumbersome construction" was all for naught and fate was left "with a furniture van on her hands and the expenses not recovered" (E375/R407-8). The second attempt is better, but still inadequate. Although in need of money, Fyodor rejects an offer to help an unknown Russian girl translate some legal documents (E82/R80). This fails, just as the first attempt did, because Fyodor does not care for the middleman in the transaction, here—the lawyer Charski. The third and final attempt admits no chance of failure. Fyodor makes the proper key move in the chess-problem story-plot. This time, fate, through the intercession of Fyodor's good friend Alexandra Chernyshevski, directly installs Fyodor in the Shchyogolev apartment. Even here fate nearly comes a cropper. When Fyodor arrives to inspect the room, Zina is not home and the poet meets only her odious stepfather. He is on the point of rejecting the room when fate, "as a last desperate maneuver" shows Fyodor a blue ball dress on a chair. The maneuver works and fate gives a sigh of relief. The stratagem is more subtle than Fyodor has realized, however, for the blue dress belongs not to Zina but to her homely cousin Raissa who has left it for alteration.

This final bit of information, only now supplied by Zina as the lovers linger over their dinner, renders Fyodor ecstatic: "What resourcefulness! The most enchanting things in nature and art are based on deception. Look, you see—it began with a reckless impetuosity and ended with the finest of finishing touches. Now isn't that the plot for a remarkable novel? What a theme! (E375-6/R407-8).

Fyodor's outline of the plot of *The Gift* in terms of the strategy and vocabulary of the chess problem refers the reader back to his earlier disquisition of the art of composing such problems. As we noted, the critical act in the solution of a chess problem lies in finding the unique proper opening move, the so-called "key" which will permit White to mate in a designated number of moves. This is precisely the process which Fyodor is going through in retrospectively seeking out the moves in his life which will provide the structural turning points in the plotting of his projected novel. As in solving a chess problem Fyodor attempts and rejects two of the false tries proffered by fate, the composer of the problem, before finally hitting upon the uniquely possible key which will produce mate and win Zina. The chess-problem plotting that Fyodor has drawn on for his novel schema conforms in broad outline to the chess problem devised and described by him at the introduction of the chess key motif: "The key to it, White's first move, was masked by its apparent absurdity—but it was precisely by the distance between this and the dazzling denouement that one of the problem's chief merits was measured. . . ." The correct key move is indeed marked by its seeming absurdity. Moving Fyodor into the Shchyogolev apartment is grossly obvious—not a desirable feature in either chess problems or in belletristic writing. It is also absurd because the apparent consequence of such a move is not proximity to Zina (of whom Fyodor is still unaware), but to the stupid and intrusive Shchyogolev.[41] The distance between living with Shchyogolev and the denouement of living alone with Zina is indeed dazzling. Equally apposite is Fyodor's observation that the most fascinating aspect of his chess problem is "the fine fabric of deceit, the abundance of insidious tries. . . , and of false trails . . ." (E184/R193). The "fine fabric of deceit" almost too perfectly corresponds to the blue ball dress which tricks Fyodor into making the correct move, the key play, for the wrong reason.

The evolution of Fyodor's relationship with Zina is not the only aspect of his life that is structured in terms of this same chess problem, for the development of his literary gift proceeds along the same lines. The first false try (corresponding to Romanov's invitation) is Fyodor's book of poems. Only later does the young writer realize that his métier is prose. The second try, better but still inadequate, is his aborted biography of his explorer father. This structurally echoes the aborted meeting with the unknown girl with whom he was to translate some legal documents. The third, successful try, the "key" to his literary future, is the Chernyshevski biography which corresponds to Fyodor's move to the Shchyogolev apartment where Zina lives. Here too deceit plays a prominent part. Just as fate had attempted to bring Fyodor and Zina together earlier, N.G. Chernyshevski had previously been suggested as a subject by Fyodor's friend Alexander Chernyshevski. (The family had adopted their name in the last century in honor the Orthodox priest, the radical critic's father, who had converted them from Judaism.) Fyodor, the aesthete, is repelled at the very thought of writing about Chernyshevski. It is only after his chance encounter with Chernyshevski in the chess magazine that, against the advice of his friends, he undertakes such a seemingly uncongenial subject. Nevertheless, the successful Chernyshevski book proves to be the key move in Fyodor's literary career just as the unpromising move to the Shchyogolevs' is the proper key move leading to his romance with Zina.

The Gift's two major plot lines, Fyodor's romance and his literary development, move in tandem in accord with the model of the chess problem composed by the hero. Each plot line has two false tries before arriving at a correct key move that is ostensibly absurd. Once found, the opening key move in Fyodor's chess problem quickly leads to the resolution of the work's two major themes: the beginning of his life with Zina and the composition of *The Gift*.[42]

Our discussion of Nabokov's longest and most intricate Russian novel has focused on its most inclusive single theme—the gift of art—and has approached its various facets through an examination of the pervasive "key/spring" motif. Keys in the most usual and literal sense play a central part in the events of the narrative. Beyond this, the *klyuch* (key/spring) motif has three metaphoric dimensions that point to and echo different aspects of the book's theme. The *klyuch* motif figures in its most evident form when Fyodor says that his burden of exile is easier to bear because he retains the keys to Russia. Fyodor has in view here the treasure house of the Russian cultural heritage, particularly the language and its literature. The novel is a discriminating critical survey of XIXth and XXth century Russian literature. This theme is evoked in explicit literary discussions, by tributes and parodies, and often by subtle allusion. Central to the book in this context is the long Chernyshevski biography which grows from Fyodor's attempt to discover where a major portion of the Russian literary heritage became mired in the muck of social utilitarianism. The cultural heritage is Russia's gift to Fyodor—a gift that he must cultivate and pass on.

The second aspect of the *klyuch* motif is paronomastically based upon a second distinct meaning of *klyuch*—a spring or fountain. This aspect of the motif pattern corresponds to a second dimension of the gift theme—that of inspiration. Fyodor finds his primary inspiration in drinking from the spring of Pushkin's writings. This is expressed in the Pushkin subtext that permeates the novel in so many ways. Not the least of these is Pushkin's Castalian Spring (*Kastal'skii klyuch*) that quenches the thirst of the young exile and which is attended by Fyodor's Muse, Zina, whose mythological geneaology we have traced.

The third and final dimension of the *klyuch* motif pattern involves a contextual shift to the world of chess. This elaborately developed aspect of the key motif serves as the basis for fate's plotting of the biographical moves which in turn provide the raw material for the plotting of *The Gift* itself. More specifically, this aspect of the motif pattern echoes the elaborate sequence of moves which bring together Fyodor and Zina and parallels the stages of Fyodor's artistic development. The chess motif is developed not as a game but as a chess problem where attention centers on finding the proper opening move, the key. The ending, which is a foregone conclusion in a chess problem, entails the mating of Zina and the composition of *The Gift* which is Fyodor's gift to Russian literature.[43]

I have remarked that the chapter of Nabokov's memoir dealing with his European exile deals (almost equally) with only two themes: writing and chess problem composition. Nabokov sees the two activities as cognate. Fyodor speaks for his author when he describes the genesis of a chess problem: "The making of . . . a problem began far from the board (as the making of verse began far from paper) . . . when suddenly, from an inner impulse which was indistinguishable from poetic inspiration, he envisioned a bizarre method of embodying this or that refined idea for a problem (say, the combination of two themes . . .)" (E183/R192). We recall here the intertwining of *The Gift*'s two narrative lines. The most critical parallel between the two art forms occurs elsewhere, however. In both, the composer is engaged in the physical realization of an abstract and ill-perceived schema—a task of enormous difficulty. So demanding is the effort that only the artist's intuition that the abstract ideal actually pre-exists gives him the strength to carry through the task. Fyodor speaks as both chess problemist and writer when he says he is "certain (as he also was in the case of literary creation) that the realization of the scheme already existed in some other world, from which he transferred it to this one . . ." (E183/R192). Luzhin, the hero of *The Defense*, senses the existence of an ideal pattern in the other world, but can not decipher it. Fyodor, Nabokov's most successful artist figure, both perceives and realizes the pattern emanating from the other world.

NOTES

Section 3

1. The problem appeared in the émigré newspaper *Rul'* (Berlin, April 20, 1923). It is reproduced in Janet K. Gezari and W.K. Wimsat, "Vladimir Nabokov: More Chess Problems and the Novel," *Yale French Studies*, 58 (1979), p. 102. In the Introduction to *Poems and Problems*, Nabokov reports that he started to devise chess problems in late 1917 (15). Andrew Field, in his *Nabokov: His Life in Part*, offers an appraisal of Nabokov as a chess player (rather than a problemist) during his European emigration. An erratic if sometimes brilliant player, Nabokov played (in simultaneous matches) against both World Champion Alekhine and Grandmaster Nimzovich, one of the fathers of "Hypermodern" chess. Nabokov was on the verge of defeating the latter "when a hand from the crowd suddenly reached out over his shoulder and moved a piece for him...Nabokov had to accept defeat, the victim of a bystander's impetuosity" (154-155).

2. From an interview with Harvey Breit, "Talk with Mr. Nabokov," *The New York Times Book Review*, July 1, 1951, p. 17. Cited from Jürgen Bodenstein, "'The Excitement of Verbal Adventure': A Study of Vladimir Nabokov's English Prose," II, notes to ch. xiii, note 67, (Heidelberg, 1977). Bodenstein provides an excellent survey of Nabokov's chess references, pp. 375-394.

3. *The Nabokov-Wilson Letters: 1940-1971*, ed. Simon Karlinsky (New York, 1979), p. 51.

4. In the Russian text Franz's moves are likened to those of a Knight (140-41); in the revised English text—to a Bishop (142-143).

5. Bodenstein, pp. 391-392. Gaston presents Humbert with a box for his chessmen which Humbert uses instead to house the gun with which he kills Quilty. This association of murder by gunshot and chess echoes that illustrated above in connection with the death of Nabokov's father.

6. J-F. Bergery, "Tandis que Lolita Fait le Tour du Monde l'Entomologiste Nabokov, l'Agronome Robbe-Grillet Échangent leur Pions sur l'Échiquier Litteraire," *Arts, Lettres, Spectacles*, 741 (Oct. 28-Nov. 3, 1959). There is an extensive literature on Nabokov's literary use of chess. The major study is the unpublished doctoral dissertation (Yale, 1971) by Janet Krasny Gezari, "Game Fiction: The World of Play and the Novels of Vladimir Nabokov." Published studies include: Edmond Bernhard, "La Thématique Échiquéenne de *Lolita*" *L'Arc*, 24 (1964), pp. 39-47; J.K. Gezari, "Roman et Problème chez Nabokov," *Poétique*, 17 (1974), pp. 96-113; Strother B. Purdy, "Solus Rex: Nabokov and the Chess Novel," *Modern Fiction Studies*, 14 (Winter, 1968-1969), pp. 379-395; David I. Sheidlower, "Reading Between the Lines and Squares." *Modern Fiction Studies*, 25, 3, pp. 413-425. The resemblance of Nabokov's novels to chess was remarked as early as 1930 by Gleb Struve who saw in their formal harmoniousness "the regularity of chess moves and the fancifulness of chess combinations." Quoted by Professor Struve in his *Russkaia literatura v izgnanii* (New York, 1956). Struve's thought is echoed by George Steiner in his essay "A Death of Kings" in *The New Yorker*, Sept. 7, 1968, p. 136.

7. Ludmila A. Foster, "Nabokov in Russian Émigré Criticism," *Russian Literature Triquarterly*, 3 (Spring, 1972), pp. 332-333.

8. Alfred Appel, Jr. in his *Nabokov's Dark Cinema* (New York, 1974) tentatively identifies the picture as a still from the 1923 Harold Lloyd film *Safety Last*, p. 161. The picture is reproduced on p. 165.

9. *The Encyclopedia of Chess*, comp. Anne Sunnuck (New York, 1976), p. 419. For a charming introduction to retrograde analysis the reader is referred to Raymond Smullyan, *The Chess Mysteries of Sherlock Holmes: 50 Tantalizing Problems of Chess Detection* (New York, 1979).

10. Janet Gezari (1971) accepts both of Nabokov's chess problem analogies. She does not, however, confront the difficulty that black Luzhin is the wrong color to commit sui-mate. Gezari's argument that the "backward" plot moves of Chapters IV, V, & VI mimic retrograde analysis seems to be based on the idea that Luzhin's present is "inevitable" in light of the past that those chapters describe (104). "Inevitability" is indeed an attribute of retrograde analysis problems in that there can have been only one particular preceding move that has resulted in the present board situation. This "inevitability" is not, however, peculiar to retrograde analysis problems but, in fact, applies to all chess problems in that only one particular key move is possible. "Inevitability" is a property of any chess problem. Consequently, the asserted close "fit" between retrograde analysis problems and Nabokov's plot mechanism seems open to question. There is, of course, a general, metaphoric parallel (just as there is for the sui-mate type) but it can be pushed too far. The "try" is seductive both because of Nabokov's preoccupation with games in art and because, as Dr. Gezari notes, Nabokov's first published chess problem (which appeared three years before *The Defense*) was of the retrograde analysis type (102).

11. Fred Moody, "Nabokov's Gambit," *Russian Literature Triquarterly*, 14 (1976), pp. 67-70.

12. A Freudian analysis of *The Defense* (but not of Nabokov's family life) may be found in Alexander Cockburn, *Idle Passion: Chess and the Dance of Death* (New York, 1974), pp. 31-40.

13. Harold C. Schonberg, *Grandmasters of Chess* (Philadelphia, 1973), pp. 62-63 and *The Encyclopedia of Chess*. Schonberg reproduces the Anderssen-Kieseritsky game. Also see Moody, p. 67.

14. Schonberg, p. 62.

15. *The Encyclopedia of Chess*, p. 260.

16. Vladimir Vukovic, *The Chess Sacrifice: Technique, Art and Risk in Sacrificial Chess*, trans. P.H. Clarke (London, 1968), pp. 45-46. Vukovic mistakenly calls the Anderssen-Kieseritsky game the *Evergreen*. According to Schonberg and other sources, this name refers to another of Anderssen's great games.

17. Schonberg, pp. 200-205. Nabokov began serial publication of *The Defense* in late 1929. He was at work on the novel by February 27, 1929, however. See the photograph and caption opposite page 256 in *Speak, Memory*.

18. John Updike in his review-essay "Grandmaster Nabokov," *Assorted Prose* (New York, 1965), p. 323 cites a letter sent to him by Mr. Hugh E. Myers of Decatur, Illinois who wrote: "The character of Turati is clearly modelled after the famous...grandmaster Richard Réti.... The description of Turati's opening... describes Réti's own favorite opening which is still known as the Réti System." Réti, like Luzhin, married a Russian girl some years younger than himself. Andrew Field in his *Nabokov: His Life in Art* reports that "the character of Luzhin is based in part, Nabokov has acknowledged, on that of the chess master Rubenstein and of another, lesser known master (177). Akim Rubenstein went mad but survived to old age.

19. Vukovic, pp. 45-48. It might be noted that Euwe was nineteen at the time and went on to become World Champion in 1935-1937. Byrne J. Horton, *Dictionary of Modern Chess* (New York, 1959), p. 61.

20. *The Annotated Alice*. Introduction and Notes by Martin Gardner (New York, 1960). The chess problem is described on pp. 170-172.

21. Field, *Art*, p. 138.

22. Vukovic, p. 44.

23. Nabokov's evaluation may be found in *Strong Opinions*, p. 13. Simon Karlinsky observes that even on the basis of the incomplete serialized version published in the thirties Nabokov admirers felt that "*Dar* was perhaps the most original, unusual and interesting piece of prose writing in the entire émigré literature between the wars." Simon Karlinsky, "Vladimir Nabokov's novel *Dar* as a Work of Literary Criticism: A Structural Analysis" in *Slavic and East*

*European Journal*, 7, 3 (1963), p. 285. Andrew Field in his *Nabokov: His Life in Art* unhesitatingly calls *The Gift* "the greatest novel Russian literature has yet produced in this century" (249). The publishing history of the novel is curious. Its initial appearance in the Parisian émigré journal *Sovremennye zapiski* in 1937-1938 was marred by the suppression (with the author's consent) of the hundred page chapter containing the derisive biographical sketch of N.G. Chernyshevski, the martyred XIXth century radical literary and social critic who was (and is) a particularly sacred cow of the Russian intelligentsia. The full Russian text of the novel appeared only after the war as *Dar* (New York, 1952), and in English as *The Gift* (New York, 1963).

24. Although the book is in part Nabokov's tribute to the classical Russian novel, it is also a parody of that genre. Note, for example, the opening sentence: "One cloudy but luminous day, towards four in the afternoon on April the first, 192- (a foreign critic once remarked that while many novels, most German ones for example, begin with a date, it is only Russian authors who, in keeping with the honesty peculiar to our literature, omit the final digit) a moving van . . . pulled up in front of Number Seven Tannenberg Street, in the west part of Berlin." The mockery of the honest Russian tradition is even more pronounced than the parenthetic insert suggests for internal evidence establishes the year as 1926. Nabokov acknowledges this in an editorial comment in *A Russian Beauty and Other Stories* where he notes the action of *The Gift* begins on April 1, 1926 and ends June 29, 1929 (254).

25. In Nabokov's Foreword to the English translation, he describes Chapter II in which Fyodor works on his father's biography as "a surge towards Pushkin in Fyodor's literary progress." Chapter III, in which Fyodor prepares his Chernyshevski study, "shifts to Gogol."

26. Published separately as a short story in *The New Yorker* (March 23, 1963) under the title "Triangle in a Circle." The circle format is also explicit in another Nabokov short story *"Krug"* (The Circle) which was a spin-off from *The Gift*. In his preface to the English version published in *A Russian Beauty and Other Stories*, Nabokov comments on its "serpent-biting-its-tale-structure" and notes its structural kinship to the Chernyshevski biography (254).

27. See particularly the imaginary dialogue between Fyodor and Koncheyev (E83-88/R81-87). The best treatment of this major subtheme is the Simon Karlinsky essay cited in note 23 above.

28. The parallel with Nabokov is striking. In an interview Nabokov remarked "I will never go back, for the simple reason that all the Russia I need is always with me: literature, language and my own Russian childhood." *Strong Opinions*, pp. 9-10.

29. Such evocations may be found on E65/R62, E71/R69, E78/R76 and E81-82/R79-80.

30. Specifically from the genitive case form *Zēnos*. N.A. Petrovskii, *Slovar' russkikh lichnykh imen* (Moscow, 1966), p. 116. The etymology of "Fyodor" as "gift of god, divine gift" may also be found here, pp. 241-15. The mythological background of Zina's name is also noted by Anna Maria Salehar, "Nabokov's *Gift*: An Apprenticeship in Creativity," *A Book of Things about Vladimir Nabokov*, ed. Carl R. Proffer (Ann Arbor, 1974), pp. 76-77. This article also contains an instructive exploration of Fyodor's love poem to Zina.

31. The word *klyuch* is used in the sense "spring" only once in the novel—albeit in a highlighted position—and this occurrence is on the same page (R176/E169) as that of an ordinary house key *(klyuch)* with which Zina's mother lets herself into the apartment while Fyodor is composing the poem. The co-occurrence of two of the three *klyuchi* of the novel's motif pattern underscores the homophony of the semantically disparate aspects of the central motif. Nabokov often incorporates clues to his puzzles in the adjacent text.

32. As the ancient Greek tribes moved about, the mountain abode appointed for the Muses did also. The earliest was Mt. Olympus, then, Mt. Helicon and finally, Mt. Parnassus. Common to all three locations is the presence of a mountain spring, the fount of artistic inspiration. Respectively, these were the Pierian Spring, the Hippocrene Spring (or Aganippe),

and the Castalian Spring. The horseshoe-shaped spring originated from a blow of the foot of Pegasus, the winged horse. Pegasus figures marginally in *The Gift* in Fyodor's imaginary dialogue with Koncheyev. In contrast to Fyodor who would accept or reject writers on an all-or-nothing basis, Koncheyev argues that one must be more selective: "we must resign ourselves to the fact that our Pegasus is piebald, that not everything about a bad writer is bad and not all about a good one good" (E83/R82). The Russian text with its *"Nash Pegas peg"* is more pungently aphoristic. See Robert Graves, *The White Goddess* (New York, 1948) for an extended discussion of the Muses, pp. 316-337.

33. Although a synonym *(istochnik)* is being used here rather than *klyuch* itself, the conceptual pattern of the motif figure remains valid even in the absence of the key word itself.

34. A suspiciously similar writer named Herman Lande is also mentioned (E222-23/R237). Delalande also figures in Nabokov's *Invitation to a Beheading* (written just prior to *The Gift*) as the author of the book's spurious epigraph and is the subject of several comments in Nabokov's preface to the English translation of *Beheading*. Chief among them is that Delalande is the sole writer whom Nabokov concedes as an influence on his own work and, further, that he is an invented figure. Delalande bears an obvious kinship to Nabokov's "philosophical friend" Vivian Bloodmark, quoted in *Speak, Memory*, p. 218.

35. The following is a partial list of the references to Pushkin in *The Gift*: E47/R42, E77/R75, E84/R83, E106-113/R108-115, E117/R119, E149-150/R154-155, E157/R165, E160-161/R167-168, E266-267/R284-285 and E378/R411. For a discussion of the influences of Pushkin on Nabokov's work, see Clarence Brown, "Nabokov's Pushkin and Nabokov's Nabokov" in *Nabokov: The Man and his Work*, ed. L.S. Dembo (Madison, 1967), pp. 196-208. William Rowe in his *Nabokov's Deceptive World* (New York, 1971) lists many Pushkin allusions culled from Nabokov's work.

36. Vladimir Markov, "Russian Poetry" in *The Princeton Encyclopedia of Poetry and Poetics*, ed. A. Preminger (Princeton, 1965), p. 730.

37. Quoted and discussed at length in D.D. Blagoi, *Tvorcheskii put' Pushkina: 1826-1830* (Moscow, 1967), pp. 147-153.

38. Acknowledged by Nabokov at the end of his Foreword to the English edition.

39. It is, of course, not by chance that the discussion of themes in chess problems echoes Fyodor's comments on the role of "themes" in the compositional patterning of the Chernyshevski biography which spirals out into the structure of *The Gift* itself. Thus the theme of "themes" joins the Chernyshevski biography, chess, and the plotting of *The Gift*.

40. This and subsequent information on chess problems is from the introduction and glossary of *101 Chess Problems for Beginners*, ed. Fred Reinfeld (No. Hollywood, 1972).

41. One chess allusion not present in the original Russian text is assigned to Shchyogolev in the English translation. Shchyogolev's speech, like his mind, consists entirely of clichés. At the farewell dinner before his departure for Copenhagen, he remarks on this sudden improvement in his fortunes with the Russian proverb *"meniaetsia sud'ba chelovech'ia, pechenka ovech'ia"* "man's fate changes like a sheep's liver" (R391). In the English text this is replaced by "one twist of fate, and the king is mate" (E360). This is an example of the tendency noted by Jane Grayson in her *Nabokov Translated: A Comparison of Nabokov's Russian and English Prose* (Oxford, 1977) for the texts to be revised such that "the mechanism of the plot is more openly exposed" (57).

42. Among the incidental occurrences of chess allusions in the novel, at least one deserves mention. Against his inclination, Fyodor is persuaded to attend a meeting of the Russian émigré writers association. At the meeting, which rapidly degenerates into a scandalous farce, Fyodor finds himself seated between the two novelists Vladimirov and Shahmatov (E322/R358). Vladimirov's Nabokov-like appearance, background, and literary career are described at some length and in the preface to the English edition of *The Gift* Nabokov

concedes the self-portrait. The not uncommon name of his colleague, Shahmatov, is derived from *shahmaty*, the Russian word for "chess."

43. A number of critics, mostly *en passant*, have taken notice of the crucial key motif. Andrew Field and L.L. Lee both remark on the missing keys as the lovers wend their way home (*Nabokov's Life in Art*, p. 248 & *Vladimir Nabokov* [Boston, 1976], p. 94). Lee also notes that they form a part of the novel's image pattern. G.M. Hyde, in addition to noting "lost keys" as a theme, makes the shrewd observation that the keys stand in the same relationship to Fyodor's autobiography as do the spectacles in the inset Chernyshevski biography (*Vladimir Nabokov: America's Russian Novelist* [London, 1977], p. 33). Only Julian Moynahan assigns a specific meaning to them when he writes that the keys Fyodor has taken into exile are the Russian language, its art, and his own recollections (*Vladimir Nabokov* [Minneapolis, 1971], p. 40). Critical response to the English version of *The Gift* was remarkably uniform on one point. It was felt that the book, although brilliantly written in its parts, was, as a whole, shapeless, or, at best, episodic and lacking in ultimate unity. See, for example, the following reviews: D.J. Segal, *Commonweal*, July 12, 1963, p. 431; Hilary Cook, *The New Republic*, July 6, 1963, p. 25; and Stephen Spender, *New York Times Book Review*, July 12, 1963, p. 4. This reaction was partially due to the fact that full comprehension of much of the book presupposes a command of XIXth and XXth century Russian intellectual and cultural history. Readers lacking this synthesizing framework failed to grasp certain deep unities embracing the various episodes. In part, however, failure to recognize the integrative *klyuch* "key/spring" motif pattern may also have contributed to this fundamental misunderstanding of what is, in fact, a highly structured novel.

## SECTION FOUR

## NABOKOV AS MAZE MAKER

Pattern, a less fashionable word for "structure," is the source of significance. It is what makes the ordered figure stand out from the jumbled background. It is the stuff of labyrinths and, equally, of their unraveling. In *Speak, Memory* Nabokov artfully interpreted his life in terms of a handful of interwoven thematic patterns. The very purpose of autobiography was, he said, to detect and trace such patterns. The final chapter of *Speak, Memory* appropriately draws upon pattern discrimination as its guiding motif. The motif is introduced in the course of Nabokov's description of his wonder at "the initial blossoming of man's mind": "It occurs to me that the closest reproduction of the mind's birth . . . is the stab of wonder that accompanies the precise moment when, gazing at a tangle of twigs and leaves, one suddenly realizes that what had seemed a natural component of that tangle is a marvelously disguised insect or bird" (298). After flickering in and out of the text in various more or less covert permutations this theme of themes culminates on the autobiography's last page. The Nabokovs with their four-year-old son Dmitri are walking in a park in St. Nazaire from where they will soon sail for America. At the end of the park path they look down toward the harbor which is largely obscured by the varied mundane sights of the city. Amidst the clutter they suddenly perceive, inconspicuously nestled beyond the buildings, the funnel of their ship like "something in a scrambled picture—Find What the Sailor Has Hidden." Once seen the figure can never again blend into the background. So it is with all of the themes, the correlated patterns, that Nabokov sees as constituting his life and from which he weaves his autobiography.

If patterns are the source of meaning in life, they are all the more so in art. A moment's reflection tells us that the reader of Nabokov's novels is in approximately the same situation as Nabokov vis-à-vis his own existence. Recognition of pattern must precede interpretation and, to some extent, the "stab of wonder" that accompanies the recognition of the marvelously concealed figure is reward enough in itself. The subsequent tracing of such emergent figures and detecting the themes they express offer their own satisfactions—although they are rarely so certain as those initial flashes of insight. The novelist has the advantage over the autobiographer in that he has a free hand in creating and imposing the pattern-forming details that give meaning to his work. Unlike the autobiographer he is not dependent upon the vagaries of reality to afford him the necessary detail. In his fiction Nabokov has even complained of the obstacles that external reality (such as wars and revolutions) impose upon the writer's freedom of imagination (*Df* 78-80). The reader of a novel (especially a Nabokov novel) is in a happier position for he is not forced to contend with reality or to sift through the random myriad of life's trivia to seek a pattern that may not be present or detectable. He knows it is there. The weaving of such patterns is one of the ways that Nabokov asserts the dominating presence of the author beyond the worlds of each of his novels.

One of the explicit thematic patterns that Nabokov develops in *Speak, Memory* is his genealogy. The family origins are traced from a late XIVth century founding father, and the XVIIIth, XIXth and XXth centuries are treated in considerable detail. Both sides of the family tree are examined as are the histories of the three family estates near St. Petersburg. Incidental family contacts with literary figures are noted. Famed explorers and musicians are catalogued, and thematic lines are drawn from them to Nabokov's own generation. Recurrences of detail are gleefully noted. In 1791 one of his remote maternal relatives, the cousin and/or sweetheart of the famed Count Axel von Fersen lent her coach and passport to the royal family for their ill-fated escape attempt from revolutionary France (56). There is "an amusing thematic echo" of this episode in the 1917 request assertedly made to Nabokov's father for a sturdy motorcar in which Prime Minister Kerenski might flee revolutionary Russia. The extended Nabokov genealogy touches upon the lives of perhaps a hundred people, offering the usual incidence of family scandal: lovers, mistresses, divorces, doubtful paternities, and homosexuality. There were family secrets aplenty.

In Nabokov's fiction he has on more than one occasion combined his artistic penchant for secret patterning and his interest in family skeletons— one of the staples of the XIXth century novel. *Ada or Ardor: A Family Chronicle* is Nabokov's most ambitious venture in this vein. The "marvelously disguised insect" is brother-sister incest which is part of a thematic pattern evolving over several generations in the novel. This theme is taken up again in *Look at the Harlequins!* in which a series of covertly incestuous marriages punctuate the life of the narrator-hero. Much, but far from all, of the pleasure of these novels lies in working out the patterns of incest. In a sense, they are puzzle novels as opposed to some of the earlier works which we viewed in the context of games, letter and word games, and to others that we saw as resembling chess problems. Incest differs from these contextual playing fields in that it is not a game. It is rather the subject of a mystery whose solution has game-like qualities. The solution of the puzzle involves the sudden transposition of foreground and field that brings out the hidden figure making it the central image of the novel. It is a literary version of "Find What the Sailor Has Hidden."

*Ada* and *Look at the Harlequins!* have more in common than meets the eye. Both involve hidden brother-sister love affairs and both are what we have termed "two world" novels in which the narrator-hero's world is an "inverted" version of the "real" world. The clues to the incest puzzles are tokens of the presence of the otherworldly author. In the following essays we examine the labyrinths of brother-sister incest in *Ada* and *Look at the Harlequins!* and explore possible meanings of that theme.

## THE LABYRINTH OF INCEST IN *ADA*

The theme of incest makes its first major appearance in Nabokov's English chef-d'oeuvre *Ada or Ardor: A Family Chronicle*. Like other "mandarin" writers, Nabokov wrote with an informed awareness of earlier literary treatments of his themes. Allusion to such predecessors, both classic and commercial, is a hallmark of his style, and *Ada* is the most allusive of all Nabokov novels—the consummate work of a writer who was also a Professor of Modern European Literature. The book's coy reference to the actions of its characters as stages in the "Novel's Evolution in the History of Literature" makes it, as Alfred Appel remarks, "a self-contained survey course."[1] *Ada*'s central theme is sibling incest, and, as might be expected, Nabokov draws heavily upon his literary predecessors in his own recreation of it.[2]

The appearance of the theme of sibling incest in modern European literature is largely coincident with the rise of Romanticism whose principal French and English avatars, Vicomte François-René de Chateaubriand (1768-1848) and Lord Byron (1788-1824) explored the forbidden theme in their works and, possibly, in their lives.[3] The presence of Chateaubriand in the thematic background of *Ada* has been widely recognized. In his early review essay, John Updike dwelt at length on the Chateaubriand echoes in the novel, noting that the thematic basis for the comparison is the 1802 novella *René* as well as certain passages from the French writer's autobiography, *Mémoires d'outre-tombe* (1849-50). As Nabokov observes in the notes to his *Eugene Onegin* translation, a "subtle perfume of incest" permeates the relationship of René and his sister Amélie, a relationship widely thought to be modeled on that of the author and his sister Lucile.[4] Chateaubriand's tale of incest was, he said, conceived under the very elm in Middlesex, England, where Byron *s'abandonnait aux caprices de son âge*.[5] Although less visible in *Ada* than Chateaubriand, Byron is also present. His relationship with his half-sister Augusta after whom he named his daughter Ada has been the subject of much speculation.[6] Byron's fascination with brother-sister incest is reflected in three of his works: *The Bride of Abydos* (1813), and the blank verse dramas *Manfred* (1817) and *Cain* (1821). In the latter the name of the stepsister-wife is Adah.

*Ada* is a literature survey course that draws its primary subject matter from the three literatures that the trilingual Nabokov saw as paramount: French, English, and Russian. In this literary triptych Chateaubriand may be said to represent the French incarnation of the sibling incest theme and Byron, the English. But what of Russian? Alexander Pushkin (1799-1837) occupies in Russian literature a position in some ways correspondent to Chateaubriand in French, and Byron in English literature. The early verse of

Russia's greatest poet is, in its themes if not in its form, very much under the sway of Byron and Chateaubriand. There can be no doubt that Pushkin was aware of the incest theme in the works of his mentors.[7] *Manfred* is specifically mentioned in the text of an early separate edition of Chapter Seven of *Onegin* and it is known that Pushkin read Byron's verse drama in a French volume that also contained *The Bride of Abydos*.[8]

There are a number of references in Pushkin's *Eugene Onegin* (1823-1831) to Chateaubriand's *René*, albeit none manifestly to its incest motif.[9] There is, however, a curious stanza in Pushkin's novel-in-verse that seems faintly to foreshadow crucial aspects of *Ada*. In Chapter III, Tatyana, newly smitten with Onegin, immerses herself in her favorite novels such as Goethe's *Die Leiden des jungen Werthers* (1774), Rousseau's *Julie, ou la Nouvelle Héloise* (1761), and Richardson's *Sir Charles Grandison* (1753). In these and other sentimental tales, Tatyana finds a misguided model for her feelings for Onegin who is, however, a man of a quite different literary generation. Pushkin then contrasts these antiquated eighteenth century novels (which, incidentally, he used to twit his sister Olga for reading)[10] with the "fables of the British Muse."[11] The stanza ends with an allusion to Lord Byron who "by an opportune caprice, / in woebegone romanticism / draped even hopeless egotism."[12] In the following stanza (XIII) Pushkin embarks upon a digression: "I", he says, shall abandon [Byronic?—DBJ] poetry and "descend to humble prose: a novel in the ancient strain / will then engage my gay decline. / There, not the secret pangs of crime shall I grimly depict, / but shall simply detail to you / the legends of a Russian family, / love's captivating dreams...." It is in Stanza XIV that outlines of *Ada or Ardor: A Family Chronicle* faintly emerge:

> I shall detail a father's, an old uncle's,
> plain speeches; the assigned
> trysts of the children
> by the old limes, by the small brook;
> the throes of wretched jealousy,
> parting, reconciliation's tears;
> once more I'll have them quarrel, and at last
> conduct them to the altar. I'll recall
> the accents of impassioned languish,
> the words of aching love,
> which in days bygone at the feet
> of a fair mistress
> came to my tongue; ... (I, p. 160).

There is, of course, nothing here suggesting incest: but when the lines are reexamined in the context of Byron and Chateaubriand on the one hand, and Nabokov's *Ada* on the other, they begin to seem less innocent.

An "incestuous" interpretation of this stanza assumes that Pushkin is being tongue-in-cheek in his hypothetical conversion from "the secret pangs of crime" characteristic of exotic Romantic poetry to the humble prose of a Russian family chronicle.[13] First, let it be noted that the stanza immediately follows a discussion of *echt* Romantic writers with their disturbing themes. In this setting "the assigned trysts of the children by the old limes" seems faintly suggestive. If, as seems plausible, the children are those of the father and uncle just referred to, they are first cousins. Their meetings among the old limes of the family estate perhaps echo the rambles of François-René Chateaubriand and his sister Lucile in their parental park and, more pointedly, those of the writer's characters René and his sister Amélie.[14] Lastly, in a discarded variant of the stanza, we find instead of "a fair mistress" the doubtful reading "the fair Amélia"—a name not dissimilar to that of René's beloved sister Amélie and, in fact, a possible Russian form of that name.[15] The case is far from conclusive, but it does not seem inconceivable that Pushkin is toying with the favorite Romantic theme of incest in his projected novel.

Pushkin did not live to enjoy a "gay decline" in which to write his fictional family chronicle, but Nabokov, born exactly one hundred years later, wrote *Ada or Ardor: A Family Chronicle*, a book that seems to echo and develop the scenario implicit in Pushkin's digressive *Eugene Onegin* stanza. The father and uncle of the *Onegin* lines might well correspond to *Ada*'s Demon and Daniel Veen.[16] Demon is the father of Van, while Dan is ostensibly the father of Ada. Thus, Demon is Ada's "uncle," and Dan is Van's "uncle." Officially, the children are first cousins as the children of Pushkin's stanza appear to be. The favorite trysting place of *Ada*'s incestuous children is the park of the family manor with its old limes and small brook, both specifically mentioned by Nabokov and quite possibly borrowed in part by both Pushkin and Nabokov from Chateaubriand. Like the children in Pushkin's projected family epic, Nabokov's Van and Ada are finally united in their love after numerous quarrels and reconciliations. A final parallel is the position of the two narrators: both are old men looking back and giving first-person accounts of family histories, although in Pushkin's case the history is fictional.[17]

Even if one doubts the presence of the incest theme in Pushkin's text, there remains the possibility that Nabokov read such an interpretation into it and then drew on that reading as a source for *Ada*. Nowhere in his massive Commentary on *Onegin* does Nabokov explicitly suggest an incestuous interpretation of the passage in question, but there is some reason to believe that he projects such an interpretation (rightly or wrongly) into his translation of the text. Nabokov's choice of terms in his translation of the lines in question is curious: "the assigned trysts of the children." The word "tryst" in both the nineteenth and twentieth centuries often has the connotation of a clandestine appointment made by lovers. Pushkin's Russian *"uslovlennye vstrechi"* (agreed-upon meetings) is much more neutral in its implication. Translation is perforce an act of critical interpretation, and the cousins' "assigned trysts" would seem to reflect Nabokov's incestuous understanding of the passage. It is, moreover, the term used by Nabokov to specify the amorous dalliances of brother and sister in Ardis Park (132). Our argument linking Pushkin's *Onegin* stanza with the sibling incest theme is tenuous, but the cited coincidences are at least suggestive. That Nabokov himself had an incestuous interpretation of the passage and drew on it for his novel is less tenuous, although still speculative. Whatever the merits of our surmise (and Nabokov's), there is no question that Pushkin's work in general, and *Eugene Onegin* in particular, loom large in Nabokov's work.[18]

This much is clear: the English Byron and the French Chateaubriand, with their fictional and biographical theme of sibling incest, are part of the literary subtext of Nabokov's *Ada*. As Nabokov documents in his *Onegin* commentary, these same figures are an informing presence in Pushkin's *Eugene Onegin*, a work which seems in certain ways to foreshadow the basic outlines of Nabokov's *Ada*.[19] Thus the Russian Pushkin, the French Chateaubriand, and the English Byron all serve as sources of literary resonance for the sibling incest theme in *Ada*, Nabokov's tribute to European Romanticism.[20]

Incest is not found as a theme in Nabokov's Russian work. He does, however, make reference to it as a theme in the work of other writers. One example is the short story *Vstrecha* (The Reunion) written in December, 1931.[21] Set in Berlin on a Christmas Eve circa 1929, it recounts the dismal encounter of two brothers separated ten years earlier by the Russian Revolution. The elder, Serafim, a Soviet engineer who is briefly in Berlin on a purchasing commission, visits the shabby room of his émigré brother Lev, a former literature student. The reunion is uncomfortable for both men as they cast about for topics of conversation. Looking over Lev's modest library, Serafim fills in the time by recounting the plot of a silly but rather entertaining German novel about incest that he happened upon in the train (E134/R137). During Serafim's account Lev ponders the absurdity of spending their brief time together discussing "some philistine tripe by Leonard Frank," but contents himself with remarking that incest is "a fashionable subject these days" (E134-5/R138). Nabokov apparently still had the Frank book in mind in 1935-37 when writing his Russian chef-d'oeuvre, *Dar (The Gift)*. The novel's poet-protagonist, Fyodor Godunov-Cherndyntsev, who lives in Berlin, writes to his mother in June of 1929: "I'll visit you in Paris. Generally speaking I'd abandon tomorrow this country, oppressive as a headache—where everything is alien and repulsive to me, where a novel about incest . . . is considered the crown of literature, where in fact there is no literature" (E326/R393).

Incest, and particularly sibling incest, was indeed a "fashionable subject" in German literature and art.[22] The national epos that underlies the Wagnerian cycle *Der Ring des Nibelungen* tells of Siegfried who (at least in Wagner's version) is the son of Wotan's offspring, the Wälsung twins Siegmund and Sieglinde. Their story is the subject of *Die Walküre*, the second opera of the Ring cycle.[23] The works of Thomas Mann, one of Nabokov's *bêtes noires*, almost constitute a survey of sibling incest in German literature.[24] The incestuous brother and sister of Mann's 1905 story *Wälsungenblut"* (The Blood of the Walsungs) echo the names (and sin) of their prototypes in the Wagnerian opera that they attend.[25] Mann's 1951 novel *Der Erwählte* (The Holy Sinner), the story of a medieval Pope born of the union of a royal brother and sister, is, says, its author, "based in the main on the verse epos *Gregorius vom Stein* by the Middle High German poet Hartmann von Aue (c. 1165-1210) who took his legend of chivalry from the French."[26]

The theme of brother-sister incest becomes especially prominent in German literature of the 1920s when Nabokov was residing in Berlin.[27] Frank Theiss gained notoriety with his 1922 novel *Die Verdammten* which portrays an incestuous brother-sister relationship as part of its picture of the decay of the Baltic German aristocracy.[28] Gunther Birkenfeld's 1929 *Dritter Hof Links* (known in English as *A Room in Berlin*), another sensational novel of the period, deals with a brother and sister who become intimate because of crowded living conditions resulting from their poverty. Yet another German bestseller of 1929, the one to which Nabokov contemptuously alludes in his 1931 short story *Vstrecha*, is Leonhard Frank's *Bruder und Schwester*.[29]

Frank's novel opens with the Berlin divorce of an extremely wealthy cosmopolitan couple—the husband, a German-American international business executive named Schmitt and his Russian wife. Their children, Konstantin, age eight, and Lydia, age three, are separated and all contact between the two sides is lost after the father's death and the adoption of the boy who retains his father's fortune but not his name. After completing Eton, he returns to St. Petersburg (where his father's business was) and spends the years of World War I, the Russian Revolution, and the Civil War there before graduating from Petrograd University. The girl, Lydia, who knows almost nothing of her father and brother, lives in Zurich at her mother's lakeside estate. By 1924, Konstantin has just returned from a three-year trip around the world gathering material for a scholarly treatise on economics. Passing through Berlin on his way to England, he encounters the unknown Lydia in an outdoor restaurant. The two virgins, endowed with great beauty, sensibility and intellect, are smitten with irresistible passion and bed within hours of meeting. They are soon wed, and the eighteen-year-old bride takes Konstantin to her mother's Swiss estate. Gradually the mother begins to suspect Konstantin's identity. She learns the truth on the night of the young couple's departure on a motor trip and informs Konstantin. Aghast, Konstantin determines to keep the secret from Lydia until an opportune moment when he hopes to persuade her that their passion far outweighs the sin of their kinship. Lydia has become pregnant by the time her mother at last locates her and apprises her of the truth before killing herself. Shaken, Lydia abandons Konstantin and goes into hiding until after the birth of their child when at last passion conquers consanguinity, and she summons Konstantin to her side. Love has overcome all obstacles, and the young couple presumably live happily ever after in a luxurious villa on an Adriatic isle.

Frank's novel, although of conventional structure, partakes of some elements of expressionism, particularly in passages of sustained emotional pitch. Exterior dialogues and interior monologues are interwoven without formal discrimination. Not atypical of its breathless prose style is the scene of the unwitting siblings' initial coupling: "Ecstasy in her heart, she shut her eyes and tasted in a swoon this weightless, hitherto unknown sweetness. Her mouth opened soft to his firm lips; they slipped down into the chasm of her wild and fainting surrender, which inflamed him ever afresh to the verge of madness" (59). It is perhaps this fever-pitch treatment of emotion that earned Frank the label of a "vulgarisator of expressionism."[30]

I would suggest that Frank's *Bruder und Schwester*, singled out by Nabokov in his early short story, may have played a role in the later genesis of *Ada*. Before proceeding to this topic, it is necessary to address a preliminary question. Nabokov often proclaimed his ignorance of German in spite of his fifteen-year residence in Berlin. Typical is his comment in the preface to the English translation of his 1928 novel *King, Queen, Knave*, which is set in Berlin and has an entirely German cast: "I spoke no German, had no German friends, had not read a single German novel either in the original, or in translation" (viii). This flat assertion should perhaps be viewed with some suspicion. Not only does Nabokov make reference to the Frank novel in his 1931 story and again in his later novel *Dar (The Gift)*, but his own 1930 novel *Zashchita Luzhina (The Defense)* contains an interesting parallel to it.

In Frank's *Bruder und Schwester* we find a scene set in the spring of 1924. Konstantin and Lydia are strolling along Berlin's Friedrichstrasse. As they pass a shop window, they see "a life-sized wax figure, a man with two heads, one face cheerful and one bitterly aggrieved, constantly draw aside the lapels of his coat, showing first a pique waistcoat stained with ink, and then—beaming—the other side, snow-white, because the fountain-pen in the pocket was of a non-leaking sort" (E48/G43). A remarkably similar description is to be found in Nabokov's *The Defense*. Grandmaster Luzhin is strolling along a Berlin street with his wife in the winter of 1929-30: "Presently he stopped stock-still in front of a stationery store where a wax dummy of a man with two faces, one sad and the other joyful, was throwing open his jacket alternately to left and right: the fountain pen clipped into the left pocket of his white waistcoat had sprinkled the whiteness with ink, while on the right was the pen that never ran" (E204/R184). The parallel is most striking especially in view of the hardcover publication dates of 1929 for Frank and 1930 for Nabokov, but the case is less than conclusive.

Judging by reviews, Frank's novel was published in late 1929. Nabokov was finishing *The Defense* in the summer of 1929 and the first portion of the novel started serial publication in the Parisian émigré journal *Sovremennye zapiski* in the last issue of 1929.[31] The wax dummy appears, however, in the second issue of 1930, presumably well after the publication of Frank's novel. The crucial issue is, of course, when Nabokov composed the passage in question. Was the manuscript complete when Frank's novel appeared? These questions remain unanswered. The available evidence shows only that it is chronologically possible for the borrowing to have occurred. It must also be considered that both authors lived in Berlin during the Twenties and could easily have seen the prototype of the figure that each man incorporated into the text of his current novel.[32] If Nabokov did adopt Frank's image, it was from the original German edition rather than the November 1930 English translation, although the English version could conceivably be the source of Nabokov's reference to Frank's novel in the December 1931 short story. In sum, it is certain that Nabokov was aware of Frank's novel of sibling incest, although it remains unclear how well he knew the book. If nothing else, the episode casts doubt upon Nabokov's assertion of total unfamiliarity with German fiction in the Twenties and Thirties. Nabokov's hostility to all things German is well known, and it may be that his blanket denial reflects a general attitude rather than particular facts.[33]

Nabokov's *Ada* does not seem to contain any allusions to German treatments of the sibling incest theme, notwithstanding its frequency in German literature. We have shown, however, that Nabokov was aware of that theme in its German variant and in particular in Frank's *Bruder und Schwester*. We must also keep in mind Nabokov's vast literary memory and such statements as, "I can always tell when a sentence I compose happens to resemble in cut or intonation that of any of the writers I loved or detested half a century ago" (SO 70). It is not "in cut or intonation" but rather in a series of coincident details and scenes that we find similarities between the

1969 *Ada* and the 1929 *Bruder und Schwester*. The major point of similarity is, of course, the brother-sister incest theme. This, however, merely relates both books to a rather select thematic genre. Beyond this, there are an impressive number of parallels in detail and in scene that occur in both books.

Both the Veens and the Schmitts are extremely affluent cosmopolitan families. Konstantin and Lydia, like Van and Ada, are possessed of physical beauty, intelligence, and a sense of honor immeasurably beyond those of ordinary mortals. The problems of the world are not their problems. Van, like Konstantin, is an athlete and sportsman. Lydia, like Ada, has mat white skin and black hair—features that serve as leitmotifs for both heroines. The lives of the polyglot families (German, Russian, English, and French) revolve about a series of estates, foreign travels, and luxury hotels. Van and Konstantin are both writer-scholars. Just as Ada has her French maid Blanche, Lydia has her Marie. Scholar Konstantin's male secretary mirrors the older Veen's Ronald Oranger. The homes have dachsunds (as did Nabokov's own family). Both pairs of brother and sister share gestures and table mannerisms that are clues to their kinship. Konstantin, like Van, is intensely jealous of rival suitors and threatens mayhem against them. Their respective rivals have attended the same posh prep schools as the heroes and discuss their terms there.

A number of scenes coincide in the two novels as well as details such as the above. Just as Van and Ada wander and declare their love in the park of Ardis Manor, Konstantin and Lydia roam and make their avowals in the Berlin Tiergarten (cf. the Chateaubriand parallel). Each book has an erotic interlude in which the heroine sits on her lover's lap while riding in a vehicle. The initial scene of intercourse takes place on divans (ottomans) which become leitmotifs throughout the respective narratives. There is in each novel a confrontation scene in which the hero is told of the incestuous nature of his relationship by a parent—Konstantin by his mother, Van by his father (although Van is already aware of the fact). The relationships are both curtailed until after the death of the parents, and in each the hero contemplates suicide by pistol. Although the protagonist of Frank's novel has no half-sister equivalent to *Ada*'s Lucette, he is followed about in his travels by a mysterious woman who is so smitten at the very sight of him that she abandons her husband and children to follow and gaze at him from afar. Like Lucette in *Ada*, this woman serves as a paranymph and brings Konstantin and Lydia back together after they lose each other—an act that leads to her own ruin. In both novels the hero wildly drives through the night toward a final reunion with his sister.

Many of the parallels that we have noted are undoubtedly functions of the incestuous relationship and the social milieu of the families. They are, so to speak, "built into" the underlying situation. The very abundance of the coincidences is, however, striking. The most suggestive similarity between the two novels is the one that opposes them to almost all other treatments of their theme. In virtually all treatments of the brother-sister incest theme, the relationship, once revealed, leads to grief, separation, and death. Perhaps the most distinctive parallel between the Nabokov and Frank novels is that the reunited sibling-lovers live happily ever after.[34]

We have noted the classic thematic prototypes for *Ada* in the works of the giants of Romanticism—the English Byron, the French Chateaubriand, and the Russian Pushkin. These authors, all frequently alluded to in *Ada*, form the literary backdrop of the sibling incest theme. The theme resurfaces a century later in a German incarnation in a series of works of less genial stature. Nabokov was in some measure aware of this resurgence and of Frank's book in particular. Could it have been Frank's book that planted the seed for Nabokov's treatment of the theme? If we entertain such a conjecture we must ponder the thirty-odd-year interval between provocation and reaction. The gap is all the more curious in that virtually all of the themes that appear in the English Nabokov are already present in his Russian works. The incest theme is the only major exception. Any answer to this question is, of course, speculative. It can be pointed out, however, that Leonhard Frank's death in Munich in August of 1961 was widely reported in the European press[35] and, doubtless, particularly so in Switzerland where for political reasons he had spent World War I and a part of the Thirties. Nabokov was a resident in Switzerland at the time of Frank's death, and in all likelihood saw the obituaries of the German novelist whose best-selling *Bruder und Schwester* he had castigated thirty years before. The news of Frank's death and the recollection of his novel of sibling incest was perhaps the grain of sand that provided the nucleus for Nabokov's major novel of the Sixties.

*Ada or Ardor: A Family Chronicle* is a family saga of an extraordinary sort. The history of the Zemski-Veen clan is presented over five generations, although the last, that of Van, Ada, and Lucette, receives by far the most attention. The family genealogy is sufficiently important (and complex) that *Ada*'s narrative is prefaced by a family tree in order to facilitate the reader's journey through the long novel.[36] The genealogical chart is helpful in some ways, but its primary purpose is to mislead the reader. It gives the "official version" of the family history, while the true history is wildly different. The disparity is most evident for the fifth and last generation of the moribund Zemski-Veen clan, and the unraveling of this situation is the major secret (and motivation) of the plot. Van Veen is ostensibly the son of Demon Veen and his wife, the mad Aqua Durmanov. Ada and her sister Lucette, no less ostensibly, are the children of Daniel Veen, Demon's first cousin, and his actress wife Marina Durmanov, Aqua's twin sister. In reality, Demon Veen is the father of both Van and Ada by Marina, while only Lucette is Daniel Veen's progeny. According to the falsified genealogical chart, Van and Ada are first cousins, whereas in truth they are full brother and sister, and Dan's daughter Lucette is their half-sister. This state of affairs has come about as follows. Marina has been Demon's mistress both before and after he marries her twin sister Aqua. Marina is pregnant with Van before her own hasty marriage to Dan. The newly married Aqua soon becomes pregnant, but suffers a miscarriage in a mental home in Switzerland. Nearby, Marina gives birth to Van. Marina (and Demon) succeed in substituting their new-born son Van for Aqua's dead child at a time when she is too disoriented to grasp the deception. Thus Van is raised by his father and initially regards Aqua as his mother, Marina as his aunt, and Ada as his cousin. He and Ada, aged fourteen and twelve, discover the truth while rummaging among family mementos in the attic of Ardis Hall. This revelation is, however, so obscured by the complexity of the narrative that many readers fail to grasp it.

Most critics have successfully unraveled this artfully tangled skein and arrived at the central secret of the novel's plot—that the turbulent life-long love affair of Van and Ada is one between full brother and sister, although Van's narrative thinly maintains the official version with occasional hints that the lovers are (at worst) half-siblings.[37] What has not been widely recognized is that the incestuous relationship of Van and Ada is but the final episode in a series of incestuous matings among Veens and Zemskis over several generations. Van, Ada, and Lucette are the fifth and final generation. The fourth generation, that of their parents, is comprised, as we have noted, of four living persons: the twin sisters Aqua and Marina (Zemski) Durmanov who respectively marry Demon and Dan Veen who are each other's first cousins.[38] The Durmanov twins are ostensibly the children of Dolly Zemski Durmanov and her husband General Ivan Durmanov who also have (officially and presumably in fact) a son, Ivan, a musical prodigy who dies before the opening of the novel. The male members of the fourth generation of the Veen family, Demon and cousin Dan, are respectively the offspring of the Veen brothers: Dedalus (married briefly to Irina Garin) and Ardelion (married to Mary Trumbull). Here again we come to a major discrepancy between the official genealogy and probable reality. There is good reason to doubt that General Durmanov is the father of Aqua and Marina, and some reason to question that Irina Garin is Demon's mother. The complex opening chapters of *Ada* include much of the genealogical data in the book, and although some sketchy information is provided on the first two generations of the Zemski family, the more detailed genealogical exposition starts (for no obvious reason) from Daria (Dolly) Zemski

Durmanov, Ada's grandmother: "Dolly, an only child, . . . married in 1840, at the tender and wayward age of fifteen, General Ivan Durmanov . . ." (3). It is then reported by nonagenarian narrator Van that "Dolly had inherited her mother's beauty and temper but also an older ancestral strain of whimsical, and not seldom deplorable, taste, well reflected, for instance, in the names she gave her daughters: Aqua and Marina. . . ." At this point her husband is brought on stage with the parenthetical thought "('Why not Tofana?' wondered the good and sur-royally antlered general . . .)" (4). Aqua Tofana is a poison used in eighteenth-century Italy by young wives (Dolly is twenty-four years her husband's junior) to get rid of their aged and "antlered" spouses.[39] Thus Dolly's fidelity and the cuckolded General's paternity of the children are both subjected to doubt at the very beginning of the narrative. These doubts are nourished in incidental asides throughout the novel, albeit never explicitly formulated or confirmed.

"Wayward" Dolly is fifteen at the time of her marriage to General Durmanov and nineteen when her twin daughters are born in 1844. That Dolly's waywardness predates (as well as postdates) her marriage to Durmanov is suggested by references to "love letters, written when she was twelve or thirteen" (374), i.e., well prior to her marriage to the General.[40] Dolly's sexual precocity is further evidenced by Ada's remark on her sixteenth birthday that she is already "older than grandmother at the time of her first divorce" (279). Dolly has been married (and divorced) prior to her marriage at fifteen to General Durmanov. We may conjecture that Dolly has also borne a son—perhaps to the unknown first husband or, more probably (as we shall see) to a lover. Two questions arise: who is the hypothetical son and who is the father?

Before addressing these questions, let us return to the third generation of the Veen family, Dedalus and his brother Ardelion. The marriage of Demon's father Dedalus to Countess Irina Garin ends in her death in the following year, 1838, the year of Demon's birth. Once again we are given reason to doubt the official version. The supposition that Irina is Demon's mother is subtly undermined when Demon casually mentions (and demonstrates) to his son Van an "ancestral mannerism" of Demon's mother that is shared by him and Ada (240). Since Demon obviously cannot remember Irina Garin, the reader might reasonably suppose that his mother is someone else.[41] A less direct bit of evidence is a passing comment made by Demon at a family dinner attended by Marina, Van, and Ada. Among the dishes is Peterson's grouse or *gelinotte* which is served, to Demon's dismay, with burgundy. Demon is moved to remark that "my maternal grandfather would have left the table rather than see me drink red wine instead of champagne with *gelinotte*" (256). Irina Garin's father is never alluded to in the narrative. It is a reference to a void. If, however, we pursue our assumption that Dolly is Demon's mother, Demon's maternal grandfather is Peter Zemski. It is probably not by chance that they are dining on *Peterson's* grouse.[42] All things considered, it seems more than likely that wayward Dolly is Demon's real mother.

Only one thing seems to weigh heavily against our supposition that Dolly is Demon's mother. Dolly would have been thirteen at the time of Demon's birth in 1838. This is not a fatal objection, however, when we recall that Dolly's romantic life started at twelve or thirteen (the love letters) and that her marriage at fifteen to General Durmanov is already her second marriage. Demon is in all probability the product of a liaison between Dedalus Veen and his sexually precocious first cousin Dolly about two years prior to her marriage to General Durmanov. If so, this makes Demon (at the least) a half-brother to Dolly's two daughters; Aqua, who becomes his wife, and Marina, his mistress and the mother of his two children, Van and Ada. We have noted that Demon's birth in 1838 is in the same year that Dedalus' wife Irina dies. Let us suppose that Dedalus takes his bastard son Demon and passes him off as the child of his just dead wife. There is yet a further possibility. Dedalus, who fathers Demon with cousin Dolly in 1838, resumes his affair with her after her marriage to the "sur-royally antlered" General Durmanov (4). The twins Aqua and Marina (b. 1844) may also be Dedalus' children. In this eventuality Demon marries one and mates with another of his full sisters.[43] Lest this line of conjecture seem altogether implausible, let it be recalled that it closely (but not exactly) parallels the events of the following generation which are far less speculative, if no less scandalous. An illicit child (Demon & Van) is taken from its real mother (Dolly & Marina) by its father (Dedalus & Demon) and is attributed to the unwitting wife (dying or dead Irina Garin Veen & mad Aqua Durmanov Veen). The "real" mothers (Dolly & Marina) subsequently marry (General Durmanov & Daniel Veen) but resume their premarital affairs which result in the birth of daughters (Marina & Ada). The older children (Demon & Van) then mate with their own sisters (Marina & Ada). Other more partial parallels include Lucette who is the loser in the incestuous triangle "Lucette-Van-Ada" as is Aqua in her own triangle "Aqua-Demon-Marina," i.e., Lucette : Ada + Van :: Aqua : Marina + Demon. In her role as half-sibling to brother and sister lovers she also echoes the position and tragic early death of young Ivan Durmanov, Marina's and Demon's half-brother. The accompanying genealogical chart is our revision of Van and Ada's family history (see page 128).

The clan's founding father, Prince Zemski, has a penchant for ever younger girls culminating in his marriage at seventy-one to the fifteen-year-old Princess Temnosiniy. Although incest is not, so far as we know, among his sins, Prince Zemski seems to look benignly upon the incestuous activities

**Revised Zemski-Veen Family Tree**

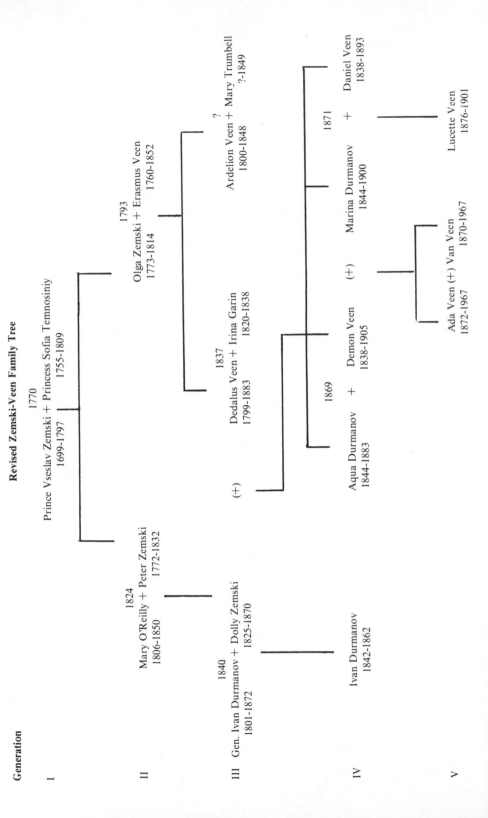

Generation

I

Prince Vseslav Zemski + Princess Sofia Temnosiniy
1699-1797            1755-1809
1770

II

Mary O'Reilly + Peter Zemski
1806-1850      1772-1832
1824

Olga Zemski + Erasmus Veen
1773-1814        1760-1852
1793

Ardelion Veen + Mary Trumbell
1800-1848          ?-1849
?

III

Gen. Ivan Durmanov + Dolly Zemski
1801-1872          1825-1870
1840

Dedalus Veen + Irina Garin
1799-1883      1820-1838
1837

Daniel Veen
1838-1893

IV

Ivan Durmanov
1842-1862

Aqua Durmanov  (+)  Demon Veen  (+)  Marina Durmanov
1844-1883              1838-1905              1844-1900
1869                              1871

V

Ada Veen (+) Van Veen
1872-1967    1870-1967

Lucette Veen
1876-1901

of his descendants. On Van's first morning at Ardis the family portraits, including that of Prince Zemski, are all "discreetly attentive" as he comes downstairs (48). On the morning after Van and Ada first couple, Van passes beneath the portrait of "a pleased-looking Prince Zemski" (124). Given the prevalence of incest in the third, fourth, and fifth generations of the family, one cannot but wonder about the earlier generations—especially that of Peter Zemski and his sister Olga. Tempting though the idea is, there seems to be little textual support for it. Further, if Dedalus Veen is the son of Peter and Olga Zemski rather than Olga and her husband Erasmus Veen, there is no Veen blood in Demon, Van or Ada. This seems unlikely because Van, Ada, and their father Demon share many physical traits and mannerisms as opposed to Lucette in whom, we are told, "the Z(emski) gene" dominates (367). The pattern of incest begins with Dedalus Veen and his first cousin Dolly Zemski who are respectively the children of Olga Zemski Veen and her husband Erasmus, and Olga's brother Peter Zemski and his wife Mary O'Reilly. Dedalus' and Dolly's children, Demon and Marina, are probably full (or perhaps half-) brother and sister while their offspring, Van and Ada, are unquestionably full brother and sister. Their sterile union marks the end of the super imperial Zemski-Veen clan.

The Zemski-Veen labyrinth of incest is, appropriately, not without its mythological antecedents and it is in part these antecedents that lend support to our argument about the extent of incest in the family's history. The names of the progenitors of the clan, Prince Vseslav Zemski (1699-1797) and his young bride Princess Sofia Temnosiniy (1755-1809) bespeak the misty mythological origins of the clan. The name "Zemski" is from the Russian root for "land, earth" and "Temnosiniy" (dark-blue) is the traditional epithet for the sky. Compare the progenitors of the Greek gods: Uranus who personifies Heaven, and his wife Gaea, embodiment of the Earth; Uranus is dethroned by his son Cronus who marries his own sister Rhea; Cronos is in turn outsted by his son Zeus who weds his own sister Hera.[44]

It is not by chance that Dedalus Veen, the initiator of Ada's Labyrinth of Incest, bears the name Daedalus, the creator of the famed Labyrinth of Crete. The association is made explicit when Dedalus Veen's son, Demon, is humorously addressed as Dementiy Labirintovich, a mock-Russian patronymic meaning "Demon, son of the Labyrinth" (523-24).[45] Further, Demon, the son of Dedalus Veen, dies in an air disaster as does Daedalus' son Icarus whose wax-sealed wings melt when he flies too near the sun. Lastly, Marina and Lucette, the sole surviving possessors of Van and Ada's secret after Demon's air death also meet mythologically appropriate ends: Marina by fire and Lucette by water (suicide by drowning).[46] The Labyrinth of Incest created by Dedalus Veen is scarcely less a maze than that of his mythological prototype Daedalus, the legendary artist-craftsman.

Incest is the most emotionally charged of all human experiences. If anthropologists are to be believed, the taboo against it underlies the organization of society and, indirectly, of civilization itself.[47] The act of incest is an attack on society; the triumph of irrational nature over rational society. This is presumably why incest, particularly brother-sister incest, becomes a central theme for Romanticism with its cult of the demonic hero in rebellion against the stifling strictures of society, i.e., the Byronic hero. Incest is the ultimate rebellion. From the viewpoint of mytho-psychology, however, incest has a quite different meaning. It is the cardinal symbol of the human urge to union, to wholeness, as reflected in the legend found in Plato's "Symposium" that all humankind are originally twins who have been separated and eternally seek their other halves. In the words of novelist John Barth, "The loss accounts for alienation...; the search accounts for ... erotic love...."[48] The "ideal" form of incest is between opposite-sex twins. The folklore surrounding such pairs in both primitive and literate societies is rich in sexual implications: "Throughout opposite-sex twin lore, the two are always seen as an original unit which has split, a unit destined to be reunited by sexual love, the ultimate symbol of conjoining."[49] In the alienated world of the Romantic vision, this urge to union is thwarted by the exclusivity of the hero whose fate it is to be tormented by the masses. So exalted is the hero in comparison with the surrounding world that only one of the same blood, someone genetically, physically, and psychically very like the protagonist is conceivable as a love object, i.e., capable of reconstituting the lost whole. The urge to wholeness can be satisfied only by sexual congress with an intimate family member—a choice which (at least in the Romantic imagination) has the added *frisson* of defying mankind's most deep-seated taboo.

The anthropological and the mytho-psychological views of incest have extensive structural but little *thematic* significance in Nabokov's novel. The anthropological incest taboo provides the novel's central plot mechanism. Were Van and Ada (and their parents) not brother and sister, there would be no plot, no need for subterfuges, no obstacles to their love. The mytho-psychological meaning of incest—the urge to wholeness—also plays a role. Because of their exclusivity, Van and Ada can find completeness only in each other.[50] All other romantic options are closed to the protagonists.

Some critics see the meaning of *Ada*'s incest theme in the area of moral philosophy. Bobbie Ann Mason avers that "*Ada* is about incest, and ... incest ... is virtually synonymous with solipsism."[51] In her view, the older Van, tormented by guilt for corrupting his sister Ada, falsely creates an idyllic past for himself and Ada in his "memoir." Van opts out of life. Mason presumes that Nabokov (who granted that his protagonists were "both rather horrible creatures") condemns Van's escape into solipsism as a means of assuaging his incestuous guilt.[52] Unfortunately for Mason's argument, there is no evidence that Van is wracked by guilt and, judging by her occasional marginal notes, Ada at eighty is no less happy with their life-long incestuous love than is Van. Further, Ada, who is the "victim" in Mason's view, is quite as aggressive as Van in initiating and pursuing their affair. Brian David Boyd, in his brilliant doctoral dissertation, also advances a moral interpretation of the incest theme: "Lucette ... is the real reason for the prominence given to incest in the book. Incest is in *Ada* not as it has generally been conceived, as an emblem of solipsism or self-love—Nabokov detests such symbols—but rather to stress the intimate interconnections between human lives, interconnections which impose on human life requirements of morality and responsibility."[53] In Boyd's interpretation, incest is an evil not so much as it pertains to Van and Ada but in that it ends in the agony and death of their vulnerable half-sister Lucette. Nabokov's theme of sibling incest inescapably has moral implications, and Boyd may well be accurate in his assessment. It does not, however, seem plausible that Nabokov's intense focus on the incest theme was more than marginally motivated by ethical rather than literary considerations. They are to be inferred from the narrative but do not underlie it.

When asked about the meaning of incest in *Ada*, Nabokov answered, or rather parried, the question with the following words: "If I had used incest for the purpose of representing a possible road to happiness or misfortune, I would have been a best-selling didactician dealing in general ideas. Actually I don't give a damn for incest one way or another. I merely like the 'bl' sound in siblings, bloom, blue, bliss, sable" (SO 122-23). If Nabokov is to be believed, his comment would seem to explode any hope of relating *Ada*'s sibling incest theme to the generalities of anthropology, psychology or philosophy—moral or immoral. The meaning of the novel's central thematic metaphor must be sought elsewhere.

Nabokov has made it abundantly clear that in his view the proper study of art is art. All of his novels in one way or another take as their main subject art and the artist.[54] *Ada* is no exception. Van, a psychologist-philosopher specializing in the study of Anti-Terra's hypothetical sibling planet Terra, finally comes to realize that the value of his writings lies not in their epistemic content but in their literary style (578). Accordingly, the meaning of *Ada*'s sibling incest theme is to be sought in the world of art rather than in the world of ideas. It is no accident that *Ada*'s only explicit extended discussion of incest takes place in the chapter which recounts Van and Ada's adventures in the Ardis Hall library only hours before their sexual initiation.[55] Twelve-year-old Ada's access to the family library is closely monitored, a situation she hotly resents. Van, via blackmail, gains unlimited and unsupervised entrée for Ada and himself to the bibliographic treasure trove of Ardis Hall. Not surprisingly, the chapter is a compendium of literary allusions, real and imaginary, ranging from the *Arabian Nights* to John Updike's *Centaur* which is transmuted into *Chiron*. Most of the works referred to deal with matters sexual and sometimes incestuous. Near the beginning of the chapter we read that Ada's newly won access to the library is due to her "intimacy with her *cher, trop cher René* as she sometimes called Van in gentle jest..." (131). The allusion soom becomes explicit in the remark that Ada had not quite understood the sentence *les deux enfants pouvaient donc s'abandonner au plaisir sans aucune crainte* when she had first read Chateaubriand's tale about "a pair of romantic siblings" (133). This is followed by a disquisition drawn from a volume entitled *Sex and Lex* on the incestuous family life of one Ivan Ivanov (the Russian version of "John Doe") who first impregnates his five-year-old great-granddaughter, Maria, and then, five years later, her daughter, Daria, who, in turn, produces a daughter named Varia. Upon his release from enforced seclusion in a monastery, Ivan, age 75, makes an honest woman of Daria. In consequence of this scandal, "not only first cousins but uncles and grandnieces were forbidden to intermarry" (135). The Ivanovs are presumably a satirically vulgarized version of the Zemski-Veens, although the detailed similarities seem to be limited to the coincidence of the names: Maria = Mary O'Reilly Zemski, while Maria's daughter Daria = Daria (Dolly) Zemski.

The children's lewd library lore is put to good use as suggested by the fact that purloined library volumes accompany them into Ardis park "whenever she and Van had their trysts" (133), and also by the couple's life-long preference for *"positio torovago"* which is first described in one of their library treasures (136). The ultimate function of the family library is not merely that of a multivolume sex encyclopedia, however. The library establishes the proper context for Nabokov's theme of sibling incest—a context that is literary rather than social, psychological, or philosophical. The link between incest and art is first formulated by Ada, seemingly quite *en passant*. To a description of the ever-fertile and ever-incestuous Ivan Ivanov as an "habitually intoxicated laborer," Ada casually responds—"a good definition...of the true artist" (134). Any literary work is the outgrowth of a complex interaction with other literary works—particularly those that are closely related in setting and theme. Given *Ada's* myriad of literary allusions and its references to stages (generations) in the Evolution of the Novel (96), it does not seem untoward to see its theme of incest as a metaphor for intercourse among kindred works of art. *Ada* is the consequence of a complex act of incestuous procreation.

Nabokov's subtexts and allusions to the literary forbears of his novel are often parodic—a literary device with evident ties to the idea of incest. Parody has always played an important part in Nabokov's writing,[56] and in part *Ada* can be seen as Nabokov's parodistic reworking of the great

Romantic theme of sibling incest.[57] It is to this parodic aspect of *Ada* that Nabokov alludes in the final passage of his "library" chapter on literature and incest: "That library had provided a raised stage for the unforgettable scene of the Burning Barn [the night of the siblings' first intercourse —DBJ]; it had thrown open its glazed doors; it had promised a long idyll of bibliolatry; it might have become a chapter in one of the old novels on its own shelves; a touch of parody gave its theme the comic relief of life" (137).

Ada is the end product of many generations of bibliolatry—taken in a specifically sexual sense. It has its thematic founding fathers (Chateaubriand, Byron, Pushkin) whose offspring are intimately and obscurely related. Its more recent, and perhaps less illustrious forebears (Frank, *et al.*) are even more dubiously intertwined. The parallel to the Zemski-Veen family is evident. It is in this connection that the incest of the preceding generations is thematically important. If the novel's incest theme were restricted to the generation of Van and Ada, the genetic parallel to the literary history of the theme would be less impressive. The elucidation of the literary genealogy of the sibling incest theme is not unlike the detection of the carefully concealed incestuous relations in successive generations of the Zemski-Veens. It is the historical depth of the Zemski-Veen family incest that establishes the parallel to the evolution of that theme in European literature. *Ada*'s theme of sibling incest can plausibly be read as a master metaphor for the creative intercourse of several generations of sibling incest novels in the three major literatures to which Nabokov's novel is heir.

George Steiner has advanced the idea of "extraterritoriality" as one of the hallmarks of twentieth century literature.[58] Noting the multilingual background of such writers as Samuel Beckett, Jorge Borges, and Nabokov, Steiner has suggested that much of the singularity of their literary styles may derive from the filtration of one language through the grammatical and cultural world-view inherent in a second language. He conjectures that their writings in each of two languages somehow may be "meta-translations" of the other—a phenomenon that presumably underlies their dazzling virtuosity.[59] Much of Nabokov's work, Steiner asserts, may be read "as a meditation—lyric, ironic, technical, parodistic—on the nature of human language, on the enigmatic coexistence of different, linguistically generated world visions and of a deep current underlying, and at moments conjoining, the multitude of diverse tongues" (8). Underlying Steiner's thesis is that Russian, English, and French are literally sibling tongues, all taking their origin from a remote common parent known as Proto-Indo-European. The interaction of the distinctive world visions (cultures) imposed by the grammatical and lexical systems of these three sibling tongues—all inhering in Nabokov's mind from early childhood—is surely not without parallel to the phenomenon of incest. Steiner speculates that this linguistic interaction is "the source of the motif of incest, so prevalent throughout Nabokov's fiction and central to Ada."[60]

Nabokov's unique literary career displays a curious interaction among its own parts. Perhaps the most striking aspect of the self-reflexiveness of Nabokov's career is his singular role as the translator of his own work from Russian into English and English into Russian.[61] Beyond this there is the even more intricate act of drawing upon his own versions of Pushkin and other writers as a basis for original creations. *Pale Fire* obviously draws its formal structure from Nabokov's massive *Onegin* translation *cum* commentaries. Far more subtle is Nabokov's practice of making allusion not so much to a "classic" source but to his own, highly idiosyncratic interpretation of that source, e.g., his "incestuous" reading of (and borrowing from) the *Onegin* stanza discussed above. Nabokov interacts with Nabokov. Further, Nabokov's English career has in some ways paralleled and replicated the earlier Russian one in that certain of the English novels re-evoke themes first enunciated in their Russian predecessors.[62] This partial mirror imaging of the English and Russian works has been accompanied by the increasingly self-referential quality of the late English novels.

Sibling incest is an apt metaphor for Nabokov's unique career and *Ada* is the most intricate elaboration of this metaphor. *Ada*, with its mirror-image patterns of incest, and its parallel relationship of the two worlds of the novel's underlying cosmology, embodies many aspects of Nabokov's life and art. Sibling incest becomes a master metaphor embracing not only his own work but the genesis of literature itself. This metaphor attains its apogee in Nabokov's novel *Look at the Harlequins!* and it is to this work that we shall now direct our attention.

# DEMENTIA'S INCESTUOUS CHILDREN IN *LOOK AT THE HARLEQUINS!*

*Look At The Harlequins!*, Nabokov's incest-suffused last novel, is a retrospective of its author's favorite themes and a meditation on the identity of its own narrator.[63] In *Ada*, the theme of sibling incest, if not its degree or extent, is readily apparent to the reader. In *LATH!*, perhaps owing to the involuted narrative, the tangled web of consanguinity enmeshing the narrator, his wives and lovers is thoroughly obscured. The novel is cast in the form of the autobiography of the distinguished Anglo-Russian writer Vadim Vadimovich N. (b. 1899). Composed in the aftermath of a mysterious paralytic stroke, VV's memoir is no ordinary one and is perhaps best described in the words of the narrator himself:

> In this memoir my wives and my books are interlaced monogrammatically like some sort of watermark or *ex libris* design; and in writing this oblique autobiography—oblique because dealing mainly not with pedestrian history but with the mirages of romantic and literary matters—I consistently try to dwell as lightly as inhumanly possible on the evolution of my mental illness. Yet Dementia is one of the characters in my story (85).

We shall see that Dementia is not merely "one of the characters" in the story but that she is the leading lady. The narrator's works and women (apart from the last) are, in the form he sees and describes them, the offspring of his Dementia who is both Mistress and Muse. The autobiography deals quite literally with "mirages of romantic and literary matters."

The narrator, Prince VV, is the putative son of an aristocratic Russian couple who assertedly abandon him to the care of relatives thanks to the frenetic pace of their divorces, remarriages, redivorces, and so on. Their neurasthenic, dreamy son is left in the custody of a grand-aunt, who resides on one of the family estates called Marevo, a Russian word appropriately meaning "mirage." It is this aunt who advises her morose seven or eight-year-old charge to "Look at the harlequins!" "Play! Invent the world! Invent Reality!" (8-9). This is just what VV does, starting, he confesses, with his grand-aunt.

Following the Bolshevik revolution, VV shoots a Red Army sentry and steals across the Polish border. He then makes his way to London where, funds soon exhausted, he discovers a patron, the Anglophilic Count Nikifor Nikodimovich Starov. The Count, who had "graced several great Embassies during a spacious span of international intercourse," is a quondam lover of VV's "beautiful and bizarre" mother (10-11). In fact we shall learn that Count Starov, by virtue of his "spacious span of international intercourse," is the progenitor of several of the characters of *LATH*. He is also the head of an anti-Soviet spy network, the White Cross, that passes itself off as a charitable organization for Russian refugees.

It is through the grace of Count Starov that his protégé attends Cambridge where, in his final term in the spring of 1922, he is invited to the newly inherited Riviera villa of his classmate, Ivor Black. Here he meets Ivor's twenty-year-old sister, Iris, who becomes the memoirist's first wife. The parentage of the fond brother and sister is no less murky than that of VV himself. Their mother, Iris says, was "American and horrible," while the businessman father had "good connections" in London diplomatic circles (29 & 177). This becomes strangely portentous when VV and Iris, newly married unbeknownst to the Count, visit him at his summer Villa on the Côte d'Azur. Upon being introduced to Iris (whom he assumes to be Vadim's fiancée) the old Count gazes at her for a time and then somewhat ambiguously tells his protégé that his fiancée "is as beautiful as your wife will be" (49). After Iris leaves the room to have tea in "an adjacent alcove (illuminated by a resplendent portrait by Serov, 1896, of the notorious beauty, Mme. de Blagidze, in Caucasian costume)," the newly enlightened Count asks VV his wife's maiden name (50). Slowly shaking his head, he then inquires the name of Iris's mother. Vadim's reply is greeted by the identical response and the conversation moves on to talk of the couple's financial future.

VV and Iris move to Paris where, during the seven years of their marriage, the narrator embarks upon his literary career, rapidly publishing three Russian volumes—*Tamara* (1925), *Pawn Takes Queen* (1927) and *Plenilune* (1929).[64] Iris, not knowing Russian, is somewhat excluded from her husband's literary milieu and it is through her unsuccessful effort to learn Russian that she becomes the (unwilling?) object of the amorous attentions of Lt. Wladimir Starov-Blagidze, the husband of her tutoress. The lieutenant, VV learns, is another "protégé" of Count Starov at whose funeral the two half-brothers first meet as pallbearers. Starov-Blagidze, three or four years senior to VV, is apparently the result of a liaison between Count Starov and the "notorious St. Petersburg courtesan" depicted in the Serov portrait mentioned above (11). The lieutenant, already half-mad from a Russian Civil War head wound and now spurned by Iris, runs amok and on the night of April 23, 1930 shoots Iris and himself in the presence of VV and Ivor, one of whom, and possibly both, are likewise offspring of the mysterious Count Starov.

After his wife's death, VV submerges himself in his writing, finishing his fourth and fifth Russian novels, *Camera Lucida* and *The Red Top Hat*. The narrator meets his second wife, Annette, (Anna Ivanovna Blagovo) when he hires the long-necked Botticellian beauty as the typist for his longest, last and best Russian novel, *Podarok otchizne* (*Gift for the Fatherland*), later known in English as *The Dare*. Notwithstanding her inept typing, her thoroughly philistine tastes and her frigidity, VV is so strongly attracted to her that he enters into his second and longest marriage. In 1939,

VV, who has now completed his first English language novel, *See under Real*, emigrates with Annette to the United States where he joins the faculty of Quirn University (Quirn = kernel = Cornell). Here VV adds to his modest reputation as an English novelist with *Esmeralda and Her Parandrus* (1942), *Dr. Olga Repnin* (1946), and the short story collection *Exile from Mayda* (1947). Meanwhile, Annette conceives, and a daughter, Isabel, is born on New Year's Day 1942. The marriage, never more than marginally adequate, comes under the blighting influence of their ex-Soviet landlady Ninel (a palindrome of Lenin) who befriends and carries off Annette and the four-year-old Isabel to her lake-side cottage while VV dallies with Dolly von Borg. The brief affair with Dolly, who successfully schemes to break up her lover's marriage, is the long delayed consummation of a series of furtive fondlings with the compliant eleven-year-old Dolly while VV had been a house guest of her Russian émigré grandparents in prewar Paris.

The covert kinship pattern that characterizes VV's first marriage is quite possibly, if obscurely, present in the second. Anna Blagovo is the daughter of a Tsarist army surgeon, who in 1907 married a provincial belle in the Volgan town of Kineshma a few miles from one of VV's most romantic estates—presumably Marevo (112). It may well occur to the reader that Count Starov, the long-time lover of VV's mother, was quite possibly a visitor to the estate and its environs. Further, there are hints that Annette herself may have been acquainted with the late Lt. Starov-Blagidze. This becomes apparent in her responses to VV's questions at the time of his proposal. Although the status-conscious Annette hesitantly agrees to marry her titled suitor, she finds him strange—unlike other men she has met. In answer to VV's query as to whom she had met: "trepanners? trombonists? astronomists?" she blandly replies "mostly military men...officers of Wrangel's army..." (108). That Lt. Starov-Blagidze, who served under Wrangel, has been subject to trepanning is quite probable (possibly at the hands of Annette's father) for we know he suffers a "terrifying tic" as a result of his head wound (58). Still more curious is VV's choice of "astronomist," for the initial syllable is the Latin root for "star" while the first five letters form an anagram corresponding to the first five letters of the name Starov.[65] In short, Anna Blagovo, like Iris Black, may be the half-sister, as well as the wife, of the narrator. Again like Iris, she is (possibly) acquainted with Lt. Starov-Blagidze.

In 1953, some seven years after Annette flees VV, she and Ninel perish in a flood, and Isabel, now eleven and a half and called Bel, returns to live with her father. For two blissful years Bel and her adoring father are inseparable companions, spending their summers idyllically wandering from motel to motel in the Far West. The intimacy of father and daughter as well as brilliant Bel's precocity lead to ugly rumors which Professor N. seeks to counter by marrying Louise Adamson, the fast young widow of the former head of the Quirn English Department. Beautiful Louise, a sexually and financially avaricious celebrity collector, is all too ready to wed the novelist who is reportedly the leading candidate for "the most prestigious prize in the world" (175). She is, however, equally quick to cool when the prize is not forthcoming. Her relationship with Bel is abysmal, and the daughter is soon packed off to a Swiss finishing school from which she eventually elopes with an American student who defects to Russia. VV finds solace for the loss of Bel by reliving their life and travels in the transmuted form of what will become his most successful (and sensational) novel, *A Kingdom by the Sea* (1962).

Louise, VV's third wife, is also implicated in the incestuous network of the author's life. She too is not without family ties to her husband's tangled past. Shortly before his marriage proposal, VV spends an evening with a number of guests including Louise and her cousin Lady Morgain, the fat and fiftyish daughter of a former American Ambassador to England (175). Fay Morgain informs VV that she had been acquainted with Iris Black in London around 1919 when she herself was "a starry-eyed American gal" (177). Louise's obscure connection with Count Starov is also hinted in another anagrammatic reference. As VV and Louise leave the gathering, she agrees to marry him: "She was gone before I could enclasp her slender form. The *star*-dusted sky, usually a scary affair, now vaguely amused me . . . I made water into a sizzle of *asters*" (182) [ my italics—DBJ].Thus Louise too may be a member of the Count Starov's consanguineal brood.

VV meets his fourth and final grand love in September 1969 on the day when the now notorious author submits his resignation to the overjoyed administration of Quirn University. As VV is leaving campus, a bulky folder under his arm spills, and he is aided in gathering up its contents by a young woman coming from the library.[66] As the girl helps VV collect his scattered papers she inquires about Bel (now in Russia). The narrator suddenly remembers her name and "in a photic flash of celestial memory" sees her and her schoolmate Bel "looking like twins, silently hating each other, both in blue coats and white hats, waiting to be driven somewhere by Louise" (226). This young woman, who is throughout referred to only as "you"[67] and who shares Bel's birthday (January 1, 1942), becomes VV's lover during his final year at Quirn while he writes his last lovel, *Ardis*. At the end of the academic year they move to the Continent.

VV is markedly reluctant to speak of the details of his relationship with "you" in his autobiographical account, saying that "Reality would only be adulterated" (226). In consequence we learn very little about the background and identity of VV's last love. She speaks a "lovely, elegant Russian," has studied Turgenev in Oxford and Bergson in Geneva, and has "family ties with good old Quirn and Russian New York" (226 & 228). She also knows butterflies and her lover's complete *oeuvre*. The question we are approaching is, of course, that of her place, if any, in the intricate network of Count Starov's progeny. The only clue to her identity is connected with her Russian background. This, together with her family association with Quirn, points to Marion Noteboke, the daughter of Professor Noteboke, the head of the Quirn Russian Department (163). Marion, however, seems to be slightly too old to be "you" who is known to be eleven years and four-odd months of age in May 1953 when Marion is described as being twelve (162). Also against Marion's candidacy is VV's passing reference to her (circa 1954) as "a depraved and vulgar nymphet" who carries tales of Bel's relationship with her widowed father home to Mrs. Noteboke (173). In sum it must be concluded that VV's final love, "you," remains both anonymous and outside the Starov family orbit. This assumption is strengthened by VV's persistent association of "you" and "Reality,"[68] an association strikingly absent from his account of his previous loves.

It is a curious and significant fact that at least two of VV's wives have the letter sequence "BL" in their names: Iris *Bl*ack and Anna *Bl*agovo. The writer's much loved daughter *Bel* also enters into this alphabetic series. The family name of Louise is unknown but one of the names from her past is *Bl*anc (181). Also of note is that Starov's other son (and Iris Black's lover) bears his mother's family name *Bl*agidze and that, on occasion, the narrator refers to himself as *Bl*onsky (232). All of these characters are related to Count Starov and it is their incestuous consanguinity that is denoted by the alphabetic emblem "BL" in their names.[69] The sound sequence is, moreover, not randomly chosen. As we have noted previously in connection with *Ada*, Nabokov denies any deep meaning in his use of the incest theme, saying merely that he likes "the 'bl' sound in siblings, bloom, blue, bliss, sable" (SO 122-23).[70] "BL" is Nabokov's private emblem for the incest theme. That VV's last love is in no way associated with the "BL" incest emblem is additional evidence of her unique reality in his "autobiography."

It is now time to consider the other "real" character in VV's autobiography—Dementia, which is the source of the other "characters." Dementia appropriately attends both the beginning and ending of VV's tale of love and prose. Indeed it predates the narrative which begins with the youthful narrator's meeting his first wife. In the memoirist's earliest reference to himself—as a child of seven or eight—he already harbors "the secrets of a confined madman," something he in fact becomes at various times in his life (8). At nine or ten, he says, his morbid childhood terrors were supplanted "by more abstract and trite anxieties (problems of infinity, eternity, identity, and so forth)" which he believes to have saved his reason (7). This belief is, as we shall see, open to question, for it is these more abstract anxieties of space, time, and identity that seem to be at the root of his psychotic episodes. In their acute phase these episodes last from several weeks to several years, and seven are severe enough to require hospitalization.

VV's mental condition, vaguely described as "a nervous complaint that skirted insanity" and as "flayed consciousness" (5 & 31), displays a number of symptoms among which the more mundane are severe headaches, dizziness, neuralgia and confusion about his surroundings.[71] Attacks are sometimes occasioned by a faint ray of light that awakens the sleeper into a state of madness. Along this narrow beam descends a row of bright dots "with dreadful meaningful intervals between them" (16). We shall see that sanity ultimately reestablishes itself in a not dissimilar pattern (250).

The most peculiar manifestation of the writer's madness is his inability to visualize left/right reversals. The problem is entirely psychological for VV is physically able to reverse his tracks and the corresponding vista without difficulty. It is the mental effort of imagining the left/right reversal of vista accompanying any such about-face that induces stress so acute that VV is literally immobilized. He likens the effort of such inversions to trying to shift the world on its axis (236). The "paralysis motif" is prefigured in VV's account of earlier fits of total cramp while swimming—fits which he describes as the physical counterpart of "lightning insanity" (36-37). Mental transpositions of any sort induce severe trauma for the narrator. So acute, for example, is VV's distress arising from the change of languages entailed in the composition of his first English-language novel that it "almost led to the dementia paralytica that I had feared since youth" (122).[72] It is, however, the purely spatial dimension of his abberation, the mental inability to translate left into right (and right into left), that most troubles VV. So obsessed is he by this seemingly inconsequential aspect of his mental state that he feels honor bound to confess it—to the exclusion of the seemingly more serious aspects of his illness—to each of his four brides-to-be.[73] These set scenes have an almost ritualistic quality.

Vadim Vadimovich's psychological malaise is rooted in his troubled sense of dual identity. He is haunted by the feeling that he is a pale shadow, an inferior variant, of another, vastly more gifted Anglo-Russian writer.[74] On one level the plot of *LATH* consists of the accumulation of evidence that this is so. The reader must regard VV's statements about his identity with suspicion for VV is yet another example of Nabokov's use of the unreliable narrator. A telling example occurs in the narrator's contradictory statements about his father. Early in the narrative VV notes he was raised by a great aunt (upon whose reality he immediately casts doubt) and saw his parents only "infrequently" due to their frenzied cycles of divorce and remarriage (8). This "infrequently" is a considerable overstatement for later VV avers that his father, Vadim, a reactionary gambler and rake nicknamed Demon, died in a duel following a card table fracas in Deauville some six months before the narrator's (and Nabokov's) birth in April of 1899 (95-96).[75] Thus VV could never have seen his "official" father. Such contradictions (quite apart from the previous strong insinuation that Count Starov is VV's father) are among those that must lead us to question the veracity of all of the narrator's account of his life.

The name of the narrator remains obscure throughout his autobiography. In the London psychiatrist's report of his case, the patient is identified as "Mr. N. a Russian nobleman" although, to VV's intense irritation, the doctor lumps his case history with that of "another" patient, a Mr. V.S., whom the reader (but not the narrator) might reasonably associate with Nabokov's Russian pen name, Vladimir Sirin (15). At a later point the tipsy narrator rhetorically addresses himself as Prince Vadim Blonsky but shortly thereafter disavows the surname as a false one used for a surreptitious trip to Russia in search of his daughter (232 & 249). His Cambridge friend, Ivor Black, once refers to him as "McNab" because he resembles an actor of that name and on a later occasion calls him Vivian (7 & 43)—the latter evoking for the reader Nabokov's own sometime anagrammatic pen names of Vivian Calmbrood and Vivian Darkbloom.[76]

The narrator's unease about his name and identity is, of course, symptomatic of his aberrant mental condition which *au fond* seems to partake far more of schizophrenia than dementia paralytica. Even the most casual reader of Nabokov will have noted that most of VV's books, in title, content, and serial order, are transparent variants and blends of Nabokov's own novels. For example, Nabokov's *Kamera Obskura*, which becomes the English, *Laughter in the Dark*, underlies the mad narrator's *Camera Lucida* and its English counterpart *Slaughter in the Sun*. It is VV's unseen and nameless double who is obviously the source of the narrator's intuition that he is a "non-identical twin, a parody." He feels that a demon is forcing him to impersonate "that other writer who was and would always be incomparably greater, healthier, and crueler than your obedient servant" (89). This feeling is reinforced in VV's conversation with Oksman, the Russian bookman, who mistakenly welcomes the author of *Camera Lucida* to his shop as the author of *Camera Obscura* and then blunders again by confusing VV's *Tamara* with a book entitled *Mary* (96-97).[77] To make matters worse the amiable bookseller reminisces that he twice saw the narrator's father, a prominent liberal member of the First Duma. On one occasion VV's father was at the opera with his wife and *two* small boys and once again, later, at a public meeting where his English *sangfroid* and absence of gesticulation was in sharp contrast to that of his fiery friend Alexander

Kerenski (95).[78] These recollections from the period between 1905 and 1917 postdate the 1898 death of VV's "father." Oksman, like a number of other characters, is seemingly party to the widespread confusion of the narrator with another, unnamed novelist.[79] This unnerving experience further intensifies VV's lurking dread that "he might be permanently impersonating somebody living as a real being beyond the constellation of ... tears and asterisks ..." This is of course precisely what VV is doing within the anagrammatic constellation of Count Starov's *tears* and *asterisks*. The "real" person (or, more accurately, persona) is "Vladimir Vladimirovich." So distraught is VV that he returns home and makes a detailed record of the meeting in cipher (96-97). He even contemplates repatterning his entire life, abandoning his art, taking up chess, becoming a lepidopterist, or making a scholarly Russian translation of *Paradise Lost* that would cause "hacks to shy and asses to kick." Realizing, however, that only his writing, his "endless re-creation of his fluid self" keeps him "more or less" sane, he finally contents himself with dropping his *nom de plume*, V. Irisin, in favor of his real (but unrevealed) name. V. Irisin, of course, evokes Nabokov's Russian-language pseudonym, V. Sirin, the initials of which we remarked in the London psychiatrist's report.

In spite of this shift from pseudonym to real name, the narrator continues to be plagued by his shadowy nemesis. Some dozen years later while motor touring in the American West, VV is overcome by a "dream sensation of having come empty-handed—without what? A gun? A wand? This I dared not probe lest I wound the raw fell under my thin identity" (156). The same page also contains an oblique reference to butterflies and it is obviously a butterfly net that VV's empty hand longs to enclasp.[80] The wonder-working wand is also, however, the omnipresent symbol of the autobiography's title motif, the Harlequin, the madcap prankster of the commedia dell-arte—another of the guises of the mysterious double. It is appropriate that the harlequin is traditionally invisible to some of the other commedia characters.

Vadim Vadimovich's sense of duality persists throughout the narrative, even manifesting itself at a particularly radiant moment in his life shortly after he has moved to Switzerland with his last love. The seventy-one-year-old author has just completed the fair copy of his last novel, *Ardis*. Louise has been blackmailed into agreeing to a divorce, and VV is contemplating a proposal of marriage to his new love. Before doing so, however, he feels once again honor bound to confess his bizarre inability to mentally invert right and left. To accomplish this painful chore he hits upon the idea of giving "you" an early manuscript-chapter of *Ardis* in which the hero discusses his own (and VV's) aberration. While his love reads his "confession," VV goes for a pre-prandial stroll. He is in a rare euphoric state that nothing can mar, not even "the hideous suspicion that *Ardis*, my most private book, soaked in reality, saturated with sun flecks, might be an unconscious imitation of another's unearthly art, *that* suspicion might come later" (234). And indeed it does. VV reaches the far end of his stroll, stands before a low parapet, and gazes at the setting sun. As he attempts to turn about and retrace his steps, he finds he can not: "To make that movement would mean rolling the world around on its axis..." (236). VV's psychological inability has become a physical reality. The dementia paralytica he has feared from youth has overtaken him.

VV awakens in a hospital, his mind racing but his body and senses all but lifeless. As he gathers his thoughts he first tries to establish his own identity. He is fairly certain that his first name *cum* patronymic is Vadim Vadimovich but is troubled by the thought that in rapid, indistinct speech the name Vladimir Vladimirovich degenerates into something very like Vadim Vadimych (the slurred form of Vadim Vadimovich). Of his family name the narrator is at first certain only that it contains the letters N and B. After trying and rejecting several possibilities such as Nebesnyy, Nabedrin, Nablidze, Naborcroft, Bonidze, and Blonsky, his "sonorous surname" finally bursts into his consciousness (248-249).

The questions of identity and reality are closely coupled. The theme of "reality" in *LATH* is, in turn, closely linked with VV's nameless fourth love. The narrator even declines to identify her or speak of their relationship for fear that it would contaminate "the reality of your radiance." "Yet," he writes, "'reality' is the key word here; and the gradual perception of that reality was nearly fatal to me" (226). As the reader knows, it is just as VV wishes to go back to his newly enlightened love with his proposal of marriage that his near-fatal seizure occurs. As VV emerges from his deathlike coma and at last recalls his surname, the door of his hospital room opens and he becomes aware of "a slow infinitely slow sequence of suspension dots in diamond type. I emitted a bellow of joy, and Reality entered" (250). Reality in the person of his ideal love has entered the room.

The identity of the narrator is that of the nameless "other" author who is the prototype of which VV and his books are flawed copies. The identity of this original has long been obvious to the reader. It has remained a secret only to the mad narrator who has vaguely sensed but not known the truth. It is only during VV's mysterious paralysis that his speeding mind has attained certain insights from its brief intimacy with non-being and "Problems of identity have been, if not settled, at least set" (239).

Vadim Vadimovich is now consciously aware of both halves of his dual schizoid being. Vadim Vadimovich and "Vladimir Vladimirovich," mad and sane, left and right, have been reintegrated. If we adopt this interpretation, and it seems fully warranted, a new question poses itself. The narrator is now whole and between his seventy-first and seventy-fourth years composes *LATH*. This "autobiography" is, however, patently fantastic. If VV is no longer mad, why does he write a largely fantastical autobiography? There would seem to be only one perspective from which all of the pieces fall into place. *LATH* is an account of the delusional world of the narrator during his existence as Vadim Vadimovich told entirely and consistently from that point of view.

In the fictional universe of Nabokov's *LATH*, there exists a Nabokovian persona who shares much, but far from all, of the biographical background of the real, extra-fictional Nabokov and who has written a series of books—*Mary, Camera Obskura, The Gift, Lolita, Ada*, etc. This Nabokovian persona whom we have termed "Vladimir Vladimirovich" suffers from periods of schizophrenia in which he is Vadim Vadimovich, the author of *Tamara, Camera Lucida, The Dare, A Kingdom by the Sea, Ardis*, etc. None of these works exist outside the mind of the mad narrator. They are simply distorted variants of the real works written by the sane half of the narrator's personality—"Vladimir Vladimirovich." The other characters know that the narrator is mad and has periods in which he is the "other" personality. The Stepanovs, for example, with whom VV stays after one of his breakdowns, refer to him as mad (87-88). Oksman, the book dealer, also knows this and humors VV by pretending that his reference to *Camera Lucida* as *Camera Obscura* is a slip of the tongue. Note that none of the characters seem *ever* to have read any of Vadim's books—only those of the "other" author.

Vadim's incestuous wives and lovers (with the exception of the last) are no more real than his books, although like the books they are presumably delusional variants of real women in the world of "Vladimir Vladimirovich." The unreality of this aspect of Vadim's life is attested by the gross improbability of the fiction that the multifarious bastards of the mythical Court Starov meet, mate, and murder. Still more implausible is that their diverse names all include the emblematic "BL." The almost ritualistic patterning in the presentation of the women is strikingly artificial. With minor variation three events must precede each new relationship. The obligatory butterfly must appear. There must be a scene in which the nude VV stands before a mirror and takes stock before making his declarations to his future brides.[81] Finally, there is the bizarre left/right confession which assumes a modicum of meaning only in the context of the narrator's schizophrenic dual identity. All this bespeaks the artifice of art rather than the chaos of reality or even fictional realism. Vadim's "autobiography" is so neatly patterned because it never happened. It is entirely the product of his disordered (or possibly his over-ordered) imagination during periods in which "Vladimir Vladimirovich" is supplanted by Vadim Vadimovich.

VV has taken the advice of his invented great-aunt in the creation of his "oblique autobiography" with its "mirages of romantic and literary matters." In obeying the injunction to "Look at thc Harlequins!" the narrator is looking at the left-handed world of Vadim Vadimovich's "motley madness" as it is set within the right-hand world of "Vladimir Vladimirovich." VV has invented his own delusional "reality" through inversion.

The incest theme that suffuses *LATH!* has obvious congruity with several aspects of the narrative. The incestuous brother-sister relationship (actually half-brother/half-sister) mirrors several crucial aspects of the narrative: the relationship of Vadim Vadimovich and "Vladimir Vladimirovich" and their respective worlds, the relationship of their respective novels, the relationship of the Russian and English parts of their careers to each other, and the left/right aberration of the narrator. In each case one half of the pairing is a reflected inverted version of the other half, a distorted mirror image, a simulacrum of the forbidden brother-sister relationship.

*Ada* and *LATH!* are united by much more than the theme of hidden sibling incest. The events of each novel take place on an inverted antiworld. In *Ada*, with its Anti-Terra, this is literally the case, while in *LATH* the antiworld seemingly consists of the hero's delusional world which coexists with the "real" world. In each case, the antiworld hero has obscure intimations of a parallel world which is a distorted mirror-image of his own. Although the heroes take their own worlds as the "real" ones, they are troubled by secret patterns that hint that their worlds are but imperfect copies of an original prototype. Much of the data testifying to the existence of the other world comes from the delusions of madmen. Vadim Vadimovich is mad, and Van Veen, a psychologist, derives much of his information about Terra from the delusions of his patients.

Each novel has a shadowy character who is a source of signs and portents: *Ada*'s Baron Klim Avidov who supplies the vatic Scrabble set that foretells the incestuous relationship of Van and Ada, and *LATH*'s Count Nikifor Nikodimovich Starov who sires Vadim and his half-sister brides. In both novels the secret pattern of sibling incest is one of the clues to the controlling presence of another world. Just as the narrators seek out covert patterns suggesting another world, the reader of Nabokov's two novels must decipher the secret labyrinth of sibling incest that lies at their center. For the voyager who discovers "What the Sailor Has Hidden," the intricate patterns of sibling incest testify to the controlling presence of Nabokov, the maze-maker.

NOTES

Section Four

1. Alfred Appel, Jr., "*Ada* described," *TriQuarterly*, 17 (Winter 1970), p. 171.

2. The author gratefully acknowedges his debt to the following colleagues for information relating to the sibling incest theme in European literature: Richard Exner, Gunther Gottschalk, Neil Granoien, Kenneth Harper, Albert Kaspin, Rolf Linn, Ursula Mahlendorf, Olga Matich, and Henry Steinhauer.

3. John Updike in his review of *Ada* offers the aphorism "Rape is the sexual sin of the mob, adultery of the bourgeoisie, and incest of the aristocracy. Romanticism, which made every ego an aristocrat, spawned Wordsworth and Dorothy, Byron and Augusta, Chateaubriand and Lucile...." "Van Loves Ada, Ada Loves Van," *The New Yorker*, August 2, 1969, p. 73. The link between the theme of incest and Romanticism is discussed in Mario Praz, *The Romantic Agony*, trans. Angus Davidson (London, 1970), pp. 111-12. Praz's index listings under "Incest" are particularly useful in documenting the association. "Incest and Romantic Eroticism," Chapter vii in Eino Railo, *The Haunted Castle: A Study of the Elements of English Romanticism* (London, 1927) also contains much helpful information, especially on Byron and Shelley, pp. 267-81.

4. *Eugene Onegin: A Novel in Verse by Alexander Pushkin*, translated from the Russian, with a commentary by Vladimir Nabokov (Bollingen Series, 72, New York, 1964), Vol. III, p. 100. Henceforth cited as *EO* I-IV. Nabokov mentions Chateaubriand's beloved sister Lucile in his trilingual pastiche of that author's poem "Romance à Hélène"(*A* 139). Lucile is identified in Nabokov's notes to the British paper edition of *Ada* (Harmondsworth, 1970), p. 467, note to p. 112. For a judicious appraisal of the relationship between Chateaubriand and his sister and its reflection in his novella *René*, see George D. Painter, *Chateaubriand: A Biography*, Vol. I (New York 1978), pp. 64-65.

5. Quoted from Chateaubriand's *Mémoires* by Nabokov in his *EO* III, p. 98.

6. For discussions of Byron and incest, see Railo, pp. 273-76, and Praz, pp. 73-77. The numerous Byronic allusions in *Ada* were first remarked by Matthew Hodgart, "Happy Families," *The New York Review of Books*, 22 May 1969, pp. 3-4.

7. One of Pushkin's few Russian precursors may have been the first to introduce the theme of sibling incest into Russian literature. N.M. Karamzin (1761-1825), the founder of Russian Sentimentalism, wrote (very guardedly) of brother-sister love in his 1798 tale "The Island of Bornholm." *Selected Prose of N.M. Karamzin*, trans. Henry M. Nebel, Jr. (Evanston, 1969).

8. See *EO* II, pp. 159-60, and *EO* III, p. 95.

9. Pushkin paraphrases an innocuous line from *René* and gives the original text in his footnote 15 (*EO* I, p. 155, ch. ii, st. 31). Discarded variants of *Onegin* also make reference to *René* (*EO* III, pp. 94-100). The index to Nabokov's translation identifies other less explicit allusions.

10. Ernest J. Simmons, *Pushkin* (New York, 1964), p. 29.

11. "The fables of the British Muse / disturb the young girl's sleep, / and now her idol has become / either the pensive Vampyre, / or Melmoth, gloomy vagabond, / or the Wandering Jew, or the Corsair, / or the mysterious Sbogar." (*EO* I, p. 155) Nabokov's Commentary identifies the works and authors as follows: *The Vampyre, a Tale*, a 1819 work attributed to Byron but written by his physician, Dr. John Polidori; *Melmoth the Wanderer* (1820) by Charles Maturin; *The Corsair* (1814) by Byron; and *Jean Sbogar* (1818) by Charles Nodier (*EO* II, p. 352-59).

12. Onegin's character is ultimately defined for the naive Tatyana by the writings of Byron and Chateaubriand with their dark Romantic heroes. After Onegin coldly rejects her and leaves his country estate, Tatyana gains access to his library where she finds well-thumbed copies of Byron. (*EO* I, p. 292-93, ch. vii, sts. 22-24) Although there is ultimately little similarity between them, it is a commonplace that the "initial impulse" for Pushkin's *Eugene Onegin* came from Byron's *Don Juan*. D.S. Mirsky, *A History of Russian Literature*, ed. Francis J. Whitfield (New York, 1958), p. 90.

13. Pushkin is not infrequently "tongue-in-cheek." In the "library" scene (ch. vii, sts. 22-24) where Onegin's character is revealed to Tatyana by her discovery of its literary prototypes, Pushkin mockingly raises the possibility that his hero is "an insignificant phantasm," "a Muscovite in Harold's mantle, a glossary of alien vagaries," in short, "a parody" (*EO*, I, 273).

14. See, for example, Painter, p. 64, and François-René Chateaubriand, *Atala & René*, trans. Walter J. Cobb (New York, 1962), p. 96.

15. *EO* II, p. 360. Nabokov reports but does not comment on the "Amalia" variant. Other commentators have suggested Amalia Riznich, who was an object of Pushkin's attentions in Odessa in 1823. The name Amalia, very rare in Russian, is of Germanic origin. The German form *Amalia* underlies the French *Amélie* and the English *Amelia* and later, Emily. E.G. Withycombe, *The Oxford Dictionary of English Christian Names*, 3rd ed., (Oxford, 1978).

16. "Demon," the name of Van's and Ada's father, has strong Romantic associations for Russians. The allusion is to the narrative poem *"Demon"* (1839) by M. Yu. Lermontov (1814-41), who is perhaps the purest representative of Romanticism in Russian literature. Lermontov is also the author of an unfinished novel *Vadim* in which the central brother-sister relationship has erotic undercurrents.

17. A more detailed discussion of the relationship between the two works may be found in my "Nabokov's *Ada* and Pushkin's *Eugene Onegin*," *Slavic and East European Journal*, XV, 3, pp. 316-23. Explication of various Onegin allusions in *Ada* may be found in Carl Proffer, "*Ada* as Wonderland: A Glossary of Allusions to Russian Literature," in *A Book of Things About Vladimir Nabokov*, ed. Carl R. Proffer (Ann Arbor, 1971), p. 251 *et passim* and in William Woodin Rowe, *Nabokov's Deceptive World* (New York, 1971), pp. 21-23. A more general consideration of the relationship between Pushkin and Nabokov may be found in Clarence Brown's "Nabokov's Pushkin and Nabokov's *Ada*" in *Nabokov: The Man and His Work*, ed. L.S. Dembo (Madison, 1967), pp. 195-208.

18. Although no Romantic, Tolstoy is also a source of major subtexts in *Ada*. Tolstoyan parodies both open and close the book. At least one of the Tolstoy allusions shows how far Nabokov is willing to go in search of incest implications—a subject relevant to our discussion of Nabokov's "incestuous" reading of the Onegin stanza. In the following passage Nabokov is describing mad Aqua's delusions; ". . . presently panic and pain, like a pair of children in a boisterous game, emitted one last shriek of laughter and ran away to manipulate each other behind a bush as in Count Tolstoy's *Anna Karenin*, a novel, and again, for a while, all was quiet in the house, and their mother had the same first name as hers had" (25). Aqua'a mother Dolly is a namesake of Dolly Oblonsky in the Tolstoy novel. The allusion is to a scene in which the distraught Dolly Oblonsky complains to Levin of the "vile tendencies" of her daughter Masha who with her brother Grisha had gone off "among the raspberry canes and there . . . I can't even tell you what she did." Later Dolly tells Levin (but not the reader) "Masha's crime." (The brother and sister are approximately ten and nine.) Tolstoy, *Anna Karenina*, trans. A. Maude, ed. George Gibian (New York, 1970), p. 545 (Part VI, ch. 15). Aqua's Tolstoyan hallucination accurately previsions the amorous activities of Van and Ada in the bushes of the family's country estate. The allusion was first identified by Bobbie Ann Mason, *Nabokov's Garden: A Guide to Ada* (Ann Arbor, 1974), pp. 25 & 176. *War and Peace* also provides fuel for Nabokov's fires of incest. Ada's mother Marina in her usual myopic fashion warns Van of the

dangers of inadvertently arousing the affections of his little cousin Lucette. In doing so she hazily refers to the French adage which in its correct form reads *"Le cousinage est un dangereux voisinage."* The adage is doubtless borrowed from *War and Peace*, Book I, ch. 5, where Countess Rostov is warned that her son Nicholas may marry his impoverished cousin Sonia (New York, 1966), pp. 42-43. Oddly, Nabokov does not make use of a much more promising incest reference in *War and Peace* where rumors circulate that the relationship between "La Belle Hélène and her equally depraved brother Prince Anatole Kuragin is closer than delicacy might dictate (p. 233 [Book III, ch. 1]). In a discarded and much stronger variant of another passage (p. 342 [Book IV, ch. 6]), the pair's father forbids them to meet in private after their mother finds Anatole sitting on his sister's bed caressing her bare arm. L.N. Tolstoy, *Polnoe sobranie sochinenii*, ed. V.G. Chertkov (Moskva, 1949), vol. XII, pp. 479-480.

19. We have noted that Byron's *Don Juan* was an impulse toward the creation of Pushkin's *Eugene Onegin*. In Nabokov's initial jottings for the novel that became *Ada*, the hero's name was Juan. (Vladimir Nabokov, "Inspiration," *Saturday Review of the Arts*, Jan. 1973, p. 30.) In the final form of the book Van is on occasion referred to as Juan and there is a Don Juan motif centering on a film entitled "Don Juan's Last Fling" in which Ada has a small part.

20. We use the term Romanticism in a broad sense. Of our three authors, only Byron (1788-1824) is unequivocally a Romantic. The older Chateaubriand (1768-1848) is "one of the great precursors of *le Romantisme.*" (*The Oxford Companion to French Literature*, comp., & ed., Sir Paul Harvey & J.E. Heseltine [Oxford, 1966], p. 126.) The case of Pushkin (1799-1837) is more ambiguous. His work of the early twenties such as "The Prisoner of the Caucasus," "The Fountain of Bakhchisaray," "The Gypsies," and the first chapters of *Onegin* are all strongly Byronic in their stance and thematic content, although their form is entirely classical in its concision and clarity. It can nonetheless be asserted that Pushkin introduced Romanticism to Russian literature and that the writings of all three men are marked by the Romantic sensibility.

21. First published in January, 1932, in the émigré daily *Poslednie novosti*, Paris, and collected in V. Sirin, *Sogliadatai* (Paris, 1938). The collection has been reprinted under Nabokov's name (Ann Arbor, 1978). Bibliographic details are from Nabokov's English translation: Vladimir Nabokov, *Details of a Sunset and Other Stories*, pp. 125-38. Quotes are from the Ardis reprint of the Russian edition and the McGraw-Hill English version.

22. Jethro Bithell provides a brief summary of novels on the incest theme in his *Modern German Literature: 1880-1950*, 3rd ed., (London, 1968), p. 33. His summary comment is "Incest becomes a favorite theme at this time." Elsewhere he remarks on "the uncanny fascination of incest for German authors—from the *Gregorius* of Hartmann von Aue onwards" (366). According to Walter H. Sokel, incest was a theme of particular fascination for German Expressionist writers and constituted "an obvious correlative of the narcissistic element in much of Expressionism." (*The Writer in Extremis: Expressionism in Twentieth-Century German Literature* [Stanford, 1959], pp. 129-30.)

23. Milton Cross and David Ewen, *Milton Cross' Encyclopedia of the Great Composers and their Music*, 2 vols. (Garden City, 1953), pp. 873-78.

24. Nabokov refers to Mann *(inter alia)* as a "puffed-up" writer of second-rate, ephemeral works in his *Strong Opinions*, p. 54. Other, equally hostile Mann references may be found on pp. 55, 57, 83, 85, 112, and 204. Although references to German authors are infrequent in *Ada*, Mann is alluded to twice. In one case, Professor Veen refers to the *Collected Works of Falkenmann* in his apartment as something "dumped by my predecessor" (371). William Faulkner (1897-1962) used sibling incest as a theme in *The Sound and the Fury* (1929) and *Absalom, Absalom* (1936). A second Mann reference is to a novel entitled *Love under the Lindens* "by one Eelmann" which is described as "One of the most tawdry and *rejouissants* novels that ever 'made' the first page of the Manhattan *Times'* Book Review" (402). In his notes to the

Penguin edition of *Ada*, Nabokov identifies Eelmann as a blend of Thomas Mann and Eugene O'Neill (1888-1953). O'Neill's play *Mourning Becomes Electra* (1931) has incestuous undercurrents between brother and sister while the 1924 *Desire Under the Elms*, with its son/stepmother affair, is "quasi-incestuous." It is perhaps of note that Mann, who received the Nobel Prize for Literature in 1929, is unceremoniously lumped together with two other Nobel Prize laureates: O'Neill—1936, and Faulkner—1949.

25. Although written in 1905, the story first appeared in 1921 as a privately printed edition intended for the author's friends (München, 1921) [Bithell, p. 314]. Reprinted in Thomas Mann, *Stories of Three Decades* (New York, 1936). Mann's story as well as those by a number of other writers on the incest theme may be found in the anthology *Violation of Taboo: Incest in the Great Literature of the Past and Present*, ed. D.W. Cory and R.E.L. Masters (New York, 1963).

26. Thomas Mann, *The Holy Sinner*, trans. H.T. Lowe-Porter (New York, 1951), p. 337.

27. Although exceptionally well represented in German literature of the period, the theme was by no means restricted to German writers. Note, for example, the above-cited works of Faulkner and O'Neill. The theme is represented in English literature by Ivy Compton-Burnett's *Brothers and Sisters* (1929, rpt. London, 1971) and W. Somerset Maugham's tale of sibling incest, "The Book Bag," in *East and West: The Collected Short Stories of W. Somerset Maugham* (New York, 1937). French literature contributes Jean Cocteau's 1929 *Les Enfants Terribles* which appears in *Ada* as *Les Enfants Maudits* written by Ada's governess Belle Larivière under the *nom de plume* Monparnasse (198). Some of her works recreate the stories of Guy de Maupassant (1865-1893) (notably *"La Parure,"* which appears as *"La Rivière de Diamants* [83] but not, strangely enough, Maupassant's only tale of sibling incest, the 1885 *"Le Porte."* Leo Tolstoy so admired the latter piece that he adapted it into Russian and published it under the title *"Frantsuaza. Rasskaz po Monpassanu"* (*François. A Tale after Maupassant*). *L.N. Tolstoy. Polnoe sobranie sochinenii*, ed. V.G. Chertkov (Moscow, 1936), vol. XXIV, pp. 251-58 (text) & 671-76 (annotations).

28. Bithell, p. 471. Thiess' novel was reprinted in 1923 and 1924 and again in 1930-33.

29. In English as *Brother and Sister* (New York, Nov. 1930). The translation went through several printings.

30. Bithell, p. 365.

31. Andrew Field, *Nabokov: His Life in Part*, p. 183 and Field, *Nabokov: A Bibliography* (New York, 1973), p. 72.

32. This possibility should be seriously entertained given Nabokov's use of automated manikins in the 1928 novel *King, Queen, Knave* in which the Berlin department-store owner Dreyer becomes involved in a scheme to develop such figures.

33. A further consideration contributing to Nabokov's dismissal of contemporary German literature and Frank's book in particular may have been Frank's identification with socialism. In the Weimar Republic there was a pronounced association between art and leftist politics that Nabokov found abhorrent. Although Frank's *Bruder und Schwester* was not political and indeed involved only the cosmopolitan haute bourgeoisie of Nabokov's own background, its passing reference to the Russian Revolution as "the willing self-immolation of a people building a new story on the edifice of human history" understandably may have annoyed a Russian émigré such as Nabokov (15).

34. In his autobiography, Frank says that in the earliest stages of writing *Bruder und Schwester* he himself did not know "whether love could overcome this greatest of all obstacles." *Heart on the Left*, trans. Cyrus Brooks (London, 1954), p. 199.

35. See, for example, *The Times*, 24 Aug. 1961, p. 10.

36. Within the framework of the novel the chart is presumably made up by Van, or, conceivably, by Ada. It is also possible, however, that it is the work of Van's obtuse posthumous editor Ronald Oranger. One notes, incidentally, the similarity of his name to that

of G.I. Gurdjieff's disciple, A.R. Orage, who extensively edited his master's writings. James Webb, *The Lives and Work of G.I. Gurdjieff, P.D. Ouspensky, and Their Followers* (New York, 1980). In the ensuing discussion the reader may find it helpful to consult the family tree at the beginning of the novel and compare it with our revised family tree on page 128 below. Lucy Maddox has suggested that Demon and Dan may actually be twins rather than cousins. I have incorporated her proposal in my revision of the Zemski-Veen family tree. Lucy Maddox, *Nabokov's Novels in English* (Athens [Georgia], 1983), p. 111.

37. Matthew Hodgart, for example, possibly misled by the Byronic parallels, saw Van and Ada as half-brother and -sister in his review in the *New York Review of Books*. Subsequent critics have generally recognized the true relationship. See, for example, Alfred Appel, Jr., "Ada described," pp. 161-62. Although there are numerous "giveaways" embedded in the text of the novel, the story of the baby switch is first told (in covert form) in the flower list (pp. 7-8).

38. It is of marginal interest that even in terms of the official genealogy the Durmanov females and the Veen males are second cousins. The Durmanovs' maternal grandfather is Peter Zemski, whose sister, Olga Zemski Veen, is the Veens' paternal grandmother.

39. *Brewer's Dictionary of Phrase and Fable: Centenary Edition*, rev. Ivor H. Evans (New York, 1970).

40. The letters are mentioned by Lucette in her childhood recollection of Van, Ada, and herself rummaging through a secretaire in the Ardis Hall library where Van, she says, expected to find "our grandmother's love letters" (374). Dolly's name is not mentioned, but she is the only grandmother shared by the three children. Cf. Count Rostov's exclamation in *War and Peace*: "Why our mothers used to be married at twelve or thirteen" (43). The remark is in the same scene as the *"Cousinage est dangereux voisinage"* comment discussed above.

41. Dolly never appears as a character in the narrative so the reader is deprived of the opportunity to observe her mannerisms. Demon, however, is thirty-two at the time of Dolly's death and would be well aware of her gestures. The mannerism, a wagging of a forefinger at temple height in "casual, pacific denial" (240), has previously been used by Ada (227).

42. Peterson's Grouse, which is described as being one of Demon's favorite dishes, does not exist. The allusion is presumably to ornithologist Roger Tory Peterson and his famed field guides as well as to Peter Zemski. Multiple allusions are frequent in Nabokov's work.

43. This may be the ultimate implication of Marina's affirmation that "in bed . . . Demon's senses must have been influenced by a queer sort of 'incestuous' (whatever that term means) pleasure . . . when he fondled . . . flesh that was both that of his wife and that of his mistress, . . . an Aquamarina both single and double . . ." (19). That Marina and Aqua are twins would not make Demon's dual relationship with them incestuous—unless he was, in fact, their brother. Nabokov readers are well advised to pay particular attention to words given "parenthetic" emphasis, e.g. "(whatever that term means)."

44. Charles Mills Gayley, *The Classic Myths in English Literature and in Art* (Boston, 1911), pp. 4-6, and Railo, p. 268.

45. Demon's name and physical image have other, non-classical, mythological associations. His name, as we have noted, is that of the hero of M. Yu. Lermontov's poem about a fallen angel. Demon's physical description, including references to his wings (appropriate to a son of Dedalus), derives from a set of pictures which are based on Lermontov's *Demon* by the Russian artist Mikhail Vrubel (1856-1910). The allusion to Vrubel's paintings was first noted by Simon Karlinsky, "Nabokov's Russian Games," *New York Times Book Review*, 18 April 1971, pp. 2-18.

46. The three deaths are described by Van in specifically mythological terms: "Three elements, fire, water and air destroyed in that sequence, Marina, Lucette, and Demon" (450). Marina dies of cancer which in Russian is *goret' rakom*, "to burn with cancer."

47. Edmund Leach, *Lévi-Strauss* (London, 1970), p. 103.

48. John Barth, "Some Reasons Why I tell the Stories I Tell the Way I Tell Them Rather than Some Other Sort of Stories Some Other Way," *New York Times Book Review*, 9 May 1982, p. 3. Barth (himself an opposite-sex twin) treats the incestuous twin theme in his novel *The Sot-Weed Factor* (New York, 1964). Another recent treatment of sibling incest is Anthony Burgess' *M/F* (New York, 1971). Although Burgess has conceded the influence of Nabokov on his work (*The Novel Now* [New York, 1970] p. 212), the more immediate "ideological" source of *M/F* is the work of the French structural anthropologist Claude Lévi-Strauss.

49. Carolyn G. Heilbrun, *Toward a Recognition of Androgyny* (New York, 1973), p. 34. Heilbrun provides a survey of opposite-sex twins in literature, pp. 34-45. Van and Ada are, of course, not twins but their resemblance to each other is often emphasized. Ada herself says, "Physically ... we are more like twins than cousins, and twins or even siblings can't marry ..." (148). Given the physical and psychic similarity of brother and sister, the relevance of the opposite-sex twin lore is apparent.

50. Walter Sokel has neatly formulated this erotic dilemma in his discussion of the Austrian poet Georg Trakl (1887-1914) whose life and work were permeated by the sibling incest theme: "One's sister is perhaps even more than one's mother ... the woman closest to oneself. If she resembles one physically and mentally ... one can see and love in her his own self disguised in the opposite sex" (p. 78).

51. Bobbie Ann Mason, *Nabokov's Garden*, pp. 13-14.

52. Nabokov's assessment is from his letter to the *New York Review of Books*, 10 July 1969, p. 36.

53. Brian David Boyd, "Nabokov and *Ada*," University of Toronto, 1979, p. 406. A similar view is presented in Sissela Bok, "Redemption through Art in Nabokov's *Ada*," *Critique*, 12, 3 (1971), pp. 110-20.

54. From among Nabokov's many statements on the subject, we cite: "Although I do not care for the slogan art for art's sake..., there can be no question that what makes a work of fiction safe from larvae and rust is not its social importance but its art, only its art" (SO 33).

55. The "library" chapter is 21 of Part I, pp. 130-7.

56. See, for example, Professor Gleb Struve's remark that it is precisely in parody that the key to much of Nabokov's work is to be found. Gleb Struve, *Russkaia literatura v izgnanii* (New York 1956), p. 284.

57. In spite of its plethora of allusions to Romantic treatments of the sibling incest theme, *Ada* cannot be accurately classified as a reincarnation of its prototypes. Neither Van nor Ada can be seen as demonic heroes in rebellion against an oppressive society. While they conform to the Romantic model in being superior creatures set apart from the mass, there is no real conflict. They are so rich, so powerful, there is no contest. If nothing else, the book's happy ending for the lovers sets Nabokov's novel outside the conventions governing the traditional Romantic classics of incest. *Ada* stands in the same parodic relationship to the Romantic theme of incest as Nabokov's early novel, *Despair*, does to the trite Romantic theme of the *Doppelgänger*—a theme which is, incidentally, not without affinity to that of sibling incest. An excellent survey of Nabokov's use of *Doppelgänger* subtexts in *Despair* may be found in Julian Connolly, "The Function of Literary Allusion in Nabokov's *Despair*," *Slavic and East European Journal* (Fall, 1982). *Despair*, however, is restricted to Russian subtexts while the later, much more complex *Ada* takes all of European literature as its field of allusion.

58. "Extraterritorial" in George Steiner, *Extraterritorial: Papers on Literature and the Language Revolution* (London, 1972), pp. 3-11.

59. Steiner's fascinating speculation remains to be proved or disproved. W.W. Rowe offers a preliminary examination of the possible influences of Nabokov's native Russian on his English prose in the second chapter of his book *Nabokov's Deceptive World* (New York, 1971).

60. Steiner's characterization of incest as being "prevalent throughout Nabokov's fiction" is exaggerated (8). The incest theme, as we have noted, is restricted to Nabokov's late English

novel. Perhaps what impels Professor Steiner to his statement is the feeling that incest 'works' so well as an interpretative metaphor for much of Nabokov's writing.

61. It is curious that *Lolita*, the only English novel that Nabokov saw fit to render into his native Russian (for an audience not permitted to read it), deals with the theme of pseudo-incest. As Humbert Humbert says, his relationship with Lolita is a "parody of incest." In this sense *Lolita* is a transitional work leading to *Ada* and *Look at the Harlequins!* wherein the theme of incest springs full-blown.

62. For a detailed exposition, see the Clarence Brown essay cited in note 17. Nabokov responded to Brown's assertion of "repetitiousness" by remarking "he may have something there." He then said, "Artistic originality has only its own self to copy" (*SO* 95).

63. We shall follow Nabokov's own convention of referring to *Look at the Harlequins!* by its punning acronym *LATH*. The lath, bat, or wand are fixed attributes of the commedia dell'arte figure of the harlequin. Information on the harlequin figure is drawn chiefly from Pierre Louis Duchartre, *The Italian Comedy* (New York, 1966). Since the surname of *LATH*'s narrator and protagonist is obscure we shall refer to him by the initials of his first name and patronymic, VV. General text references are by Part and Chapter number, e.g., VI, 4.

64. All of VV's books have patent connection with those of Nabokov. For an able discussion of this aspect of the novel, see Richard Patteson, "Nabokov's *Look at the Harlequins!*: Endless Re-creation of the Self," *Russian Literature Triquarterly*, 14 (Winter, 1976), pp. 84-98.

65. The suspicion is strengthened by the fact that Nabokov made a similar play on this same root in *Pale Fire*, where the character Starover Blue is a Professor of Astronomy (56 & 256). An equally mysterious Dr. Starov figures in *The Real Life of Sebastian Knight*.

66. VV also meets his earlier lover Dolly as she comes from a library (136-137). The narrator's loves and books are indeed "interlaced monogrammatically like...(an) *ex libris* design."

67. As we have noted, Nabokov uses this same device in *Speak, Memory* where he occasionally addresses as "you" an unknown person who proves to be his wife.

68. The textual associations of "you" and "Reality" are summarized below.

69. There is one further possible member of Count Starov's ubiquitous clan. It is VV's "Russian Zoilus," Demian Basilevski, who follows the narrator from Paris to New York where he founds a Russian-language journal (130). Basilevski could, in principle, be the father of VV's last love who has ties with "Russian New York." Basilevski, however, is not known to have either a daughter or connections with "good old Quirn."

70. Although Nabokov does not include it, the word "*blood*" (in the sense of consanguinity) also belongs in this series and might well underlie it.

71. These confusions persist even in VV's recollection of certain scenes many years later. See, for example, the account of a visit to a French psychiatrist's office which blends surreally (and perhaps drunkenly) with a house party and a dentist's waiting room (17-19). Similarly, a social gathering thirty-odd years later, also preceded by one of VV's "black headaches," seems to take place at two different locations simultaneously (175-182).

72. VV twice refers to his illness as "dementia paralytica" (122 & 242) and also, skeptically, refers to a medical diagnosis of his final attack as "general paresis" (239). Strictly speaking, these synonymous terms refer to a dread complication of syphilis involving inflammation and degeneration of the brain. Symptoms usually begin to appear from ten to twenty years after primary lesion and end in paralysis and death within three years. Although VV appears to be mad and his behavior sometimes displays such standard symptoms of dementia paralytica as megalomania, impaired memory, depression, paranoia, and hallucination (*Cecil Textbook of Medicine*, P.B. Beeson et al [Philadelphia, 1979]), it does not seem likely that his madness is syphilitic in origin since his attacks date from early childhood. Dementia paralytica *per se* is not congenital nor is the narrator's recovery from his final paralytic seizure consistent with such a diagnosis. It seems probable that VV's madness is not

organic in origin and that Nabokov seized upon the terms as a matter of thematic convenience.

73. The confession scenes are as follows: Iris - Part I, 7; Annettte - II, 7; Louise - IV, 4; "You" - VI, 2.

74. The identity of this "other" Anglo-Russian writer is at once obvious and not so obvious. The ultimate prototype, as the following discussion will show, is, of course, Nabokov himself. It is important to understand, however, that it is a Nabokovian persona and *not* Nabokov, the author of *LATH*, who is the shadowy original of whom Vadim Vadimovich is the flawed copy. We shall refer to the Nabokovian persona as "Vladimir Vladimirovich" (in quotes) to distinguish him from Vadim Vadimovich, on the one hand, and Nabokov, on the other.

75. Vadim's "father" died on October 22, 1898. The six-month interval would place VV's birthdate in late April of 1899. That the exact date is April 23 (Nabokov's birthday) is strongly hinted in that VV goes out to a formal (birthday?) dinner on the night of 23 April 1930 when Iris is shot (65).

76. Andrew Field, *Nabokov: His Life in Art* (Boston, 1967), p. 54. Another Cantabrigian link is VV's passing allusion to "one of his Cambridge sweethearts Violet McD., an experienced and compassionate virgin" (28) who suggests the Violet of Nabokov's long, autobiographical work "A University Poem" (82-85).

77. The "double" episode with Oksman echoes another such situation with the Russian bookseller Weinstock in Nabokov's 1930 *The Eye* (New York, 1965), a novella that has strong thematic affinities with *LATH* (52-53 & 63). See my "Eyeing Nabokov's *Eye*" in the special Nabokov issue of *Canadian-American Slavic Studies* (1984).

78. Love for the opera and the "English style" of oratory are two of the attributes that Nabokov assigns to his father in *Speak, Memory* (178-179).

79. The narrator's second wife, Annette, mistakenly presents her parents with copies of "another man's novel because of some silly similarity of titles" (101). Oleg Orlov, a minor émigré writer, who has turned Soviet agent and follows VV on his clandestine trip to Leningrad, confuses VV's *A Kingdom by the Sea* with a book not unlike *Lolita* (218).

80. Butterflies, toward which VV (in contrast to lepidopterist Nabokov) professes indifference, if not distaste, (34) form their own thematic subpattern in the narrator's story. They are at one point identified with the harlequin motif (108) and appear in scenes depicting the onset of VV's love for three of his wives and also for Bel: Iris—34-36, Annette—108-109, "You"—226 and Bel—156 & 163. It is not by chance that Louise is missing from the pattern.

81. These scenes are as follows: Iris—31, Louise—174, "You"—227. The parallel "Annette" scene exists only in embryo on p. 88.

# SECTION FIVE

# NABOKOV AS LITERARY COSMOLOGIST

Much of Nabokov's fiction displays an underlying "two world" cosmology. Both worlds are imaginary but one is relatively like our own, while the other, often patently fantastic, is an anti-world. Either may be the scene of the novel's action, but the other is never far away. Signs and portents of the other world leak through, influencing, and sometimes controlling, the events of the novel's "primary" world. Nabokov's two world cosmology first appears in the fiction of the early thirties and becomes increasingly prominent in the late English work. Although the two world cosmology is more or less a constant, the novels display two major subtypes depending in part on which world, the more real or the less real, is foregrounded. *Invitation to a Beheading, Bend Sinister,* and *Ada* are novels in which the world of the hero is fantastic and in which he detects hidden patterns attesting to the existence of a "real" world to which he aspires. A second set of novels, including *Solus Rex, Pale Fire* and *Look at the Harlequins!,* is basically set in a "real" world, but the heroes, who are (apparently) mad, carry within themselves a second, fantastic world which they superimpose on the "real" one. Whereas the heroes of the first type of novel strive to discover and enter the "real" world whose existence is affirmed by secret patterns, the heroes of the second type try to dwell exclusively in their fantasy worlds and are distressed by intrusions from the circumambient "real" world that suggest their fantasy worlds are just that. *The Eye* and *Despair* with their schizoid heroes, also fall into the second category, although the delusions of the protagonists are not explicitly cast in the form of alternative worlds.

Even those Nabokov novels that do not display the two world cosmology have traces of another world, one on the far side of death. Taking his cue from Brian Boyd's massive study of *Ada,* W.W. Rowe has shown that all of Nabokov's novels (with the possible exception of the first, *Mary*) contain, quite literally, ghosts.[1] These ghosts, the souls of deceased characters, appear covertly and influence, for better or worse, the actions of the surviving characters who may or may not take note of the spectral intrusions. On rare occasions the intrusion may be explicit as in the acrostic woven into the last paragraph of "The Vane Sisters." More commonly, the presence of ghosts is signaled by certain natural background elements such as wind, fog, lightning, sunlight or water, or by descriptions of sunsets, stained glass windows, butterflies and moths, or by sudden shifts in scene perspectives. Such ghostly presences, whether or not in the formal context of "another world," testify to existence of a second world in the background of the novels.

It is tempting to assume that Nabokov's two world cosmology is simply an extension of the obvious: the real world of the author and the fictional world of his characters. This is a model that applies to all fiction and particularly to that of such authors as Nabokov who make no pretense that their fictional worlds are hermetic. Nabokov's two world cosmology is a more sophisticated phenomenon. His novels, as we have seen, often contain two fictional worlds—one primary and one secondary. Although the two worlds are separated by some fundamental boundary, usually death or insanity, they interact in mysterious ways. Nabokov's ghosts form one of the secret patterns that links the two fictive worlds. Author Nabokov presides equally over his created worlds and often lends an anagrammatic persona to one of them. Nabokov and his world, however, stand apart from both of his fictional universes.

The two world theme is perhaps most apparent in two Nabokov novels published at an interval of nearly forty years: *Invitation to a Beheading* and *Look at the Harlequins!*, two extremely different books, each exemplifying one of the major subtypes of the two world cosmology. Cincinnatus, the sane third-person hero of *Invitation to a Beheading*, is caught in a nightmare fantasy world from which he longs to escape. Vadim Vadimovich, the schizoid first person narrator of *LATH!*, physically lives in a "real" world, but mentally in a fantasy world which he imposes on the real world. The "real" world that discordantly intrudes upon his fantasy world is sensed as a twin world in another galaxy. In both novels the heroes are trying to flee from a less desirable world into a more pleasant one. In spite of the importance of the two world cosmology in both novels, the "other" world (whether real or fantastic) lies in the background, an object of occasional, murky, and apparently metaphorical allusion. Nabokov has provided for the reader a more tangible, more readily apparent analogue of each of the two worlds. These analogues permeate their narratives much more comprehensively and explicitly than do the two worlds themselves. In *Invitation to a Beheading*, the structural analogue of the two worlds is the binary pair *tut* and *tam*, "here" and "there." In *Look at the Harlequins!* the parallel terms are "left" and "right." Almost everything in these books is in one way or another aligned with one or the other of these fundamental thematic guideposts that reflect the two worlds underlying the narratives.

## THE TWO WORLDS OF *INVITATION TO A BEHEADING*

Among his many novels Vladimir Nabokov singled out *Invitation to a Beheading* as the one that he held in "the greatest esteem" (SO 92). He also remarked that in contrast to his usual snail-paced rate of composition, the original draft was written "in one fortnight of wonderful excitement and sustained inspiration" (SO 68). It is perhaps due to the temporal intensity of its composition that *Invitation to a Beheading* is the most compact and the most densely written of his works, showing a compression of stylistic virtuosity and theme that might have been etiolated by a more leisurely mode of writing. Whatever the reason, *Invitation to a Beheading* is the most structurally stark and artifice-saturated of Nabokov's works.

The surface plot of the novel is simple. Cincinnatus, a young teacher of defective children, has been convicted of a capital crime. Although his offense is cryptically called "gnostical turpitude," its essence is that Cincinnatus is different from the Philistine citizens of the mythical totalitarian state in which they dwell. Virtually all of the novel's (in-)action takes place in the prison-fortress where Cincinnatus awaits his beheading. He sits in his cell writing in his journal and meditating on his plight—both metaphysical and all too real. He is attended by Rodion, his jailer, Roman, his attorney, and the prison director Rodrig, whose small daughter Emmie sometimes visits the prisoner. In a nearby cell, Pierre, Cincinnatus' executioner-to-be, plays the role of a fellow prisoner in order to befriend his future victim in accord with the bizarre custom of the land. Apart from these characters, Cincinnatus also receives visits from his faithless wife Marthe, and his mother whom he scarcely knows. The plot, such as it is, features two escape attempts, but both turn out to be hoaxes staged by his jailers. In the end, after numerous unexplained postponements, Cincinnatus is duly executed. The novel is surrealistic in tone.[2] Both the prison and the society it represents are fragile stage props that disintegrate at the end. Further, the characters wear makeup, costumes, and wigs, and occasionally interchange roles, while their actions are often accompanied by stage directions. The events of the novel span the nineteen days between the pronouncement of the sentence and the beheading. Each chapter, apart from the last two, occupies one day, usually from Cincinnatus' awakening to lights-out.

The central theme of the novel is the plight of the artist, specifically the writer, a man with his personal vision of the world and his unique way of conveying it to others. The writer lives at the center of a paradox; he possesses his own tongue, the only language adequate to the expression of his vision, but it is incomprehensible and hence suspect to his audience, his fellow citizens. Cincinnatus' prison is thus dual. On the surface level he is in a very real prison for a crime against the totalitarian state. On a deeper level he is in what we have previously termed the prison-house of language.

Cincinnatus' prison world is only one world of the novel, for he visualizes another, an ideal world in which he is a free citizen among people who speak his tongue. The structure of the novel is cast in terms of the opposition of these two worlds: the "real" world of the prison and the totalitarian society it represents, and Cincinnatus' ideal world, the world of his imagination. Throughout the book the contrast between the two worlds is manifested through a series of thematic oppositions. One member of each opposition characterizes the prison world, while its opposite member typifies the other, the ideal world. From the point of view of formal structure, however, the thematic oppositions are an overlay, a super-structure, that rest on a foundation which is one of the basic lexico-grammatical categories of language itself—the phenomenon of deixis.

*Invitation to a Beheading*'s initial thematic opposition, "transparent/ opaque," is associated with Cincinnatus' inherent criminality, with his "gnostical turpitude" (*gnoselogicheskaia gnusnost'*) (R80/E72). So terrible is this offense in Cincinnatus' world that it is referred to only by euphemisms such as "impenetrability," "opacity," and "occlusion." Cincinnatus has been born into a world in which beings are transparent to each other. Cincinnatus, however, is opaque to the optical rays of others and produces the bizarre impression of "a long dark obstacle that seems pitchblack to his fellows" (E24/R36). Raised in an orphanage, the protagonist becomes aware of his criminal defect while a young child and teaches himself to feign translucence by a system of optical illusions. Although constantly on guard, Cincinnatus has occasional lapses in his self-control and his secret is discovered.

Cincinnatus' opacity is but a surface manifestation of another, more fundamental defect—his unique perception of the world and his ability to synthesize that perception. As Cincinnatus remarks: "I am the one who is alive—not only are my eyes different, and my hearing, and my sense of taste—not only is my sense of smell like a deer's, my sense of touch like a bat's—but most important, I have the capacity to join all of this into one point" (E52/R62). Further, and often reiterated in variant form, is Cincinnatus' statement that "I know a paramount thing that no one here knows" (E189/R193 & E96-96/R100). Cincinnatus's uniqueness of perception, that is, his gnostical knowledge (or turpitude from the viewpoint of his authoritarian society), is accompanied by his inability to communicate this knowledge to others. The language of Cincinnatus' society is hermetic and incapable of expressing new thoughts or assigning new names for things. Within the confines of their language the citizens understand each other "at the first half-word" (*s poluslova*), but novelty remains forever beyond their ken for "*That which does not have a name does not exist.* Unfortunately everything had a name" (E26/R38). Cincinnatus' isolation is underscored by his realization that his world contains "not a single human who can speak my language" (E95/R100). The implication, amply borne out in other passages, is that there exists another world in which people do speak Cincinnatus' language and share his perceptions. Thus parallel to the "transparent/opaque" opposition we have "open language," the language of art—that ideal tongue by which Cincinnatus may share his unique perceptions, and "hermetic language," the self-circumscribed, banal tongue of a philistine society.

Cincinnatus feels that he catches glimpses of his ideal world in dreams and gradually comes to the idea that "what we call dreams is semi-reality," that is, a glimpse of that ideal world (E92/R97). On the other hand, our "vaunted waking life" is a semi-sleep in which only perverted and distorted mockeries of the real (ideal) world filter through. The assumption that the worlds of sleeping and waking are reversed, and that Cincinnatus is in the wrong one, finds reinforcement in the fate of the town statue of Captain Somnus (sleep), who in the disintegrating world of the novel's end is mysteriously shattered by lightning—thus marking the end of the reign of sleep.

Perhaps the most pervasive manifestation of Cincinnatus' doubts about the fundamental reality of the prison world as opposed to his intuited ideal world is to be found in the "theater/reality" opposition.[3] In virtually every chapter the stage motif is prominent. In one not atypical scene Rodion, the jailer, is suddenly transformed into an opera rake in an imaginary tavern, who at the end of his rollicking drinking song, dashes his stein to the floor. On another occasion, Rodion brings into the cell "a lilac letter on a silver salver as they do in plays" (E68/R76). As Rodion leaves he collides with Rodrig, the prison director, who has been waiting impatiently in the wings and "appears just a split second too early." The actor has jumped his cue. Upon entering, the director repeats aloud the verbatim text of the letter—a stock theatrical device to inform the audience of the contents. The prison director is persistently cast in the role of stage director of life in the prison, responsible for lighting effects and props. Two of the props deserve special mention. Cincinnatus' cell is equipped with a spider that is fed a daily diet of flies and moths by Rodion. At the play's end the spider is knocked down by a broom and proves to be a "crudely but cleverly made object consisting of a round plush body with twitching legs made of springs" (E210/R205). The spider, like much else in the novel, enters into an emblematic opposition. The spider, the traditional companion of the imprisoned, is contrastively paired with a large beautiful moth, a Nabokovian emblem of freedom and art, that escapes both the mandibles of the spider and the confines of the cell at the end of the book (E211/R211). The moth, unlike the stage-prop spider, is real, thus continuing the "theater/reality" opposition. The culmination of this motif comes in the final chapters when, as Cincinnatus is being taken to his place of execution, the entire stage set of the novel disintegrates, slowly at first, and then more rapidly as the moment of the beheading draws near.

Mirrors, or more accurately, the opposition "distorted mirror image/true image" are another of the book's thematic dichotomies. This motif is developed in the vignette about *"nonnons"* or, in the Russian text, *netki* (E135-6/R136-7). These are toys consisting of sets of objects or images so grotesquely distorted as to be unrecognizable. The objects are accompanied, however, by special correspondingly deformed mirrors that while giving only contorted unrecognizable images of ordinary objects, yield perfectly reconstituted images of the *"nonnons."*[4] The parallel to the "sleeping/waking" opposition is apparent with the pristine images of the ideal world being grotesquely perverted in their reflection in the "real" world.

Apart from Cincinnatus himself the ideal world has one undistorted projection into the prison world of the novel. Tamara Gardens, the large city park that is the scene of Cincinnatus' few happy memories, is in counterpoint to the grim prison-fortress in which he awaits death. In the first mention of the Gardens, the imprisoned protagonist recalls them as the place "where, whenever life became unbearable, one could roam, with a meal of chewed lilac bloom in one's mouth and firefly tears in one's eyes" (E19/R32). So intense is Cincinnatus' longing for the Gardens where he and Marthe had their first trysts that Cincinnatus vainly attempts to catch a glimpse of the park from his cell window. Some days later as Cincinnatus wanders along a prison corridor, he encounters a lighted diorama set into the stone wall mimicking a window overlooking the Tamara Gardens. The Gardens are specifically linked with Cincinnatus' ideal world in which are to be found the "originals of those gardens where we used to roam and hide in this world" (E94/R99). The Gardens are also the locus of groves of oak trees which echo another important symbol in the novel.

To pass his time in prison Cincinnatus reads a three thousand page contemporary novel entitled *Quercus*—the Latin generic name for oak. The book is a biography of a 600-year-old tree, or rather a record of all of the events that have transpired in its immediate vicinity. As in *Moby Dick*, dramatic incidents are interspersed with essays on every aspect of the oak— dendrology, coleopterology, mythology, folklore, and so on. The work is "unquestionably the best that his age had produced" (E123/R126). As Cincinnatus lies abed reading *Quercus*, he asks himself "Will no one save me?" (E125/R128). In reply, a draft (which serves as the leitmotif of the chapter) wafts through the cell and drops on the bed "a large dummy acorn, twice as large as life, spendidly painted a glossy buff, and fitting its cork as snugly as an egg" (E125/R128). In the preceding chapter, Cincinnatus, when asked about the possibility of escape and the identity of a possible savior, replies with the single word "imagination" (E114/R117). Here again the ideal world in which art and imagination flourish momentarily intrudes into Cincinnatus's prison world with a hint of salvation through the intercession of art. Still other minor thematic oppositions parallel the "this world/that world" dichotomy. The world of here and now is characterized by roughness and friction. In Cincinnatus' ideal world, however, "everything gravitated toward a kind of perfection whose definition was absence of friction" (E50/R60). Another such contrast is to be found in the opposition "present/non-present." The odious present is contrasted both with an idealized (although possibly mythic) past and a glittering future (E27 & 50/R39-40 & 60).

We have now briefly surveyed the thematic oppositions that characterize the two worlds of the novel. In résumé they are: "transparent/opaque," "hermetic language/open language," "dreaming/ waking," "theater/reality," "distorted mirror image/true image," "prison-fortress/Tamara Gardens," "friction/fluid," and "present/non-present." In each of these pairs, the first is an attribute of the authoritarian, philistine society in which Cincinnatus lives, while the second characterizes Cincinnatus' intuited ideal world.

The above oppositions are thematic in nature and, as we have said, collectively constitute a description of the two worlds of *Invitation to a Beheading*. These thematic polarities acquire their significance within the text from being mapped onto the novel's underlying metaphysical geographic opposition—"this world/that world" (*etot svet/tot svet*). Although less explicit than the thematic oppositions, the "this world/that world" polarity has its own emotive coloration stemming from the religious and moral connotations of the contrasting pair. The "this world/that world" antithesis traditionally refers to earthly existence as opposed to the delights of heaven. The boundary between them is death. It is this deeply rooted religious mythology that makes the binary figure such an attractive and effective subtext for the plight of Cincinnatus who is imprisoned in this wretched world while longing for the next, but fearing the unknown quantity of death which is the point of transition. There is also a moral dimension that makes the "this world/that world" figure especially appropriate: *this* world is evil; *that* world is good. The opposition thus supplies the moral cosmology as well as the major structural axis of Nabokov's novel. Within the novel, however, the primary resonance of the binary pair is metaphysical rather than religious, and the most appropriate correlates of the opposing poles might be "materialistic/idealistic" or, perhaps still more simply, "real/ideal."

The key phrases "this world/that world" (*etot svet/tot svet*) are liberally scattered throughout the novel, although infrequently juxtaposed in a physical sense. Explicit juxtaposition of the contrastive pair is not necessary for they are fixed antonymic expressions that are defined and comprehensible only in terms of each other.[5] The mention of one member of the pair without at least the tacit presence of the other is unthinkable. It is the bound nature of the pair, a stock opposition embedded in the very language, that, taken together with their religious and moral connotations, makes the "this world/that world" pairing an ideal template for the alignment of the more loosely paired thematic oppositions. The "this world/that world" opposition is at the heart of the novel and represents a synthesis of the previously outlined thematic oppositions. From the purely formal point of view the difference between *etot svet* and *tot svet* lies in the demonstrative pronouns which are members of the linguistic class called "deictics"—words that have no intrinsic lexical meaning of their own, but serve to orient an utterance in terms of the location and temporal setting of the particular speech act in which they occur. Most such words form correlative pairs in privative oppositions, that is, they share some common feature (*-tot*) and are simultaneously opposed by some other feature (*e-*).

An examination of *Invitation to a Beheading* shows that many of the more restricted thematic polarities discussed above are also opposed by their modifying deictics and that the formal basis for assuming certain thematic elements to be opposed (or correlated in privative oppositions) is the presence of the deictic particles. To illustrate: in examining the above-mentioned diorama of Tamara Gardens, Cincinnatus muses that it is as if one were looking "from *this* very prison, at *those* very gardens" (*iz etoi temnitsy, na te sady*) (R83/E76), thus underscoring the opposition "prison-fortress/Tamara Gardens." Another example entails the use of only one member of a deictic opposition which, as we have noted, tacitly implies the presence of the absent member. As Cincinnatus visualizes the soon-to-be-staged execution scene he wonders why he should so fear the moment: *Ved' dlia menia eto uzhe budet lish' ten' topora, i nizvergaiushcheesia 'at'' ne etim slukhom uslyshu* (R97). "For me will this not be simply the shadow of an ax, and I shall hear the descending 'thud' not with *this* ear." (My translation and italics—DBJ.) For the Russian reader the *ne etim slukhom* "not with this ear" is automatically projected against the background of *ne etot svet* "not this world" and its counterposed *ne tot svet*, or, to transpose the pair into their respective positive counterparts—*tot svet* and *etot svet*. In other words the Russian reader intuitively understands the phrase as "I shall hear the falling 'thud' of the ax not with the ear of *this* world but of *that* world," i.e.,

Cincinnatus' ideal world on the far side of death. This interpretation is borne out by Nabokov's English translation which reads "shall I not hear the downward vigorous grunt with the ear of a different world?" (E92).

Etot (this) and tot (that) are but two of a number of deictic elements. Perhaps the most frequent are tut and tam, "here" and "there." These are respectively identified with etot svet and tot svet and contrast in the same way.[6] In the following passage Cincinnatus contrasts the ideal world of his dreams with the fearsome world of his waking hours.

> There, tam, là-bas,[7] the gaze of men glows with inimitable understanding; there the freaks that are tortured here walk unmolested; ... there everything strikes one by its bewitching evidence, by the simplicity of perfect good; there everything pleases one's soul ...; there shines the mirror that now and then sends a chance reflection here ... (94).

> Tam—nepodrazhaemoi razumnost'iu svetitsia chelovecheskii vzgliad; tam na vole guliaiut umuchennye tut chudaki; tam vse porazhaet svoeiu charuiushchei ochevidnost'iu, prostotoi sovershennogo blaga; tam vse poteshaet dushu ...; tam siiaet to zerkalo, ot kotorogo inoi raz siuda[8] pereskochit zaichik ... (99-100).

The tut/tam opposition is not only maintained throughout the book but is used (sometimes in variant forms) more pervasively than any other manifestation of the "this world/that world" dichotomy. Further, it serves as the basis of a motif of phonetic and iconic symbols that are associated with some of the thematic polarities outlined above. The more frequent of the two terms is tam "there" which is identified with Cincinnatus' ideal world. It is, however, further and more specifically linked with the most prominent projection of that other, ideal world into the authoritarian world of the novel—the Tamara Gardens (Tamarinye sady)—a name that is phonetically built upon the word tam.[9] They are the "There Gardens," projections of the gardens of Cincinnatus' ideal world. This identification is made explicit in Cincinnatus' characterization of his ideal world: Tam, tam—original tekh sadov, gde my brodili, skryvalis'. "There, there are the originals of those gardens where we used to roam and hide in this world" (R99/E94). It is of interest that Nabokov has found it necessary in the English translation to counterpoint the English equivalents of tam "there" and tex "those" by newly inserting a counterbalancing "in this world" in the English sentence. Although the passage just cited is the most explicit identification of the ideal world of tam with the Tamara Gardens, the interplay of the two elements is introduced much earlier. In the opening chapter, well before the introduction of the "this world/that world" (tut/tam) opposition we find the following bit of phonetic pyrotechnics underlining the equation of tam and Tamara Gardens as the imprisoned Cincinnatus takes an imaginary stroll through his beloved park:

Now and then a wave of fragrance would come from the Tamara Gardens. How well he knew that public park! *There*, where Marthe, when she was a bride, was afraid of the frogs and cockchafers... *There*, where whenever life seemed unbearable, one could roam... *That* green turfy *tamarack* park, the langour of its ponds, the *tum-tum-tum* of a distant band... He turned on *Matterfact* Street... (19).

Izredka naplyv blagoukhaniia govoril o blizosti Tamarinykh sadov. Kak on znal eti sady! Tam, kogda Marfin'ka byla nevestoi i boialas' liagushek, maiskikh zhukov... Tam gde, byvalo, kogda vse ostanovilos' nevterpezh i mozhno bylo odnomu... Zelenoe muravchatoe *Tam*, tamoshnie kholmy, tomlenie prudov, tamtatam dalekogo orkestra... On povernul po *Matiukhinskoi*... (32).

In addition to its occurrences in the word itself and as a part of Tamara Gardens, *tam* and its variants are woven into the texture of this lyrical flight in still other ways. Among these are the *tamoshnie kholmy* "the hills over there," based on the adjective form of the adverb *tam*, and the onomatopoeic *tamtatam* of the distant orchestra. Also echoing Cincinnatus' idealized *tam* is the *tomlenie* "languor" of the ponds. A direct equivalent of the *tamoshnie kholmy* is missing from the English since the English counterpart lacks the *tam* element which is the phonetic (and semantic) focal point of the passage. *Tomlenie* (pronounced *tamlyéniye*) is translated but the phonetic echo is lost. The English attempts to offset the lost and weakened *tam* components by inserting "*that*... park" using the deictic element *that* to stress the "other worldly" quality of Tamara Gardens and more directly by the introduction of "*tamarack*" in the same sentence. After Cincinnatus has left the idyllic Gardens, he turns onto *Matiukhinskii* Street which brings him back into "this world." Most striking here is that the first three letters of *Matiukhinskii* are a mirror-image reversal of *tam*.[10] From this it is but a step to the realization that semantically a reversed *tam* is its antonym *tut* which is indeed the location of *Matiukhinskii* (Matterfact) Street. Also interesting are the semantic associations of the oddly named street: *Matiuk*—1) "the sound of an axe blow" and 2) *zanimat' matiuki* "to engage in cursing utilizing the word 'mother'." The deliberateness of Nabokov's choice of the Russian street name is affirmed by his English substitute "Matterfact Street" which retains the inverted phonetic play of the Russian (although it is wasted on the English reader) and tries to capture some of the thematic implications, i.e., Cincinnatus leaves the Tamara Gardens, the projection of his ideal world, and reenters the banal, philistine, matter-of-fact world of his own society on Matterfact Street. The studied inversion of *tam* in *Matiukhinskii* is indistinctly echoed in Nabokov's choice of name for Cincinnatus' odious wife Marfin'ka or Marthe. Also implicit in the use of *mat* as the perverted mirror-image of *tam*, the ideal world, is its association with *materiia* "matter," *material'nost'* "materiality," an attribute of the prison society.

Subsequent mentions of the Tamara Gardens also involve anagrammatic play yielding the word *tam*. From Cincinnatus' prison tower, he looks down on the *TuMAn TAMarinykh sadov, na sizye, TAiushchie kholMy* "the haze of the Tamara Gardens and at the dove-blue melting hills" (R54/E37). Not only does *TuMAn* "haze," a frequent attribute of the Gardens, contain in scrambled form *tam*, but the following phrase with its *TAiushchie kholMy* "melting hills" echoes the key word. The same device is used somewhat more obtrusively in *Ia nikogda ne vidal imenno TAkiMi etikh kholmov, TAkiMi TAinstvennyMi* "I have never seen those hills look exactly like that, so mysterious" where the normal word order is violated by the positioning of the first *takimi* in order to accentuate the anagram (R54/E37). A similar example occurs in a passage where Cincinnatus has momentarily escaped his prison via a tunnel. As he stands outside the prison wall looking down at the city and the Gardens, he watches how *tam, tam, vdali, venetsianskoi iar'iu vspykhnul porosshii dubom kholm i medlenno zatmil'sia* "yonder, yonder, an oak-covered hill flashed with Venetian Green and slowly sank into shadow" (R164/E165).

The identification of *tam* with "that world" is established early in the novel. Only after this aspect of the polarity is firmly established do we see the introduction of the counterpointed *tut*, symbolizing "this world," the world of the prison. In order that the reader be made aware of the antithetic relationship, the initial presentation of the *tut* motif is set in the same paragraph as the most elaborate of the *tam* references. This paragraph, which is partially reproduced above, is the only passage in the book in which the juxtaposition of *tut* and *tam* is made explicit. Cincinnatus is writing in his prison journal of his vain efforts to describe his vision of the ideal world but laments that he lacks the artistic gift requisite for his task, a task, as he says, "of the not now and not here" (*nesegodniashnei i netutoshnei . . . zadachi*) (E93/R98). Cincinnatus' task requires, *inter alia*, a more favorable setting. He continues:

Ne tut! Tupoe "tut" podpertoe i zapertoe chetoiu "tverdo", temnaia tiur'ma, v kotoruiu zakliuchen neuemno voiushchii uzhas, derzhit menia i tesnit.

Not here! The obtuse *tut* (here) propped up and locked in by its pair of T's, the dark dungeon in which a relentlessly howling "uuu" of horror is entombed, confines and constricts me. (My translation—DBJ.)

This is the key passage in the introduction of the *tut* member of the central deictic opposition. We have already seen that this passage, in addition to establishing the counterpoised polarity, presents an elaborate array of phonetic and iconic devices suggestive of Cincinnatus' plight.[11]

The members of the *tut/tam* opposition also confront each other in the episode treating Cincinnatus' abortive escape, although *tut* appears only anagrammatically. Cincinnatus has heard digging sounds for several nights. Finally his cell wall breaks open and there appear his mock saviors, Pierre the executioner and Rodrig the prison director, much amused by their cruel hoax. To celebrate their feat, Cincinnatus is forced to enter the newly dug tunnel and crawl to a neighboring cell to join the executioner in a cup of tea. The journey is described as follows:

> Spliushchennyi i zazhmurennyi, polz no karachkakh Tsintsinnat, szadi polz m-s'e P'er, i oTovsiudU Tesnia, davila na khrebet, kolola v ladoni, v koleni, kromeshnaia t'ma, polnaia osypchivogo treska, i neskol'ko raz TsintsinnaT UTykalsia v TUpik, i Togda ms'e P'er TianUl za ikry, zasTavliaia iz TUpika piaTiT'sia i ezheminUTno Ugol, vysTUp, neizvestno chTo bol'no zadevalo golovU, i voobshche Tiagotela nad nim Takaia Uzhasnaia, besprosveTnaia Toska, chTo, ne bUd' szadi sopiashchego, bodUchego spUTnika,—on by, TUT zhe leg i Umer. No voT posle dliTel'nogo prodvizheniia v Uzkoi, Ugol'no-chernoi T'me (v odnom mesTe, sbokU, krasnyi fornarik TUsklo obdal loskom chernoTU), posle TesnoTy, slepoTy, dUxoTy,—vdali pokazalsia okrUgliavshiisia blednyi sveT: TAM byl povorot i nakonets—vyxod (159).

> Flattened out and with eyes shut tight, Cincinnatus crawled on all fours, M'sieur Pierre crawled behind, and the pitch darkness, full of crumbling and cracking, squeezed Cincinnatus from all sides, pressed on his spine, prickled his palms and his knees; several times Cincinnatus found himself in a cul-de-sac, and then M'sieur Pierre would tug at his calves, making him back out of the dead end, and every instant a corner, a protrusion, he knew not what, would brush painfully against his head, and all in all he was overcome by such terrible, unmitigated dejection that, had there not been a wheezing, butting companion behind, he would have lain down and died then and there. At last, however, after they had been moving for a long time through the narrow coal-black darkness (in one place, off to the side, a red lantern imparted a dull lustre to the blackness), after the closeness, the blindness, and the stuffiness, a pale luminosity expanded in the distance: there was a bend THERE, and finally came the exit (159-60).

The pitch black confines of the tunnel are a distillation of the world of the prison and the society it bespeaks. Although the key word *tut* occurs only once in its pristine form, its anagrammatic echoes are everywhere as we have graphically indicated in the Russian text. (Nabokov has not attempted to duplicate the encrypted anagrams in his English translation.) It is also of note that at the end of the section the opposition of the two deictic terms is evoked by the presence of *tam* which signals the light at the end of the tunnel, at the exit.

In the early part of the narrative the *tam* allusions predominate. As the hour of Cincinnatus' death approaches, the *tam* occurrences recede and *tut* allusions become ever more prominent. In the early morning hours before his beheading Cincinnatus tries to sum up his reflections in a final entry in his journal. He now realizes the falsity of all of the things that had given him hope of salvation in the world of "here." He understands that he has permitted himself to be duped and writes: *Vot TUpik TUToshnei zhizni—i ne v ee tesnyk predelakh nado bylo iskat' spaseniia* "This is the end of this life, and I should not have sought salvation within its confines" (R200/E205). It is of course significant that at this moment of revelation the *tut* motif is reintroduced and reiterated several times in the passage.

The deictic terms, *tut* and *tam*, are, as we have noted, emblems of the antithetic worlds of the novel. This being the case, it is not surprising that the events of the narrative should find their denouement mirrored in the resolution of the tension between the deictic emblems. Indeed, as we shall see, the denouement of the novel is signaled more unambiguously by the deictics than by the events themselves. As the novel draws to a close, i.e., the execution scene, the world of "here," a world of theatrical sets, literally begins to disintegrate. This process accelerates as Cincinnatus ascends the scaffold and places himself on the block. As he counts to ten, the shadow of the falling axe runs along the floor boards: "...one Cincinnatus was counting, but the other Cincinnatus had already stopped heeding the sound of the unnecessary count which was fading away in the distance..." (222). Cincinnatus then gets up and walks away from the scaffold through the crumbling stage set, ignoring the protests of the increasingly transparent crowd and of his former jailers. Although there is one additional suggestion that the beheading has occurred ("through the headsman's still swinging hips the railing showed"), the ending is somewhat ambivalent. Who dies? Cincinnatus or the world? A less ambiguous conclusion is projected by the resolution of the *tut/tam* polarity. As he lies spread-eagled on the headsman's block, Cincinnatus suddenly asks himself, *Zachem ia tut? Otchego tak lezhu?* "Why am I here? Why am I lying here like this?" (R217/E222). He answers his own question by getting up and walking away as the world of "here" disintegrates around him. The final resolution of the *tut/tam* conflict comes in the novel's last line: *Tsintsinnat... napravliaias' v tu storonu, gde, sudia po golosam, stoiali sushchestva, podobnye emu* "Cincinnatus...made his way in that direction where, to judge by the voices, stood beings akin to him" (R218/E223). *Napravliat'sia v tu storonu* "to make one's way in that direction" is a periphrastic deictic expression that is patently modelled on the stock phrase *otpravliat'sia na tot svet* "set off to that world" i.e., to die, which is, of course, part of the *etot svet/tot svet (tut/tam)* opposition that lies at the heart of the novel. Cincinnatus has at last attained his ideal world.

In addition to the basic manifestation of the "this world/that world" opposition through the deictic elements *tut/tam*, the contrast is also expressed through a number of other deictic and semideictic formulations. Among those belonging to the "this world" group, we find *zdes'* and *zdeshnii* which are synonyms of *tut* and *tutoshnii; siuda* "hither," *otsiuda* "hence," and *otkuda* "whence." A more varied group of synonyms attach themselves to the *tam* set. Many of these express their opposition to the contextually implicit *tut* by the word *drugoi* "other, another, different." In one case the opposition is explicit: *glavnaia ego chast' nakhodilas' sovsem v drugom meste, a tut, nedoumevaia, bluzhdala lish' neznachitel'naia dolia ego* "the greater part of him was in a quite different place, while only an insignificant portion was wandering, perplexed, here" (R123/E120). Other such *tam* paraphrases are: *v drugom klimate* (R122) "in another climate," *v drugom izmerenii* (R61) "in another dimension," *perexodil v druguiu ploskost'* (R123) "crossed over to another plane," *v drugoi stixii* (R124) "in another element," *v druguiu glubinu* (R124) "to another depth," as well as the *v tu storonu* "in that direction" discussed above.

We have established at some length the two worlds of *Invitation to a Beheading* and their schematized opposition through the deictic *tut/tam* opposition. The novel's plot centers around Cincinnatus' relationship to the two worlds and his ultimate translation from one to the other after an agonized lifetime of tantalizing foreglimpses. After our detailed examination of the schematization of the "this world/that world" opposition through the use of the abstract deictics, it should not come as a surprise that the role of Cincinnatus, the protagonist, is no less schematized. Above, in another context we quoted Cincinnatus' journal entry in which he wrote, *Ja ne prostoi. . . , ia tot, kotoryi zhiv sredi vas . . . Ne tol'ko moi glaza drugie, i slukh, i vkus . . . no glavnoe: dar sochetat' vse eto v odnoi tochke . . .* "I am not an ordinary—I am the one [*tot*-DBJ] among you who is alive—Not only are my eyes different, and my hearing, and my sense of taste . . . but most important, I have the capacity to conjoin all this in one point . . ." (R62/E54). Cincinnatus, in referring to himself as *tot* in opposition to all the citizens of *etot svet* "this world" is proclaiming himself a citizen of that other, better world, i.e., *tot svet*, just as he has previously rejected "this world" in his statement that "I am here through an error—not in this prison specifically but in this whole terrible, striped world." '. . . *v etot strashnyi, polosatyi mir'* (E91/R96). More significant for present purposes is Cincinnatus' statement that he can draw together all of his otherworldly perceptions into a single point *(tochka)*. Cincinnatus seizes upon the word *tochka* as a symbol of his unique, irreducible essence and in his journal writes of a strange sensation in which he gradually strips away layers of himself, *do poslednei, nedelimoi, tverdoi siiaiushchei tochki, i eta tochka govorit: 'ia esm'!* 'until he arrives at the final indivisible, firm radiant point, and this points says: "I am!"' (R95/E90). Later, during Cincinnatus's interview with his mother he suddenly perceives in her gaze *tu posledniuiu, vernuiu, vse obiasniaiushchuiu i oto vsego okhraniaiushchuiu tochku, kotoruiu on i v sebe umel nashchupat'* "that ultimate, secure, all-explaining and from-all-protecting spark that he knew how to discern in himself also" (R137/E136).[12]

Nabokov's choice of the word *tochka* for Cincinnatus' innermost essence and allegiance is ingenious, for while it is not etymologically akin to the deictic particle "*t-*" which is common to all of the keywords (*tot, etot, tut, tam*), it is alliteratively related to those terms which demarcate the moral geography of the novel. Cincinnatus, whose essence is summed up in the word *tochka*, is in transit between *etot svet* and *tot svet*. He believes that he is in *etot svet* by mistake and properly belongs in *tot svet*, his ideal world. *Tochka*, signifying Cincinnatus' essence, is evidently closer to the *tot* of *tot svet* than to the *etot* of *etot svet* with its extra *e-*[13]. The loss of the *e-* involved in Cincinnatus' translation from *etot svet* to *tot svet* is iconically suggestive of the beheading of Cincinnatus which marks his passage from "this world" to "that." All of this is part of Nabokov's novelistic strategy to demonstrate Cincinnatus' sense of identity with *tot svet*, the world of *tam*, through the very term that specifies his most intimate being. Also of note is that in conformity with his central abstract polarities of *etot/tot* and *tut/tam* Nabokov has chosen the equally abstract *tochka* as the mediator between them. When Cincinnatus arises from the executioner's block here in "this world," he does so in order to join his fellow beings in "that world."[14]

*Invitation to a Beheading* is Nabokov's earliest major statement of the two world theme that characterizes so much of his *oeuvre*. The embodiment of each of the two worlds in one of two opposed key terms (*tut/tam*) and the alignment of each with a series of thematic oppositions affords an almost schematic view of Nabokov's fictional cosmology. Precisely because of the intricate artificiality of the novel, the two world theme stands out more sharply than in many of its later appearances. The two world cosmology of *Invitation to a Beheading* is the context for two of Nabokov's reigning themes: the intermediary role of art and the artist, and the meaning of death.

## THE AMBIDEXTROUS UNIVERSE OF *LOOK AT THE HARLEQUINS!*

Space is a swarming in the eyes; and time, / A singing in the ears." These lines are a part of John Shade's meditation on death and the hereafter in his poem "Pale Fire" in Nabokov's novel of the same name (40). They also bespeak Nabokov's interest in questions of space and time in relation to man's fate. Some two years after the appearance of *Pale Fire*, Martin Gardner, perhaps best known as the long-time mathematical games editor of the *Scientific American*, published a volume entitled *The Ambidextrous Universe: Left, Right and the Fall of Parity.*[15] The book is a popular account of one of the major scientific breakthroughs of our time—the physicists' overthrow of parity, a phenomenon which is shown to be "intimately connected with left and right and the nature of mirror reversals" (16). In his discussion of space and time Gardner compares these concepts to the two lenses in a pair of glasses without which we could see nothing. The external world is not directly perceivable and can be apprehended only through these lenses which, however, shape and color all of our perceptions (149). It is in this context that Gardner aptly quotes the above lines from "Pale Fire" which he jokingly attributes to poet John Francis Shade. Only the imaginary poet (and not Nabokov) is cited in the index.

Nabokov was apparently bemused by Gardner's incarnation of his invented poet and retaliated in his 1969 *Ada*. In the "Texture of Time" section in which Van ruminates on the mysteries of space and time, he links space with the senses of sight, touch, and kinesthesis; time, on the other hand, is more closely associated with hearing. Van then quotes the line "Space is a swarming in the eyes, and Time a singing in the ears," attributing it to "John Shade, a modern poet, as quoted by an invented philosopher ('Martin Gardiner') in *The Ambidextrous Universe*, page 165" (542).

When *Look at the Harlequins!* appeared in 1974 no mention was made of either John Shade's lines or of Martin Gardner. To Nabokov readers not familiar with Gardner's book it might have appeared that the humorous exchange had come to an end. To those knowing Gardner's book, however, it was apparent that the exchange not only had not ended but had entered another, more serious dimension, for Nabokov's last novel has obvious (albeit tacit) affinities with the central thesis of Martin Gardner's *Ambidextrous Universe*. The final episode in the exchange came only with the 1979 revision of Gardner's volume, newly re-subtitled *Mirror Asymmetry and Time-Reversed Worlds*. In the revised edition Gardner briefly discusses *Look at the Harlequins!* and asserts that "questions about the symmetries of space and time are so essential to the plot that I like to think that the book was influenced by Nabokov's reading of the first edition of this book"

(271). We shall examine the interrelations of the two books and show how Nabokov adopted a cosmology expounded in Gardner's *Ambidextrous Universe* and adapted it to conform to the two world model that underlies a number of his major fictions.

*Look at the Harlequins!* is, as we know, the autobiography of the eminent Anglo-Russian writer Vadim Vadimovich N. Composed following the seventy-one-year-old author's miraculous recovery from a mysterious paralytic stroke, the autobiography is a highly selective one focusing upon three aspects of the writer's life: his wives, his books, and his Dementia (85). Although it is the four wives and, to a lesser degree, his books that provide the narrative framework, it is Dementia, that is VV's true Mistress and Muse. Our earlier reading of the memoir argued that VV's account of his wives and books is in large measure the product of his dementia. The present discussion is directed toward the cosmology implicit in the narrator's lunacy.

Vadim Vadimovich suffers prolonged sieges of insanity throughout his life. Even as a child of seven or eight he harbors "the secrets of a confined madman" (8), something he becomes at least seven times. Nor is his lunacy confined to those intervals of hospitalization. He is intermittently afflicted by *kegelkugel* headaches and confusion about his surroundings. VV describes his illness as "a certain insidious and relentless connection with other states of being which were not exactly 'previous' or 'future,' but definitely out of bounds, mortally speaking" (7). This haunting sense of other states of being is manifested in various ways. One of these is termed the "numerical nimbus" by Moody, a London psychiatrist (Moody = mood = joy = Freud) who briefly treats VV. The "numerical nimbus" attacks are sometimes occasioned by a faint ray of light falling upon the sleeper which awakens him into a state of madness. Along this narrow beam descends a row of bright dots "with dreadful meaningful intervals between them" (16). These intervals must be measured and calculated so that their secret message is revealed. Successful decipherment will allow the dreamer to escape a horrible death and flee into a region resembling landscape vignettes (a brook, a bosquet) like those surrounding a Gothic B commencing a chapter in a frightening old book for children. It seems obscurely important that in this region "the brook and the boughs and the beauty of the Beyond all began with the initial of Being" (16).[16]

The foregoing symptoms of his mental illness are not those considered the most grave by the narrator. Vadim Vadimovich is most tormented by what would seem to be an inconsequential quirk—his inability to mentally transpose left and right. So distraught is he by this apparently trivial inability that he feels honor bound to confess it to each of his four brides-to-be. The compulsion seems all the stranger in that it does not extend to the revelation of seemingly much more serious aspects of his dementia. The narrator's preoccupation with his left/right aberration is obscurely linked with another oddity which, while not openly associated with the former, proves to be closely connected with it. Each of VV's four confessions is preceded by scenes in which the autobiographer becomes auto-voyeur standing nude before a mirror taking physiological and psychological stock before committing himself to each new relationship (31, 174, 227). Typical of these narcissistic exercises is the first in which "a warning spasm" shoots through VV's "flayed consciousness" as he gazes at the reflected "symmetrical mass of animal attributes, the elephant proboscis, the twin sea urchins" (31). Two things are to be noted about the mirror scenes. One, overt, is the emphasis on bilateral symmetry; the other, tacit, is the mirror's property of reversing left and right—a capability that mocks the narrator's own mental inability to visualize this mundane act.

Vadim Vadimovich's confessions to his prospective brides, although they range in time from 1922 to 1970 and are set in varied formats, display a remarkable uniformity. As Vadim and his first bride-to-be, Iris, lie on the Côte d'Azure beach, he asks her to visualize the two hundred pace tree-lined lane running from the village post office to the garden gate of her villa. As they walk (in imagination) they see a vineyard on the right and a church graveyard on the left. Arriving at the villa, Iris suddenly recalls that she has forgotten to buy stamps. At this point in the scenario Vadim asks Iris, with eyes closed, to imagine herself turning on her heel "so that 'right' instantly becomes 'left'" with the vineyard now on her left and the churchyard on the right (41). Iris visualizes the left-right reorientation as easily as she would make the about-face in life. Vadim, however, cannot. Some "atrocious obstacle" prevents him from mentally transforming one direction into its opposite. As he says, "I am crushed, I am carrying the whole world on my back in the process of trying to visualize my turning around and making myself see in terms of 'right' what I saw in terms of 'left' and vice versa" (42). For VV, any given stretch of space is either permanently right-handed or left-handed and any attempt to mentally reverse the two brings him to the brink of madness. Iris pragmatically suggests that they should simply forget what seems to her "a stupid philosophical riddle—on the lines of what does 'right' and 'left' *mean* in our absence, when nobody is looking, in pure space, and what, anyway, is space..." (42).

Since the narrator's left/right quirk is wholly one of visual imagination and does not have immediate physical consequences, his preoccupation with it would seem to be warranted only in that he believes it to be a forewarning of the so-called dementia paralytica that finally strikes him down. This fear becomes reality soon after the seventy-one-year-old VV arrives in Switzerland with his last love. In order to ease the awkwardness of his ritual pre-marital confession he hits upon the expedient of asking her to read an early chapter of his just completed *Ardis* manuscript in which the hero describes his (and VV's) "tussles with the Specter of Space and the myth of Cardinal Points" (231). While "you" reads, VV takes his preprandial stroll down a lane ending at a parapet from which he gazes at the setting sun. As he turns to retrace his steps that which has happened so often in thought becomes a reality: "I could not turn. To make that movement would mean rolling the world around on its axis and that was as impossible as traveling back from the present moment to the previous one" (236). VV falls into a paralyzed trance from which he gradually emerges with a new understanding of certain central questions of his existence.

We now come to the question of why VV's madness takes such a strange form—the mental inability to transpose left and right. In addition to the bizarre symptoms already outlined, VV has yet another oddity—one that would seem to be much more fundamental than those already mentioned. Throughout his long life the narrator is haunted by the feeling that he and his works are but pale shadows, inferior variants of another, vastly more gifted Anglo-Russian writer and his works. VV's madness, misdiagnosed as dementia paralytica, is obviously dementia praecox, now better known as schizophrenia. *LATH* is the fanciful "autobiography" of the narrator's mad half. Glimmers from his sane half occasionally filter into the narrator's mind giving him inklings of his other self—the self which is the original of which VV is the paler, flawed copy. The identity of the original (who never overtly appears in the narrative) is more or less of an open secret. He is, of course, another Nabokov figure whom we shall refer to as "Vladimir Vladimirovich" (in quotes) as opposed to the narrator, Vadim Vadimovich. VV's strange inability to mentally transpose left and right is perhaps symtomatic of his inability to evert himself into his "other," i.e., to integrate the halves of his split personality and to merge his delusional world with its "real" world counterpart.

There is reason to suppose, however, that there is yet another dimension to VV's duality. The deranged narrator is on several occasions badly shaken by intrusions into his delusional world of bits of evidence that things are not what they seem. These encounters lead him to reflect on his troubled sense of identity. It is not by chance that these musings on his identity are often cast in terms of "another world." VV's fantasy world is not a haphazard patchwork but a hermetic system, its own reality. Incursions from ordinary reality seem to him to be dementia-tinged images from a distorted twin world with its own VV. This is the basis of *LATH*'s two world cosmology.

There is much evidence connecting VV's sense of personal duality and the other world. On one warm wet Paris night as VV walks to a meeting with the Russian bookseller Oksman, he is especially oppressed by his recurrent feeling of duality. He senses that his life is "an inferior variant of another man's life, somewhere on this or another earth,"—a life which the narrator is condemned to impersonate (89). During his talk with Oksman he is further shaken by the bookseller's reminiscences about VV's father at a time when the father was, according to VV, long dead. Also distressing is that Oksman (and several other characters) confuse VV's novels such as *Tamara* and *Camera Lucida*, with those of another writer, the author of *Mary* and *Camera Obskura*. Later that night, the emotional pressure of these "coincidences" bring VV near the point of breakdown. Most traumatic, VV says, is that events seem to "establish a sudden connection with another world, so soon after my imagining with especial dread that I might be permanently impersonating somebody living as a real being beyond the constellation of my tears and asterisks—*that* was unendurable, *that* dares not happen!" (96-97). The "other world" motif is echoed in other passages. The sight of a woman's bare back "recalled something from a parallel world..." (74). Many years later, VV is tormented by the suspicion that *Ardis*, his most private book, "might be an unconscious imitation of another's unearthly art..." (234). The most significant of these "other world" references occurs near the end of VV's narrative as he describes his awakening from his three-week-long coma. His first concern is establishing his identity: "...my family name began with an N and bore an odious resemblance to the surname or pseudonym of a presumably notorious (Notorov? No) Bulgarian, or Babylonian, or maybe, Betelgeusian writer with whom scatterbrained *émigrés* from some other galaxy constantly confused me" (248-49). Suddenly his name flashes into his mind. To be noted here is the "B" which echoes the "enchanted region" of brooks, bosquets, and the Beyond—all guarded by the Gothic "B" in VV's "numerical nimbus" nightmares (16). This region of the Beyond would seem to be associated with the other world sensed and now perhaps glimpsed by the narrator. During his trance VV's speeding mind has seemingly experienced that which lies beyond death. As he says: "Problems of identity have been, if not settled, at least set. Artistic insights have been granted. I was allowed to take my palette with me to very remote reaches of dim and dubious being" (239). The very last lines of VV's story reassert the two world theme. As the convalescing author drifts off to sleep, thoughts of the tea with rum which had earlier been promised hypnogogically float through his mind—"Ceylon and Jamaica, the sibling islands...."

In the inverted world of *LATH!* "our" reality has become the "other" world. The relationship of the two sibling worlds which is emblematized in VV's left/right aberration derives from an elaborate hypothetical cosmology that has its origins in Martin Gardner's *Ambidextrous Universe*.

The most obvious point of intersection between Nabokov's *LATH!* and Gardner's *Ambidextrous Universe* is in their shared preoccupation with left and right as fundamental categories. Gardner's book is an examination of one of the most basic of all natural laws—the conservation of parity. This law holds that the universe and the laws that govern it display a fundamental, invariable mirror symmetry with no preference for either right or left (182).[17] The universe is, in Gardner's felicitous phrase, "ambidextrous" and his book is, *inter alia,* a fascinating survey of the myriad ways in which symmetry permeates the universe at all levels: animals and plants, art and illusion, astronomy, chemistry and physics. The starting point and guiding metaphor is, however, mirror imagery—a subject long dear to Nabokov and of immediate import in *LATH.* Even at the most superficial level we need point only to VV's recurrent mirror fetish prior to his ritual left/right confessions and to his mirror-image initials.

Gardner's discussion of left and right shows these concepts to be more elusive than they might seem at first blush. Consider the following questions. What would happen if the entire universe were instantly transposed so that left became right and vice versa? (146-47). Put in another way—if the cosmos were completely empty (observerless) save for a single human hand, would it be possible to determine whether the hand is the left or the right? (141). These questions are closely akin to that raised by Iris in response to VV's confession:"what does 'right' and 'left' *mean* in our absence, when nobody is looking, in pure space" (42). As Gardner notes, Iris dismisses the question as "a stupid philosophical riddle" (2nd ed., 271). We shall, however, see that the riddle is far from stupid and that it opens the door to a much larger issue that is crucial to our understanding of Nabokov's novel.

The above paradoxes dealing with the consequences of instant total reversibility and with the hand in empty space are respectively drawn from Leibnitz and Kant by Gardner and are utilized by Nabokov in both *Ada* (373) and *LATH.* Of the greatest moment for our argument is that they are introduced in the course of Gardner's explanation of the fourth dimension, or, more precisely, any spatial dimension higher than three. Gardner demonstrates that in each spatial dimension certain operations that are manifestly impossible in that dimension are easily performed in the next higher dimension. Consider, for example, that in two dimensional space the mirror image figures ⅃ and L are not superimposable even though they are identical in every respect apart from handedness, i.e., they are enantiomorphs. If, however, the two figures are allowed the advantage of a third dimension, depth, then one may be picked up and turned over, i.e., moved through 3-space, and be superimposed on the other. Their left/right asymmetry disappears in the next higher dimension. By projection, the same applies to 3-dimensional enantiomorphic solids with regard to 4-space and so on *ad infinitum*. Unfortunately it is impossible, or nearly so, for 3-space beings to visualize objects in 4-space just as it would be impossible for 2-space beings to imagine the superposition of the above-mentioned J and L since it entails a higher dimension.[18] The left/right reversal of mirror imagery exists on every dimensional level and the enantiomorphs of each level become identical and superimposable only on successively higher levels.

The idea of the fourth dimension is beloved by science fiction writers. One of the first writers to base a science fiction story on the idea of the left/right reversal of an asymmetric object by moving it through 4-space was H.G. Wells, a particular favorite of Nabokov.[19] In "The Plattner Story," a tale which is no less permeated by the left/right opposition than *LATH*, the hero, a young chemist, inadvertently blows himself into the fourth dimension where he spends nine days before a second explosion returns him to ordinary 3-space, with the difference that the left and right sides of his body are reversed and he writes a mirror-image script with his left hand.[20] During his sojourn in 4-space Plattner discovers that he is living in a dark "Other World" inhabited by the souls of those who formerly lived on earth.

Well's fictional use of the right/left mirror-image idea in the context of another world has strong resonance with the use of this theme in Nabokov's novel. There can be no doubt of Nabokov's awareness of the story since Gardner specifically discusses it (148). Although Nabokov makes no specific mention of "The Plattner Story," there are a number of references to Wells' work in *LATH*. In reply to Iris' "I adore Wells, don't you," VV affirms Wells as "the greatest romancer and magician of our time," but rejects his "sociological stuff." Both of the lovers are much moved by a shared detail in Wells' 1913 novel, *The Passionate Friends* (22).[21] Iris also makes passing reference to the minor Wells' character Mr. Snooks (22) and is chillingly entranced by the early science fiction tale *The Island of Dr. Moreau* (88).[22]

The interrelations between the cosmology of Nabokov's *LATH!* and Gardner's "ambidextrous universe" are not limited to those outlined above. Gardner's far-ranging survey touches upon the foregoing matters as preliminary to his main topic—the fall of parity and closely related ideas in theoretical physics. Strangely enough some of these recent advances seem to parallel earlier, often fanciful, speculations such as Wells' and to argue at least the theoretical possibility of twin worlds. In the late fifties physicists determined that virtually every subatomic particle had an anti-particle twin (196). It is now thought that an anti-particle may be a mirror image reflection of a particle opposed to its twin counterpart only in electrical charge, which distinction in turn signals some type of asymmetric spatial structure in the particle itself (201). In other words, a particle and its anti-particle differ from each other only in terms of "handedness"—left versus right—as a mirror reverses the image it reflects. These mirror image particles, just like their counterparts, can, in principle, combine to form anti-atoms and anti-molecules—in short, anti-matter, which, apart from its opposite handedness, displays the exact structure of its counterpart in "our" world. Anti-worlds and even anti-galaxies populated by anti-people are, in principle, perfectly possible and are hypothetically related to their counterparts on our world in terms of left/right mirror imagery.

Let us now return to the world of *LATH!*. We have noted the book's use of the left/right opposition as a metaphor for VV's apparent schizophrenia, his sense of being an impoverished non-identical twin of another, more gifted Anglo-Russian writer. On several of the occasions that the non-identical twin is mentioned (non-identical because left and right are interchanged), it is suggested that he lives in another world, possibly even another galaxy. It seems probable that as well as borrowing the left/right opposition from Gardner, Nabokov also borrowed a cosmology for VV's dementia. Vadim Vadimovich, an anti-person corresponding to "Vladimir Vladimirovich," lives on an anti-world that mirrors, in a distorted fashion, the other VV's world. VV, perhaps due to his peculiar madness, has intimations of his counterposed twin and his world. The fictional universe of *LATH* and its narrator is a twinned anti-world opposed to "Vladimir Vladimirovich's" world, just as the fictional universe of *Ada*, Anti-Terra, is opposed to the "mythical" Terra, i.e., our world. Terra is mentally accessible to anti-Terrans only in states of madness, just as VV is most susceptible to his feeling of the other world and his other self in periods of severe mental distress.

Although the exact nature of the physical relationship between VV's two worlds is not critical to an understanding of *LATH*, it is worth pointing out that they are not necessarily remote from one another. As we have observed, the resolution of the problem of the left/right reversal of asymmetric objects lies in the fourth dimension which subsumes the three spatial dimensions of the ordinary world. Thus one of VV's worlds may be contained within the other just as the world of plane, 2-space geometry is contained within that of solid, 3-space geometry. Further, Gardner points out that it has been (half seriously) proposed by physicists that reversed mirror-image worlds might coexist in the same segment of space-time. Although the physicist's two worlds could not interact, it is, Gardner says, conceivable that they could interpenetrate each other somewhat like a pair of checker players playing one game on the black squares while a second pair simultaneously plays another game on the red squares (259). This sort of

imagery is also evoked by the interlaced black and white diamond pattern of
the harlequin costume depicted on the dust jacket of Nabokov's novel. This
pattern neatly symbolizes the intra-adjacent worlds of Vadim Vadimovich
and "Vladimir Vladimirovich." In any case, the "other" fourth-dimension
world may be identified with that "other state of Being" that VV senses in
his madness.[23]

The pervasive left/right opposition that characterizes *LATH* is an
analogue of the two opposed worlds implict in VV's cosmology. Not only is
the hero haunted by the idea of a mirror image double but so is his entire
world. We shall see that symmetric left/right imagery provides a framework
for a number of other incidents and themes in the book as well as those
fundamental ones just discussed. These minor left/right symmetries seem
to observe the pattern described by VV as he awakes from his final seizure of
dementia paralytica. At first, physical sensation returns in a pattern of
left/right symmetry; then within the left and right panels of imagination,
and, finally, further paired images occur within each of the panels:
symmetries within symmetries within symmetries (242-43).

First among the left/right symmetries that afford *LATH!* its formal
structure, we have the names (and initials) of its characters. Most central, of
course, is the opposition of the anti-world's Vadim Vadimovich to the "real"
world's "Vladimir Vladimirovich." Nor is it by chance that within each of
the opposed twin universes the names of each of the protagonists are, in
turn, doubled, i.e., Vadim, son of Vadim; Vladimir, son of Vladimir.
Within the fictional anti-world the name of Vadim's real father also offers a
doubling, albeit a partial one, Nikifor Nikodimovich. Also of note is that
the V of Vadim Vadimovich can be viewed as a slightly skewed, truncated
derivative of the N of the father's names much as Russian aristocrats gave
their bastard children truncated family names based on their own. Compare
Nabokov's *Pnin* and VV's *Dr. Olga Repnin.*

The narrator's six Russian and six English novels are, as we have noted,
distorted reflections of Nabokov's own Russian and English books. It is
thematically appropriate that as VV undertakes his last self-evaluation in his
mirror before deciding to join his life to that of this last love, he looks "into
another, far deeper mirror," where he sees and contemplates first his
Russian and then his English *oeuvre.* The two symmetrical sets are explicitly
described in terms of two worlds (228-29). It will be recalled that this
transition between languages and literary worlds occasioned an extended
period of madness coincident with VV's arrival in "the new world," a
journey that physically duplicated his linguistic migration from Russian to
English.[24]

There are still other odd examples of handedness in connection with
VV's writing. In his early pocket diaries he notices that among his accounts

of events "factual or more or less fictional" he sees that "dreams and other distortions of 'reality'" are written in a special left-handed slant (19-20). Another curious detail surfaces in VV's account of the genesis of his novel, *See under Real.* The conception of the book comes to him as he lies in bed. His first English novel appears to him under his right cheek "as a vari-colored procession with a head and a tail, winding in a generally westerly direction..." (123). There is then a correlation of Russian with left and English with right, an appropriate simulation of VV's life and career and, secondarily, of the translation process to which each of his Russian works is eventually subjected.

All four of VV's premarital confessions of his left/right spatial aberration are described in circumstantial detail in terms of short walks from one landmark to another and back.[25] It is curious that either directly or inferentially each of these meticulously described walks proceeds in an east/west direction (or its reverse) but never north/south or in an indeterminate, unspecified direction. All of VV's journeys, starting from his youthful escape from Russia, are marked by this left/right bi-directionally. The East/West contrast is yet another analogue of the left/right opposition that structures the worlds of *LATH!*

The incest theme, which we have previously discussed at length, also has obvious congruity with the left/right symmetry of the narrative. The narrator, his wife Iris, her brother Ivor Black, and Wladimir Blagidze all appear to be the children of the master spy, Count Starov, as is, in all probability, VV's second wife Anna Blagovo. The incest theme is sounded once again in the episode with Bel, the narrator's daughter. Here a particularly marked left/right symmetry develops which seems to be reflected in both of the novel's worlds. It would seem to be beyond coincidence that Bel and VV's ultimate love, "you," are both born on the same day. "You" is regarded as the intrusion of "Reality" into the writer's dualized existence (226 & 250). This situation yields a remarkably elegant equation bridging VV's twin worlds: Bel is to "you" as Vadim Vadimovich is to "Vladimir Vladimirovich." Another such equation involves the narrator's pen name: V. Irisin : Vadim Vadimovich : : V. Sirin : "Vladimir Vladimirovich." On the most abstract level it would not seem inappropriate to see incest as a metaphor for the interaction of VV's Russian and English works.

The ambidextrous universe model in which one world is a flawed mirror image of another world in a higher dimension has been used by Nabokov in a number of his fictions, albeit not in the configuration suggested by Martin Gardner's book. One of the earliest uses of the cosmology was in *Invitation to a Beheading,* written in 1934. The theme is further developed in Nabokov's *Bend Sinister* from the early forties. *Ada,* the work that occupied Nabokov throughout much of the sixties, is explicitly formulated in terms of a world and an anti-world, Terra and Anti-Terra. The events of the novel take place on Anti-Terra (or Demonia) where the hero, Van, devotes his professional life to the exploration of the existence of Terra, a distorted mirror image of his own Anti-World.[26] Here again, madness and death are the transition zones between the two worlds.

Nabokov's last novel, *Look at the Harlequins!*, is the culmination of his development of the ambidextrous universe theme which provides an underlying cosmology for a number of his major works. The events of these novels all take place on Anti-Worlds. Their plots hinge upon the strivings of the anti-world hero to apprehend the parallel real world of his double or his creator. In each case, gleams and glimmers of the "real" world are uniquely afforded to the anti-world hero in dreams and/or madness, although full realization comes only at death, the transition point between the two worlds. There is, however, another source of evidence for the existence of the "real" world that is available to Nabokov's anti-world protagonists and to his readers. This is the elaborate and intricate set of patterns and clues that are implanted in the text(ure) of the fictional anti-world. It is the growing awareness of these allusions and patterns that often leads the hero (and the reader) to divine the existence of the other world.

In each of his twin world novels Nabokov provides the hero (and the reader) with some fundamental opposition, a bipolar metaphor that demarcates each of the paired worlds. In *Look at the Harlequins!* Nabokov has drawn upon the fundamental left/right opposition of Martin Gardner's *Ambidextrous Universe* to supply the emblematic structure for his fictional cosmology.

NOTES

Section Five

1. See the unpublished doctoral dissertation of Brian David Boyd, "Nabokov and *Ada*," University of Toronto, 1979, and W.W. Rowe, *Nabokov's Spectral Dimension* (Ann Arbor, 1981). Our comments on ghosts are drawn from Rowe.

2. This aspect of the novel has been explored by Ludmila Foster, "Nabokov's Gnostic Turpitude: The Surrealistic Vision of Reality in *Priglashenie na kazn'*," *Mnemozina: Studia litteraria russica in honorem Vsevolod Setchkarev*, J.T. Baer and N.W. Ingham, eds. (Munich, 1974), pp. 117-29.

3. A detailed examination of the theatrical element in the novel may be found in Dabney Stuart, *Nabokov: The Dimensions of Parody* (Baton Rouge, 1978), pp. 55-85.

4. Mirror image anamorphic art is surveyed in Fred Leeman, *Hidden Images: Games of Perception, Anamorphic Art, Illusion from the Renaissance to the Present* (New York, 1976). In this passage Nabokov would seem to be attacking mimetic "realistic" art and making the counter argument that art is the mirror that unscrambles the distorted images of the mundane world and gives a true image of reality. Similar ideas have been advanced in recent years by certain French writers who have seized upon anamorphism as a metaphor for art in general. For references, see Jurgis Baltrušaitis, *Anamorphoses: ou magie artificielle des effets merveilleux* (Paris, 1969), p. 6.

5. See, for example, *Frazeologicheskii slovar' russkogo iazyka*, ed. A.I. Molotkov (Moscow, 1968), in which *etot svet* is defined as "The earthly world, life in opposition to the world beyond the grave. Antonym: *tot svet.*" *Tot svet* is conversely defined as "The world beyond the grave in opposition to the earthly world, life. Antonym: *etot svet.*"

6. The identification of *tam* (there) and *tut* (here) with *tot* (that) and *etot* (this) is more than metaphoric. In Ozhegov's standard Russian dictionary, *Slovar' russkogo iazyka*, the former are defined in terms of the latter: *Tam. V tom meste, ne zdes'. (There.* In that place, not here.) The *tut* entry refers one to the synonymic *zdes'* (here) which is defined as *V etom meste* (in this place.)

7. Much of the force of the Russian *tut/tam* opposition is lost in the English translation. Since this opposition is fundamental to the novel, Nabokov introduces certain innovations into the English to foreground the opposition. Among these is the italization of "there" and its repetition in English, Russian and French at the beginning of the cited passage. Neither device is present in the original. For a study of Nabokov's attempts to capture the complex interplay of *tut* and *tam* in his English translation, see Robert P. Hughes, "Notes on the Translation of *'Invitation to a Beheading'*," *TriQuarterly*, 17 (Winter, 1970), pp. 284-92. Since many of the devices Nabokov uses to incorporate his *tut/tam* opposition into the texture of his novel are language-specific and sometimes expressed only weakly or not at all in his English translation, we shall give both the Russian and English texts in parallel throughout.

8. *Siuda* "hither" is a synonym of *tut* "here" used after verbs indicating motion. Together with *tuda* "thither," it constitutes a correlative pair parallel to *tut/tam.*

9. The *tam* syllable signifying Cincinnatus' ideal world appears in many guises throughout the book, and its echoes reverberate in other of Nabokov's works. In Nabokov's autobiography his first adult love is given the pseudonym *Tamara* signifying in part the author's beloved, irretrievable Russia.

10. A similar inversion is found in Nabokov's 1925 story *"Putevoditel' po Berlinu"* ("A Guide to Berlin") in which the *top* of *utopia* "utopia" is tranformed into the *pot* of *potoplennyi* "drowned" and *pot* "sweat." Further, the short sketch makes use of anagrammatic key words interlaced into the text—a phenomenon also present in the Russian text of *Invitation to a*

*Beheading*. The earliest incarnations of several of the Nabokovian word games that abound in *Priglashenie na kazn'* are to be found in this story. For a brief survey, see my "A Guide to Vladimir Nabokov's *'Putevoditel' po Berlinu'*," *Slavic and East European Journal*, 23, 3 (Fall 1979), 353-61.

11. For a detailed discussion of these devices, see pages 36-38 above.

12. In the English version done by Nabokov and his son, the *"tochka"* in the original of this passage has been replaced by the word "spark" which, while perhaps more semantically satisfactory from the point of view of the English reader, obscures the thematically important connection between *tochka* and *tot svet* which is discussed below. The following sentence equating the loss of the reverse **E** ( Ɛ ) in the transition from *etot svet* to *tot svet* ('this world' to 'that world') to the loss of Cincinnatus' head evokes Nabokov's remark about a French politician "whose macrocephalic initial in Russian, the reverse E, had become so autonomous . . . as to threaten a complete rift with the original Frenchman" (*The Gift*, p. 48/*Dar* pp. 43-44.)

13. Russian morphophonemics also provides support for a subliminal alliance of *tochka* with *tot svet* through the existence of a standard t/ch alternation, e.g., *tratit'/trachu*. Thus, if the *tot* of *tot svet* had a nominal diminutive, it would be *tochka*.

14. Our structural analysis of Nabokov's *Invitation to a Beheading* is based in part on ideas advanced by the Soviet semiotician Iu. M. Lotman. See his *"O metaiazyke tipologicheskikh opisanii kul'tury,"* in *Trudy po znakovym sistemam*, 4 (1969), p. 463. Also available in English as "On the Metalanguage of a Typological Description of Culture," *Semiotica*, 14:2 (1975), 99. For a discussion of the relationship between my analysis and Lotman's theory, see the latter portion of my "Spatial Modeling and Deixis: Nabokov's *Invitation to a Beheading*," *Poetics Today* (Tel Aviv), 3, 1 (Winter, 1982), 81-98.

15. New York, 1964. Page number citations show that this is the edition utilized by Nabokov. Our citations are to the Mentor paperback edition (New York, 1969). We shall also have occasion to cite the new "Second revised, updated edition": *The Ambidextrous Universe: Mirror Asymmetry and Time-Reversed Worlds* (New York, 1979).

16. Martin Gardner has proposed (in correspondence with the author) that the "B"-motif of Nabokov's novel (see also pp. 248-49) may be connected with the "B"-motif in Lewis Carroll's *The Hunting of the Snark*. See *The Annotated Snark* with introduction and notes by Martin Gardner (Harmondsworth, England, 1975 rpt.). The reader's attention is directed to Gardner's comments on pages 28-31, 52, 77, and 102. I should like to thank Mr. Gardner for his suggestion and for his reading an earlier version of this chapter.

17. The law of conservation of parity was thought to be absolute until 1957 when it was shown that in weak interactions at the subatomic particle level there is indeed a slight preference for right-handedness, although at the macrolevel the law continues to hold. See Gardner, chapter XX.

18. The art of computer graphics is now beginning to create visual models of what were formerly abstract mathematical constructs. For a survey, see Kenneth Engel, "Shadows of the Fourth Dimension," *Science 80*, I, 5 (July/August, 1980), pp. 68-73.

19. Nabokov, who was not known for the generosity of his critical judgments, once described Wells as a "writer for whom I have the deepest admiration." In a 1970 interview with Alfred Appel, he singled out the science fiction "romances": *The Time Machine, The Invisible Man, The Country of the Blind, The War of the Worlds*, and *The First Men on the Moon (SO* 175). "The Plattner Story," discussed below, may be found in H.G. Wells' *Tales of the Unexpected* (London, 1970). In addition to Wells, Nabokov shares another favorite author with Martin Gardner. Cf. Nabokov's 1923 translation *Anya v strane chudes* "Alice in Wonderland" reissued by Dover (New York, 1976) and Martin Gardner's *The Annotated Alice* (New York, 1960).

20. VV's meeting with the bookseller Oksman triggers particularly severe distress about the narrator's other-worldly double. After this meeting he returns home and records the

encounter in an undescribed cipher (97). It would be thematically appropriate if that cipher were a mirror image one such as that used by Leonardo da Vinci in his notebooks: *The Literary Works of Leonardo da Vinci*, compiled and edited by Jean Paul Richter, 3rd. ed. (New York, 1970).

21. Given Nabokov's (and VV's) distaste for Wells' "sociological" literature, their affection for *The Passionate Friends* is curious for the book, especially in its latter part, is basically a feminist tract. Perhaps Nabokov's fondness for it is due to its earlier part which describes the developing romance of Steven and Mary on an idyllic English country estate not unlike that of the Nabokov family near St. Petersburg on which Nabokov had his first romance. The power of the book over Nabokov's imagination is attested by his response to a *Times Literary Supplement* query on the most underrated books of the last seventy-five years. Nabokov cited Wells' *The Passionate Friends* as "my most prized example of the unjustly ignored masterpiece" and describes how at age fourteen or fifteen he went through all of Wells' fiction in his father's library. His claim that he never reread *The Passionate Friends* finds some support in that he slightly misquotes a favorite line that he uses in *LATH* and cites again in his *TLS* response made some sixty years after his reported reading of the book: *TLS*, January 21, 1977, p. 6, and a corrected version in the issue of January 28, 1977, p. 106.

22. *The Island of Dr. Moreau* (1896) is brought to VV's mind by his reference to the bookseller Oksman (oxman) for his name evokes the half-man, half-beast creatures fashioned by Wells' mad vivisectionist. No "ox-man" appears in the Wells' story, however. Mr. Snooks is to be found in the satirical story "Miss Winchelsea's Heart" in *Twelve Stories and a Dream* (London, 1905). The schoolteacher heroine who rejects Mr. Snooks' proposal out of snobbery over his name gets her just deserts when he marries her friend and changes his name back to its elegant ancestral form "Sevenoaks".

23. So far as I know, Nabokov has never explicitly mentioned the fourth dimension in his work. The concept was, however, extremely popular among Russian intellectual, artistic and spiritualistic circles during the early years of the century. The origin of this interest may be traced to the works of an American mathematician, Charles Howard Hinton, who is briefly discussed by Gardner (228-30). Gardner quotes a passage from *A Picture of Our Universe* in which Hinton discussed mirror-image positive and negative electric charges and the fourth dimension. In the course of illustrating a point Hinton urges the reader to conceive of our world as if "there were to be for each man somewhere a counterman, a presentment of himself, a real counterfeit, outwardly fashioned like himself, but with his right hand opposite his original's right hand. Exactly like the image of the man in the mirror" (230). Hinton's *The Fourth Dimension* (New York, 1904) and other of his works appeared in Russian circa 1915 but their contents had earlier been popularized by P.D. Ouspensky in his *Chetvertoe izmerenie, Opyt issledovaniia oblasti neizmerimogo "The Fourth Dimension: An Attempt to Investigate the Region of the Unmeasurable"* (St. Petersburg, 1909) and *Tertium Organum, Klyuch k zagadkam mira "Tertium Organum: A Key to the Mysteries of the World"* (St. Petersburg, 1911). For a survey of the importance of these ideas to Russian avant-garde art circles, see Charlotte Douglas, "Views from the New World: A. Kruchenykh and K. Malevich: Theory and Painting," *Russian Literature Triquarterly*, 12 (Spring, 1975), pp. 353-70. I am indebted to Douglas for much of the above information.

24. Nabokov has used mirror imagery as an emblem of the two linguistic worlds of his own literary career. We recall in the Russian and English versions of his autobiography the palindromic "rainbow words" BЁEΠCK3 and KZSPYGV, which chromesthetically spell out the primary and secondary mirror image rainbows that respectively symbolize Nabokov's Russian and English works. Mirror imagery (with its inherent left/right inversion) is also used as a metaphor for the translation process in the cover design of Nabokov's own Russian translation

of *Lolita* where the Cyrillic title word is printed in spectral colors once from left to right and then once again in inverted letters, from right to left.

25. The four "confession" scenes are as follows: Iris—Part I, chapter 7; Annette—II, 7; Louise—IV, 4; and "you"—VI, 1.

26. For an interesting exploration of the science fiction aspects of *Ada*, see Roy Arthur Swanson, "Nabokov's *Ada* as Science Fiction," *Science-Fiction Studies*, II, pt. 1 (March, 1975), pp. 76-88.

# SECTION SIX

## NABOKOV AS GNOSTIC SEEKER

In her preface to the posthumous edition of her husband's Russian poems, Vera Nabokov sets forth what she calls Nabokov's "principal theme"—a theme that permeated his writings like a watermark, but which remained undetected by his readers. Termed *potustoronnost'*[1] or "the hereafter," this theme is found as early as the 1919 poem "I Still Keep Mute" and ends only with his last poem "Being in Love" (*Vlyublyonnost'*), attributed to Vadim Vadimovich in the 1974 *Look at the Harlequins!* (25-26).[2] Its most direct statement is the 1942 poem *Slava* "Fame." In the poem's first section the writer is confronted by a Gogolesque phantom-dummy who harries him as an exile without audience or prospect of enduring fame. In the second section the author banishes his tormentor and affirms his happiness that Conscience, the procurer of his sleepy reflections, "did not get at the critical secret."

> That main secret tra-tá-ta tra-tá-ta tra-tá—
>   and I must not be overexplicit;
> this is why I find laughable the empty dream
>   about readers, and body, and glory.

Even without these things the poet thrives because "with me all along is my secret." By substituting letters for stars he has learned to decipher the night and to transcend the self. The poem concludes:

> But one day while disrupting the strata of sense
>   and descending deep down to my wellspring
> I saw mirrored, besides my own self and the world,
>   something else, something else, something else.

The never-to-be-revealed secret, according to his wife, gave Nabokov "his imperturbable *joi de vivre* and clarity" in the face of life's innumerable onslaughts. For elucidation Mrs. Nabokov refers the reader to a passage in *The Gift* in which Fyodor Godunov-Cherdyntsev tries to capture the essence of his late beloved father, an explorer and lepidopterist: "I have not said everything yet; I am coming to what is perhaps most important. In and around my father, around this clear and direct strength, there was something difficult to convey in words, a haze, a mystery, an enigmatic reserve which made itself felt sometimes more, sometimes less. It was as if this genuine, very genuine man possessed an aura of something still unknown but which was perhaps the most genuine of all. It had no direct connection either with us, or with my mother, or with the externals of life, or even with butterflies (the closest of all to him, I daresay)..." (E126/R130). Fyodor can not discover a name for the secret which is the source of his father's solitude. Perhaps, he concludes, the lightning-singed old estate watchman (the only local peasant who could catch and properly mount butterflies) was right in saying that Fyodor's father "knew a thing or two that nobody else knew." The appeal to gnostic knowledge is reminiscent of Cincinnatus' cry "I know a paramount thing that no one here knows" (E189/R193).

Nabokov's paramount secret assumes somewhat different forms in different works. In the novels Nabokov's heroes are often confronted with an ill-defined cosmic riddle whose solution promises to explain "all the secrets, all the mysteries" (BS 137-8). In the 1928 novel *King, Queen, Knave,* Franz, the knave who conspires with his uncle's wife to kill his benefactor, begins to sleep badly: "Horror and helpless revulsion merged in those nightmares with a certain nonterrestrial sensation (*nepotustoronnee chuvstvo*—DBJ) known to those who have just died or have suddenly gone insane after deciphering the meaning of everything" (E202/R195). In one such dream the uncle stands on a ladder winding a red phonograph: "Franz knew that in a moment that phonograph would bark the word that solved the universe after which the act of existing would become a futile, childish game..." (202). The gentle Pnin, no less than the odious Franz, is visited by the same sensation. After a depressing visit from his ex-wife, Pnin is in despair at the thought that Liza's vapid soul might be reunited with his in heaven. Suddenly, he seems to be "on the verge of a simple solution of the universe" (58). The revelation is curtailed, however, by a squirrel in need of a drink. A variant of the crucial question is found in *Transparent Things.* In Hugh Person's *Album of Asylums and Jails,* a dying madman ("a bad man but a good philosopher") writes: "It is generally assumed that if man were to establish the fact of survival after death, he would also solve, or be on the way to solving, the riddle of Being"—an assertion that the mad philosopher immediately subjects to doubt (93).

It is not in the poem or in the above-mentioned novels that we find the most fully elaborated embodiments of Nabokov's cosmic riddle. The theme comes to the fore in a group of novels written from the end of the thirties through the mid-forties, a time of immense strain in the author's life. Although the theme figures in works both before and after this time, its focal point may be seen in two works of this transitional period: the unfinished last Russian novel *Solus Rex* and the first American novel *Bend Sinister.* It is to these that we now turn.

# THE MYSTERY OF INFINITE CONSCIOUSNESS IN *BEND SINISTER*

*Bend Sinister* was Nabokov's first novel to be written in the United States. The earliest reference is in a November 1942 letter to Edmund Wilson in which Nabokov mentions that he has applied for a Guggenheim grant and as a part of the application has "made a (rather silly, I'm afraid) synopsis" of a novel-in-progress called *The Person from Porlock*.[3] This was the first of a number of titles considered and rejected by Nabokov before settling on *Bend Sinister*. At various intermediate stages the work was also entitled *Solus Rex, Vortex*, and *Game to Gunm*.[4] Work proceeded slowly and on May 25, 1946, Nabokov triumphantly wrote to Wilson:

> *Ia konchil roman*. I have just finished the novel...I do not know whether the thing is likeable but at any rate it is honest i.e., it comes as close as humanly possible to the image I had of it all along. I do hope...somebody will buy it because I am horribly short of money...But I *am* glad the obsession and burden are gone.

The setting of the novel is a small imaginary European country that has just experienced a Communnazi revolution installing as dictator one Paduk, the founder of the Ekwilist (Equalist) Party. The protagonist of the narrative is Adam Krug, Paduk's erstwhile schoolmate, now a world-famous philosopher who teaches at the national university. The time setting appears to be vaguely contemporary with the composition of the novel. Its events span the brief period from late November when Olga, Krug's wife, dies, through the following January when Krug himself, maddened by grief at the government's bungling murder of his eight-year-old son David, tries to attack Paduk and is killed. The plot centers on the resistance of Krug, the country's only internationally known intellectual, to increasingly brutal government pressure to gain his public support of the new regime. Because of his international stature, Krug thinks himself invulnerable to such pressures, but he is wrong. Following his rejection of such blandishments as the presidency of the university, a motor car, a bicycle and a cow, Krug sees the arrest and disappearance of his friends one by one: first, the Maximovs, the elderly Russian couple to whose county dacha Krug and David retreat after Olga's death; then Ember, Krug's translator and friend, a Shakespeare specialist; and, finally, his colleague Hedron, the mathematician. When these measures fail to gain Krug's acquiescence, he, too, is arrested and his son is taken hostage. Krug immediately capitulates but too late, for the neophyte tyranny has through administrative error let David be killed in an experimental psychiatric therapy program. The state makes a final attempt to suborn Krug by giving him the power to save twenty-four of his friends, relatives and colleagues from being shot, but with David's death the government has lost its only hold on Krug who has gone mad and is at last truly invulnerable. His author-induced madness takes the form of the realization that he and his world are merely the inconsequential creations of the author who is shaping the narrative.

*Bend Sinister* is unique among Nabokov's works in that in his "Introduction" to the Time Reading Program edition he has provided his readers with annotations explaining various aspects of the book. We shall see, however, that useful as these notes are, they leave many matters untouched and are in some ways misleading.[5] In his introductory essay Nabokov is at pains to point out that his novel is not *au fond* about "life and death in a police state" i.e., that he has not written a novel of social or political commentary (xii-xiii). The main theme of the work is, Nabokov says, "the beating of Krug's loving heart" and the torture it is subjected to by Paduk's use of the son as a lever against his otherwise invulnerable father. It is, Nabokov continues, for the sake of this relationship that the book was written and should be read. Considering Nabokov's own recent narrow escape from Nazi Europe with his Jewish wife and their small son, this assertion has particular plausibility but, in point of fact, the relationship between Krug and his son, while tender and intense, occupies a very small portion of the narrative. It is critical only as a motive force in the plot. It is the state's lever to the apolitical Krug whose only desire is to pursue his philosophical studies and his personal concerns. Nabokov's perhaps ingenuous assertion should be accepted only with reservation. Two secondary themes are also acknowledged by Nabokov. One is the stupidity of a tyranny that, having finally stumbled on the only means of achieving its goal, blunders and destroys David; the other is Krug's "blessed madness" in which the horror of his plight is suspended by his realization that he and his world are but bits of auctorial stagecraft.

Although Nabokov terms all of the above "themes," it might be more accurate to see them, particularly the first two, as contextual dimensions of the novel bearing more on its plot than its ultimate theme. The father-son relationship might best be viewed as the human dimension of the novel and the bungling brutality of the police state as the politico-satiric dimension. It is only with the third and last dimension—that of Krug's inklings and ultimate revelation (via insanity) that he and his world are but fictional creations—that we approach a central theme to be found in a number of Nabokov's novels. We say "approach" for the idea of art as a self-conscious artifice is but an aspect of what we shall argue to be the true theme of *Bend Sinister*—the mystery of Consciousness. Nabokov's use of the "artificiality of art" idea (i.e., we are all characters in a novel) is part of an extended metaphor for a statement about the nature of Consciousness.[6]

Consciousness is the crux of the philosophical antagonism between Krug and Paduk. The philosophical foundations upon which Paduk has built his victorious revolutionary party are those advanced by an elderly crank named Skotoma (cf. the Russian *skotina* "beast, brute") whose name, not incidentally, contains the Greek root for "darkness" which in its Anglicized form (scotoma) is the medical term for "loss of vision in a part of the visual field; a blind spot." Skotoma's philosophy of Ekwilism (Equalism) far surpasses the relatively modest egalitarianism promised by socialism with its commitment to economic uniformity, or by religion with its auguries of spiritual equality beyond the grave. Skotoma's philosophy promises an ultimate equalitarianism—that of consciousness itself. Obviously neither of the aforementioned traditional panaceas is viable so long as some people are more richly endowed with consciousness than others. There exists, says Skotoma, a fixed computable amount of consciousness in the world. Society's woes proceed from its unequal distribution. This error, however, can be rectified by regulating the capacity of the human vessels. Equitable distribution can be achieved "either by grading the contents or by eliminating the fancy vessels and adopting a standard size" (66). Skotoma, the theoretician, does not suggest any way of implementing his scheme. This is the chosen task of Paduk who wishes to attain and enforce this ultimate ekwilism in the distribution of human consciousness.

Philosopher Krug, while repelled by Skotoma's theory, is not initially interested in the problem of Consciousness. As a philosopher Krug has never engaged in the traditional search for the "True Substance, the One, the Absolute" (152). He feels too strongly the "faint ridicule of a finite mind peering at the iridescence of the invisible through the prison bars of integers." Rather than being a seeker or a synthesizer, Krug has devoted his career to "creative destruction" (154). In the course of events, however, Krug begins to question his self-imposed limitations and tries to visualize a world which lies outside the scope of physics, beyond the measurable, one in which "barefooted Matter *does* overtake Light" (152).

These musings follow the death of Olga, and Krug is at first too benumbed to pursue his new line of thought. Slowly, however, the creative urge returns, but the topic itself remains beyond explicit formulation. He looks over some notes from an earlier time but cannot recollect the idea that united them, their secret combination. He sits at his desk thinking that if only he had a new pen, a bouquet of sharpened pencils, or "a ream of ivory smooth paper instead of these, let me see, thirteen, fourteen more or less frumpled sheets . . . I might start writing the unknown thing I want to write; unknown, except for a vague shoe-shaped outline, the infusorial quiver of which I feel in my restless bones . . . (140). Troubled by his lack of focus and by sexual stirrings triggered by Mariette, the new maid, he abandons his efforts. As the weeks pass he again unsuccessfully tries to seek out his elusive topic (XV). Finally, in late January while putting David to bed Krug is suddenly overcome by a welling forth of love for his son:

> ...what agony, thought Krug the thinker, to love so madly a little creature, formed in some mysterious fashion ... by the fusion of two mysteries, or rather two sets of a trillion of mysteries each; ... the whole suffused with consciousness, which is the only real thing in the world and the greatest mystery of all (168).

Without realizing it Krug has found the focal point for his long-sought new philosophical inquiry. After an early dinner he goes to sleep in his armchair. When he awakens (sexually aroused) he feels that something "extraordinary" has happened. He knows that he can write (170). Following a cold shower, he begins:

> In this preliminary report on infinite consciousness a certain scrumbling of the essential outline is unavoidable. We have to discuss sight without being able to see. The knowledge we may acquire in the course of such a discussion will necessarily stand in the same relation to the truth as the black peacock spot produced intraoptically by pressure on the palpebra does in regard to a garden path brindled with genuine sunlight (172).

As he writes he is distracted by Mariette who is attempting to seduce him. She weans him away from his train of thought and just as he is about to possess her, the doorbell rings. The police have come to arrest him and take David. Just as Krug has regained his powers and embarked on a radically new area of thought, the mystery of infinite consciousness, his nascent intuitions are abruptly curtailed. The "Person from Porlock" (Nabokov's original title for his novel) has arrived and Krug's emergent revelation is shattered.[7]

Nabokov's novels are characterized by a cunning integration of theme, plot and motif. Having identified *Bend Sinister*'s theme we may now turn to an examination of its realization within the framework of the novel's plot and motif structure. The work is conceptually organized in terms of two worlds: the fictive world of Krug and Paduk on the one side, and, on the other, that of the omnipresent author-persona that Nabokov refers to in his Introduction as "an anthropomorphic deity impersonated by me" (xviii).

Krug is consciously aware only of his own (and Paduk's) world. The plot of *Bend Sinister* is the account of his gradual gropings toward the realization that his, Krug's world, is but a creation in the consciousness of an author figure, the anthropomorphic deity who lives in a "real" world. For Krug, the attainment of infinite consciousness, the explanation of all that befalls him, proceeds from his realization of this situation. On one level the plot consists of a series of intimations ending in full revelation of the controlling presence of the anthropomorphic deity. Like Krug's, the reader's understanding of events depends upon his or her realization of the existence and relationship of the two worlds of *Bend Sinister*. First we shall examine the gradual emergence of the anthropomorphic deity and then the intricate pattern of motifs he has left upon his created world as faint footprints testifying to his presence.

The first inkling of the presence of the anthropomorphic deity in Krug's world comes in a long, complex dream that Krug has during the night following his wife's death. The dream centers around Krug's years as a schoolboy. Its description is prefaced by a discussion of the relationship between dreams and conscious memory. This disquisition on the nature of dreams is, like certain other parts of the narrative, partially couched in terms of play production with its producers and stagehands. Among these, Krug senses

> a nameless, mysterious genius who took advantage of the dream to convey his own peculiar code message which... links him up somehow with an unfathomable mode of being, perhaps terrible, perhaps blissful, perhaps neither, a kind of transcendental madness which lurks behind the corner of consciousness and which cannot be defined more accurately than this, no matter how Krug strains his brain...(56).

Later, looking back on his dream, the dreamer senses the presence of an intruder, "of someone in the know" (56). Hints of another world also are to be found in the description of Krug's old friend, the elderly, unimaginative Maximov whose sturdy, pragmatic view of life is saved from vulgarity only "by a moist wind blowing from regions which he naively thought did not exist" (77).

As the events of the narrative draw to their terrifying close, tormented Krug's intuition of "someone in the know" who has hitherto lurked on the edge of his dreams now bursts full-blown into his conscious mind. Imprisoned, and grief-stricken by the ghastly death of his son, Krug has slipped into a fitful, dream-ridden sleep. As he awakens he sees in his cell "a pale gleam like a footprint of some phosphorescent islander... The pattern of light was somehow the result of a kind of stealthy, abstractly vindictive, groping, tampering movement that had been going on in a dream, or behind a dream." The luminous pattern is likened to a sign warning one of an explosion but one conceived "in such cryptic or childish language that you wonder whether everything... has not been reproduced artificially, then and there, by special arrangement with the mind behind the mirror" (209). Just before the full weight of his grief can redescend on the awakened Krug, the "mind behind the mirror" emerges to rescue him. Here the anthropomorphic deity appears for the first time in its own voice: "... it was then that I felt a pang of pity for Adam and slid towards him along an inclined beam of pale light causing instantaneous madness, but at least saving him from the senseless agony of his logical fate" (210). This is the quite literal Epiphany in which Krug learns that he and his world are artifices in the mind of their creator in another world. Both Krug's world and his mind are shattered, but the novel is not yet at an end. Although Krug has learned the secret of infinite consciousness, his fellow characters have not, and the action continues, albeit on a very different basis. The barrier between the two worlds is broken, and Krug's consciousness has at least partly merged with that of his creator, for he is now aware of events in both worlds. As he lies in his cell listening to the night sounds of the prison he hears "the cautious crackling of a page which had been viciously crumpled and thrown into the [author's—DBJ] wastebasket and was making a pitiful effort to uncrumple itself and live just a little longer" (210). The novel-world in which Krug is a character does "live just a little longer" in one final scene.

On the following morning there is a carefully staged public "confrontation ceremony," replete with printed program, in which twenty-four of Krug's friends are to plead with him to endorse Paduk who will then spare their lives. Krug confusedly tries to explain his nocturnal "haloed hallucination," assuring his friends that there is nothing to fear, that their desperate plight is no more than a "silly theatrical" (213 & 215). The horrified hostages attempt to explain Krug's madness to Paduk's guards but Krug, suddenly coalescing present and past, reverts to his youth and tries to rally his friends for a charge against Paduk on their old school playing field. As Krug charges amid a hail of bullets toward the increasingly transparent Paduk, the scene vanishes like "a rapidly withdrawn slide, and I stretched myself and got up from among the chaos of written and rewritten pages to investigate the sudden twang that something had made in striking the wire netting of my window" (126). As the author-persona inspects his nocturnal visitor, a large moth, he gazes beyond the screen down into the street where he sees the puddle which Krug views in the novel's opening scene. The two worlds of *Bend Sinister* have merged.[8]

The theme of an omniscient author-narrator entering the world of his fictional characters is uncommon but by no means unheard-of. Nabokov makes Hitchcock-like walk-on appearances in many of his novels. In the case of *Bend Sinister*, however, this theme is inverted for the focus is rather upon the fictive character's apperception of and penetration into the world of his creator. This violation of the conventions of fiction is much more massive and infinitely more rare.[9] There is evidence that Nabokov saw this unusual inversion as central to his conception of the novel for on January 18, 1944, Nabokov wrote to Edmund Wilson saying that "Towards the end of the book . . . there will be the looming and development of an idea which has *never* been treated before." This somewhat cryptic utterance is not mentioned again by Nabokov but it is apparently the topic of a later parenthetical remark by Wilson (January 30, 1947) that he is "sorry you gave up the idea of having your hero confront his maker." This remark suggests that Wilson, who did not like the novel, perhaps did not fully understand it for the confrontation does take place, albeit not in the explicit form that the critic seemingly had in mind. It is, however, only through madness and then death that Krug crosses over from his own dimming world to that of the "comparative paradise" of his creator (217).

It is not by chance that *Bend Sinister* both begins and ends in death, for death is the point of transition between the two worlds of the novel. It is the death of Krug's wife, Olga, that leads the philosopher to the following meditation: "What is more important to solve: the 'outer' problem (space, time, matter, the unknown without) or the 'inner' one (life, thought, love, the unknown within) or again their point of contact (death)?" (154-155). These reflections lead to a more formal disquisition on death in the following key passage:

> It may be said with as fair an amount of truth as is practically available that to seek perfect knowledge is the attempt of a point in space and time to identify itself with every other point; death is either the instantaneous gaining of perfect knowledge (similar say to the instantaneous disintegration of stone and ivy composing the circular dungeon where formerly the prisoner had to content himself with only two small apertures optically fusing into one; whilst now, with the disappearance of all walls, he can survey the entire circular landscape), or absolute nothingness, *nichto* (155-56).

Death is the point of transition between two worlds but the question posed here concerns the nature of the 'other' world: is it an "absolute nothingness" or the "instantaneous gaining of perfect knowledge?" Krug's meditation on death is leading him to his major theme, for what is "the instantaneous gaining of perfect knowledge" if it is not the attainment of infinite consciousness which, in the context of the novel, we have seen to be the merger of Krug's mind with that of his maker? Only his death will bring about the melting away of his cranial prison cell with its circumscribed angle of vision and permit him to grasp the all-encompassing Absolute.

We have examined Krug's growing awareness, through dreams and finally madness, of the presence of the Nabokovian anthropomorphic deity who is creating Krug's world. This is, we have argued, the real plot of the novel as opposed to the more evident story line that follows the struggle between Krug and Paduk. There is, however, another dimension to the two world theme, for the controlling presence of the narratorial deity is further manifested in an elaborate pattern of motifs and hidden allusions. Although these cryptic patterns are manifestations of the author-persona, they are of equal consequence from the point of view of Krug, for it is in part his tacit recognition of them that is the basis for his effort to transcend the limited consciousness of his world and seek the world of his Creator.

The most critical of these patterns is the complex of images evoked by the footprint-shaped puddle into which Krug gazes in the opening scene and the Nabokovian author-persona in the closing scene. This small pool of water in its manifold permutations is *Bend Sinister*'s master motif and it relates to the theme in a complex and peculiarly appropriate way. The recurrences and general significance of the puddle are pointed out by Nabokov in his Introduction. Having noted it as the initial breeding point of the plot, Nabokov goes on to say that its repeated appearances evoke for Krug "my link with him: a rent in his world leading to another world of tenderness, brightness and beauty" (xv). Krug's dim awareness of the nature of the puddle is suggested by his mental imagery as he gropes to identify the elusive "unknown thing" he wants to write about, "unknown except for a vague shoe-shaped outline" that arouses in him an "infusorial quiver" (140). The puddle is the point of contact, the gateway between Krug's world of limited consciousness and the world of infinite consciousness inhabited by Krug's creator.

The puddle assumes a number of guises throughout the book, each of which relates to a different aspect of the theme. Two are foreshadowed in the initial description of the puddle. In the opening scene, Krug, in the hospital with his dying wife, numbly stares through a window at "An oblong puddle inset in the coarse asphalt; like a fancy footprint filled to the brim with quicksilver; like a spatulate hole through which you can see the nether sky" (1). The "fancy footprint" is that of the narrative's anthropomorphic deity and serves as a metaphor for the numerous allusions and patterns throughout the narrative. Equally important in establishing the meaning of the pool's imagery is the reference to quicksilver or mercury, the element that transforms transparent glass into mirrors. The quicksilvered pool is a two-way mirror: one through which the author-persona sees clearly, but in which Krug sees only the reflection of his own world except in certain lights, at certain times, when he senses a shadowy form behind the mirror's surface.

The small pool of rainwater has, however, a still more important dimension. The gateway between the two worlds is associated with death both in Krug's philosophy and in the book's imagery. As Olga lies dying and Krug gazes at the autumnal poolet below, "two triskelions, like two shuddering three-legged bathers coming at a run for a swim" blow into the puddle (2). The dead leaves are from a nearby tree on which the remaining leaves number "hardly more than thirty-seven or so"—a curiously precise figure which later proves to be the age of Krug's wife (27). Having passed through the spatulate hole linking Krug's and "Nabokov's" worlds, Olga's soul-symbol reemerges as a moth outside of the writer's window on the novel's final scene (xviii). The kidney-shaped puddle has a still more specific metaphoric link with Olga's death for she dies of a kidney ailment. Nabokov hints at such an association in a scene depicting an ominous interview between Krug and Paduk in which the latter spills a glass of milk leaving "a kidney-shaped white puddle on the desk" (133), perhaps intimating his complicity in Olga's unexpected death. In his Introduction Nabokov specifically acknowledges this last as one of the subthematic incarnations of the ominipresent puddle (xiv).

Not even the auctorial footprint image is free of sinister associations, for David's death is foreshadowed when he steps into a rain puddle and complains that his "left shoe is full of water" (143). Another rather vaguely puddle-shaped image of death occurs when the arrested Krug is marched through a prison courtyard with chalked outlines on its bullet-pocked wall. The sight prompts him to think of the bit of popular folklore that the first posthumous sight seen by a firing squad victim is "a welcoming group of these chalked outlines moving wanly like transparent Infusoria" (188). Finally, Krug's two old friends, the Maximovs, are arrested at their dacha near the inkstain-shaped Lake Malheur.

Yet another set of associations is linked with the puddle. Doctor Alexander, the young Assistant Lecturer in Biodynamics and government agent in charge of bringing the university to heel, badly botches his signature on the loyalty oath form signed by all of the staff apart from Krug. As the philosopher idly looks over at Alexander's document, he notices blotted remains resembling "a fancy footprint or the spatulate outline of a puddle" (48). Alexander will be one of the party that arrests Krug and David. Peter Quist, the antique dealer cum government agent who entraps Krug by offering to smuggle the philosopher abroad, leaves a large blot on his letter. Paduk, the Tyrannosaurus, is likewise inkstained. The dictator's father was a minor inventor whose sole successful creation was the so-called padograph—a custom-designed typewriter-like device that mechanically mimics the handwriting of its owner. The first model is produced as a gift for his teen-age son. Since "infantile inkstains" are characteristic of his son's script, the father adds additional keys, one for an hourglass-shaped blot and two for roundish splotched ones. One suspects that this remarkable affinity between villainy and inkblots is in aid of a latent thematic pun: a blot on the escutcheon of the heraldic design obliquely referred to by the book's title.

The heraldic escutcheon implicit in the title *Bend Sinister* may be plausibly viewed as the super eidelon that subsumes all of the above-mentioned permutations of the puddle motif. The escutcheon is the field for the bend sinister which, as Nabokov remarks in his preface, is "commonly but incorrectly" regarded as a mark of bastardy, being tacitly opposed to the "legitimate" bend dexter. Although cautioning the reader against seeing the title as having "general meaning," Nabokov says that its use is intended to suggest "an outline broken by refraction, a distortion in the mirror of being, a wrong turn taken by life, a sinistral and sinister world" (xii). The terms of references here have an obvious resemblance to those appearing in connection with the various manifestations of the central puddle image. The heraldic escutcheon, however, has additional reverberations that are uniquely its own. Although illegitimacy is indeed not the correct meaning of "bend sinister," Nabokov clearly had it in mind, for the authorized translations into German (*Das Bastardzeichen*), Dutch (*Bastaard*), and Italian (*I Bastardi*) all focus precisely upon this aspect of the title's meaning, even, in the latter two cases, foregoing the heraldic context.[10] The association of "sinister" with "left," although of broader implication than the merely political, could not have been entirely absent from Nabokov's mind. The narrative is bestrewn with incidental and not so incidental references to "left," but none to "right."

Like the puddle-escutcheon itself, the "bend sinister," in which "bend" means a diagonal band or bar, flickers in and out among the book's pages in various permutations. The puddle of the opening scene reflects *inter alia* "the brown sinus of a . . . limb which is cut off by the rim of the pool" (2). Bars, both real and metaphyscial, abound as in the image of "a finite mind peering . . . through the prison bars of integers" (152). These are dark bars of sinister meaning. Just as the puddle has opposed meanings, death in Krug's world versus intimations of transcendent life in the world of the author-persona, the bend/bar too has dual opposed meanings. The dark bend/bar has an antonymic light-colored form. Krug awakes in his barred prison cell to see a luminous pattern produced by an oblique ray from an arc light in the prison yard. It is by sliding along this "inclined beam of light" that the author-persona rescues Krug via insanity (210). The origin of the "inclined beam" may be a street light outside the window of the author-persona, the shredded ray of which he sees as he gazes down into the "special puddle" in the book's final lines.[11]

The seemingly contradictory character of the heraldic bend is puzzling but Nabokov's penchant for optical illusions suggests a possible answer. The escutcheon is a mirror-window between the two worlds—Krug's dark fictional universe and the bright "real" one of the author-persona. The two characters look from opposite sides at the heraldic puddle that simultaneously separates and joins their two worlds. From Krug's position the bend sinister is just that—a sinister black prison bar proscribing entry into the world of his creator. From the viewpoint of his author, however, looking at the heraldic image from the other side, the charge is a bright "bend dexter," a token of the "comparative paradise" of his own world. The bend sinister which bars the passageway between the worlds of life and death might also evoke Tennyson's 1889 "Crossing the Bar" whose closing stanza strikingly parallels the end of *Bend Sinister*: "For though from out our bourne of Time and Place / The flood may bear me far, / I hope to see my Pilot face to face / When I have crossed the bar."

Moving from signs and symbols associated with the point of contact between the novel's two worlds, we turn now to those internal to the fictive world, the arena of the unequal struggle between Krug and Paduk. Each character in the two opposing camps is accompanied by a number of motifs and allusions. This is most elaborate for Krug and Paduk. Adam Krug's first and last names have obvious significance. Adam, meaning "man" in Hebrew, stands in the same relation to the anthropomorphic deity of the book as does the biblical Adam to his Creator. The philosophical and moral geography of the two situations is also parallel—at least for the Postlapsarian period: Krug's world is evil; his creator's—good. This is an important subtext in the novel for it echoes the basic theme—a created character striving to (re-) enter the world of his maker. There is yet another biblical echo in the book's "apple" motif, particularly in the expression "Adam's apple" which alludes to the legend that a piece of the fruit offered by Eve became permanently lodged in Adam's throat.[12]

The hero's surname proves to be of great importance for both theme and structure in *Bend Sinister*. Krug means "circle" in Russian and "mug" or "jug" in German. The latter meaning, that of a container with a handle, plays a metaphoric plot role. Krug's plight comes about in part because of his illusion that he is invulnerable to the pressures of Paduk's regime. In a fateful interview Paduk tells him "All we want of you is that little part where the handle is." To which Krug vehemently (and wrongly) replies: "There is none..." (130-31). Later, after his arrest and David's abduction, Krug reflects that "he had not thought they would find the handle. In fact, he had hardly known there was any handle at all" (182).

The "circle" meaning of Krug's name resonates in many different dimensions of the novel. Krug is, of course, a small circle within his own circular universe which is in turn encircled by the world of the author-persona. Krug's name also betokens his supposed invulnerability. In the faculty loyalty oath meeting, Krug's friend, the mathematician Hedron, urges him" "Affix your commercially valuable scrawl. Come on! No one can touch our circles—but we must have some place to draw them" (50). The punning reference is to Archimedes' *Noli disturbare circulos meos* which was supposedly uttered by the mathematician when his study was invaded by Roman soldiers during the sack of Syracuse. Finding Archimedes in his study drawing geometric figures and failing to obtain satisfactory answers to his questions, a soldier put him to death.[13] Archimedes is, then, the paradigm of the scholar-intellectual who, like Krug, wishes only to be left alone by the state so that he might pursue his studies. Also like Krug, Archimedes, whose triumphant "Eureka" has become the symbol of sudden profound insight, was a seeker after the secrets of the universe. It is significant that the geometer's major works deal with the properties of circles and spirals, for these figures prove to be crucial to our understanding of the worlds of *Bend Sinister*.

All of the members of Krug's small family are encompassed by the circle symbol. It is surely no accident that Krug's deceased wife is named Olga with its initial stressed O, nor that Olga, who dies of a kidney malfunction, is persistently associated with Hamlet's Ophelia who dies a watery death. Not only is Olga a circle within a circle *(Krug)* but both her name, by virtue of the O, and her husband's, by virtue of its meaning, hint at a secret affinity with the roundish puddle linking them with the infinite consciousness of the author-persona's universe. Also of interest is that in Nabokov's alphabetic synesthesia, the white O evokes the image of an oval mirror (SM 34)—an artifact that figures some five times in one of Krug's dreams in which Olga sits before a mirror divesting herself first of her jewelry and then, surreally, of her head and other body parts (V). Similarly, the name of their son DaviD displays evident iconic imagery. The D's that begin and end his name are each half O's for if the final D is folded over so that its vertical bar matches that of the initial D with the respective curved portions tending left and right, a perfect O is obtained, echoing the meaning of "Krug" and the shape of Olga's initial. This iconic alphabetic fusion echoes the fusion of the parents' names as well as the joining of their genes, "the fusion of two mysteries, or rather two sets of a trillion mysteries each" (168).

One of the characteristics of the circle is reversibility, a property that is also typical of some of Krug's actions and observations. Returning home from the hospital on the night of his wife's death, Krug must pass over a bridge guarded at both ends by rag-tag revolutionary soldiers. Upon approaching the north end of the bridge, Krug is detained by the illiterate guards. One takes Krug's pass and then, holding it out to him upside down, demands that the scholar read it aloud. Krug, in a reply that sets the theme of the chapter, remarks "Inversion does not trouble me" (8). Unfortunately, Krug's glasses are broken as he rummages for them and he is unable to read the contents of his safe conduct pass to the suspicious guards. Krug finally bluffs his way across by striking up a conversation with the dimwitted head guard, Gurk. At this point, as Nabokov tells us in the Introduction, we should be bemused by the palindromic opposition of a Russian circumference *(krug)* and a Teutonic cucumber, for "gurk" is a form of the Germanic root for cucumber. This purely verbal palindrome soon takes on a life of its own. After Krug is finally permitted to cross the bridge, he is turned back at the south end for want of a signature from the guards at the north end. The philosopher crosses back to seek the signature of the illiterate Gurk. The palindromic nature of the names of the opposed characters, Krug and Gurk, literally reproduces the crossing and recrossing of the bridge, and mirrors in miniature Krug's absurd plight. The inversion has still other echoes within the episode. As Krug traverses and re-traverses the bridge, he comes to see himself as "an hourglass which somebody keeps reversing, with me, the fluent white sand, inside" (14). He mentally likens himself to an ant running up a blade of plucked grass. No sooner does he get to the top of the stalk than it is turned upside down so that the grass blade's *"tip"* becomes its palindromic opposite, a *"pit,"* and the performance must be repeated.

Paduk's name, like Krug's, displays a wide range of thematic resonance. It is the Shakespearian "paddock," literally meaning "toad," a term of monstrous abuse applied by Hamlet to his stepfather King Claudius, the murderer of his father. Paduk is not, of course, the murderer of Krug's father but rather his son David. This aspect of Paduk's role is alluded to in references identifying him with Goethe's *Erlkönig* (perhaps best known from Schubert's *lied*) in which a small boy being carried through the night in the arms of his mounted father is lured to his death by the King of the Elves (130 & 208). Paduk's name also is based on the Russian root *pad* "fall" as in *upadok* "decay, decadence." It is, however, the Shakespearian "paddock" that presumably supplies Paduk's schoolyard nickname, "The Toad," which has still another sinister bilingual connotation: the German *Der Tod* "death." Paduk, the dictator, has been Krug's *bête noire* since their school days when Krug, something of a bully, made a practice of sitting on Paduk's face. Notwithstanding Krug's evident loathing, Paduk, perhaps due to his homophilic nature, secretly adores Krug and once kissed his hand in a darkened classroom: "The Kiss of the Toad," Krug later calls it, perhaps alluding to the German *Todeskuss*, the kiss of death, an allusion that is prophetic (77).[14]

At forty both Paduk and Krug have grown into heavy men, although in all other respects they are sharply opposed. Paduk remains "chill, commonplace and insufferably mean" (60) while Krug, the brilliant master of "creative destruction," is described as robust, virile, and with a craggy brow resembling that of Beethoven (174). This opposition is reflected in a very curious way. While still a schoolboy, Paduk propounds an Ur-Ekwilist theory that "all men consist of the same twenty-five letters variously mixed" (60). Two lines of thought evolve from this dictum. The first and lesser stems from the missing twenty-sixth letter. The absent letter is obviously "I" referring to Adam Krug, Paduk's enemy and the only great man his country has produced. Krug's identification with the letter-symbol "I" is attested by utterances by and about him elsewhere in the text such as "The square root of I is I " (6), or in the parenthetical "Oh, that cramped uncomfortable 'I', that chess-Mephisto concealed in the *cogito!*" (154).[15] Just as the revolutionary state of the average man has no need of the egoistic letter/pronoun "I," it has no place for Krug, who, like the letter, is eliminated.

Paduk's enlistment of the alphabet in his pursuit of egalitarianism is also manifested in his practice of calling his school fellows by perpetually shifting anagrammatic scrambles of their names. Adam Krug becomes, *inter alia*, Gumakrad, Dragamuk, Gurdamak and Madamka. Unbeknownst to Paduk, his alphabetic games spiral into a very different dimension at the hands of the author-persona who regulates the roles of the book's characters. The denizens of the fictional world speak a *gemischte Sprache* with elements of Russian, German, and a mythical Kuranian (=cur?).[16] As well as the koine, some characters seem to speak pure Russian, others pure German. Presumably each is written in its usual alphabet, Cyrillic or Latin. This surmise is important in what follows for by means of selective transliteration of individual letters we can show the names Paduk and A. Krug to be perfect cross-alphabetic anagrams of each other. Further, their relationship can be shown to be that of near but imperfect palindromes. In their English forms the two names share the letters A, U and K. It so happens that the English  P  represents the sound value /r/ in Russian. This gives an overlap of four of the six elements in the two names leaving only the D of Paduk and the  G  of A. Krug unaccounted for. This missing link is filled in when it is realized that the miniscule script form of the English  G, e.g.,  *g*  represents the sound value /d/ in Russian. Thus the admirable Krug and the odious Paduk are equally inter-alphabetic scrambles devised and introduced by the narrative's anthropomorphic deity. In terms of the imperfect palindrome, "Paduk" misses being "Krug, A." only by the  r  (mis-)placed at the end rather than after the K, e.g., Kug, A + r. This same strange intermixture of the protagonists occurs in the name of the capital city Padukgrad.

Paduk is opposed to Krug in still another way for each has his own distinctive emblem. We have discussed the role of the circle figure in connection with Krug. Paduk's emblem is the gammadion or swastika which, like Krug's circle, is interwoven into the text in various ways. The gammadion first appears in the episode in which Krug is trying to cross the bridge. Although he talks his way past the guards at the entry point, he is sent back by the exit guards to get a signature. Krug, knowing the guards can not read, much less write, hands over his pass saying "Scrawl a cross, or a telephone booth curlicue, or a gammadion, or something" (14). The allusion, lost on the guard Gurk, is twofold. The immediate reference is to Gurk's initial ( Г in Cyrillic), for the gammadion derives its name from the four joined Greek Gs or gammas that constitute it, e.g., ⊹. The more remote reference is that the gammadion is the emblem of Paduk's new regime. This emerges only indirectly when an official car arrives for Krug, flying on its hood a red flag with an emblem resembling "a crushed dislocated but still writhing spider" (31). Any doubt that the "writhing spider" is the gammadion or swastika is removed by two highly relevant facts. Particular reference is made elsewhere to Paduk's "arachnoid scrawl" (51) and it is no fluke that the name Paduk differs from the Russian word for "spider" by only a single letter, e.g., *pauk*. The opposition of the two protagonists is thus symbolized by the contrast of the circle versus the gammadion, figures which embody the two most fundamental contrastive elements in graphic design—the curve versus the straight line.[17]

Nabokov's novels abound in allusive subtexts which, through their resonance, enrich the characters and plot events to which they are attached. Some subtexts, such as that tacitly identifying Mariette with Catullus' *Lesbia*, are localized, restricted to particular scenes (175). Others are more far-reaching and echo themes fundamental to the novel a whole. Perhaps the most extensive subtext permeating *Bend Sinister* is the theatrical one focusing on Shakespeare's *Hamlet* (VII). Krug visits his friend Ember, the Shakespeare translator who is involved in a new, "revolutionary" production of *Hamlet*. The Shakespeare theme is introduced by three engravings hanging on Ember's bedroom wall. The first shows "a sixteenth-century gentleman in the act of handing a book to a humble fellow who holds a spear and a bay-crowned hat in his left hand" (93). The second shows the rustic now dressed as a gentleman stealing the headgear, a kind of "shapska," from the gentleman who is writing at a desk. In the third, the thief, wearing his new hat and apparel, is walking toward High Wycombe, i.e., the road to London. The "shapska" (cf. Russian *shapka* "cap") and the "spear" are among the more obvious clues that the rustic is Shakespeare. The identity of the writing gentleman is given away by the inscription on the first picture which reads "Ink, a Drug." This has been transposed by an unknown hand to read "*Grudinka*," the Russian word for "bacon." (Curiously, the inscription also yields Ad. Krug—plus an extraneous "in".) The second engraving has the scholium "*Ham-let, or Homelette au Lard*," i.e., the Little Man in [Sir Francis] Bacon. This sequence sets the scene for the chapter in which Ember regales Krug with his account of the bizarre version of Hamlet which is being staged. The interpretation, ostensibly based on the work of a Professor Hamm, makes the forthright man-of-action Fortinbras the true hero, opposing him to the neurasthenic, doubt-tormented Hamlet. This and numerous other bits of Shakespearean nonsense are drawn from the commentators (mostly German) summarized in the Furness Variorum edition of Hamlet.[18] Ember's account is countered by Krug's story of a Hamlet film scenario proposed to him by an American professor. This leads Krug and Ember into a flight of absurd intepretations, based largely on Joycean word play, centering on the letters of Hamlet's and Ophelia's names. Ophelia's drowning scene features "a phloating leaph . . . her little white hand, holding a wreath trying to reach, trying to wreathe a phallacious sliver" (101). Ember proposes deriving her name from that of the Arcadian river god Alpheios: "the lithe, lithping, thin-lipped Ophelia, Amleth's wet dream, a mermaid of Lethe . . . a pale-eyed lovely slim slimy ophidian maiden." The echoes of Joyce are too strong to be ignored and Nabokov confirms his presence both in his Introduction and, indirectly, in the text: "(cp. Winnipeg Lake, ripple 585, Vico Press edition)" [102]. The friends' conversation, like Krug's essay on consciousness, is terminated by a knock at the door as the secret police arrive to take Ember away.

The Shakespeare/Hamlet motif is to be found at other points in the book: most specifically in Paduk whose very name is apparently derived from Hamlet's "paddock" and who is persistently associated with theatrical effects. On occasion he lapses into Elizabethan English or blank verse (135 & 207-08). His interview with Krug is accompanied by explicit stage directions and instructions to the speakers. The final public confrontation scene which gathers together all of the surviving characters and which presumably ends in a slaughter is patently designed as a piece of stagecraft.[19]

The most critical issue raised by the Shakespeare/Hamlet subtext is its *raison d'être*. Perhaps the most obvious reason is a very general one. Nabokov uses such subtexts in his Russian novels and has transferred the device to his English work. In his Russian novels, although the range of literary allusion is immense, pride of place goes to Pushkin, the father of modern Russian literature. For *Bend Sinister*, Nabokov's first novel composed in an English-speaking country, Shakespeare seems the most directly analogous figure in evoking comparable cultural resonance. The extensive Joycean subtext set within the Shakespearean one sounds a modernist note in Nabokov's tribute to the literary tradition of his new language.

The Shakespeare/Hamlet subtext is part of a larger theatrical motif that pervades the novel in many ways. The text constantly and deliberately displays its contrived artificial character depicting not a "real" world but an artificially created one—a theater-in-the-round. The theater motif is particularly appropriate because it mimics one of the basic ideas of the novel, i.e., that Krug's world is the artificial creation of an author-persona, a master playwright. The theatrical subtext is a metaphoric restatement of the two world theme. Further, the anagrammatic Shakespeare-Bacon allusions evoke the "Who wrote Shakespeare?" motif that parallels Krug's search for his real author.

At one point during the composition of *Bend Sinister* Nabokov remarked "I am almost sure now that my novel will be called *Game to Gunm*."[20] Alone of the five known titles considered for the novel, this, the penultimate, is the only one that does not have obvious relevance to the theme. The origin of the tentative title is obscure but it would seem to be beyond the realm of coincidence that "Game to Gunm" is the title of Volume X of the *Encyclopedia Britannica*.[21] The significance of using the *Encyclopedia* label as the novel's title may lie in something as obvious as the thematic resonance of the "Game" of thought being engulfed by the violence implied by "Gunmetal," the final entry in the volume. Thoughtful perusal of the "Game to Gunm" volume, however, shows two entries that seem more specifically relevant to theme and realization in *Bend Sinister*: "God" and "Geometry".

The "Author as God" metaphor is explicitly stated in Nabokov's Introduction and its development is, indeed, one of the major dimensions of the novel's plot. The author is the anthropomorphic deity that creates fictive worlds. The characters in their constructed world enjoy only that degree of consciousness delimited by the bounds of their universe, although certain auctorial favorites have inklings of another world beyond. From the point of view of the created world, "all secrets, all mysteries" are to be revealed in the unlimited consciousness of their creator. The seemingly omnipotent deity, however, is in the same position in his "real" world as his characters are in their created world. While he is omniscient with respect to his created world, he is, in his own universe, possessed only of limited consciousness and, like his characters, strives toward the Absolute: infinite consciousness. His "success," like that of his characters, can be fully realized only at the relevatory moment of death which will prove to be but the next higher level of an infinitely large number. Each world is a level of consciousness subsumed within a larger one that creates and contains the smaller one. Although *Bend Sinister* seems to be explicitly predicated upon only two worlds, the number ultimately implied by the scheme is limitless. The regression is infinite. The deity becomes an ultimate abstraction subsuming and transcending all of the successively layered levels of consciousness. It is "Infinite Consciousness," or "Consciousness Itself."

The "Geometry" article in the "Game to Gunm" *Britannica* volume relates to *Bend Sinister* in less elusive ways. In the historical portion of the article considerable attention is devoted to Archimedes. We have previously noted the allusions linking Krug with the geometrician

Archimedes, the discoverer of pi, the ratio necessary to compute the area of the circle, and the scholar who cautioned his slayers "Don't touch my circles." We have also noted at length the circle imagery spiraling out of Krug's name and somehow hinting at his unique affinity to the world of his creator. This is, however, not the only connection between *Bend Sinister* and the contents of the encyclopedia article. In the same section of the article we find a reference to the Ahmes or Rhind papyrus, circa 1600 B.C., which, *inter alia*, contains a method for determining the area of the circle. This papyrus also figures in *Bend Sinister*. As the bereaved philosopher Krug tries to find the "unknown thing" he wishes to write about, he comes across a number of random notes in his desk drawer. Most of these mysteriously involve the circle image. First among them is a note on the Rhind papyrus which promises "to disclose 'all the secrets, all the mysteries'" but which turns out to be merely a school text with blank spaces that some "unknown Egyptian farmer in the seventeenth century B.C. has used for his clumsy calculations" (137-38). The ancient document does not yield the promised revelations, but hints at a connection between mathematics and the disclosure of "all the secrets, all the mysteries." Thus of the two *Bend Sinister*-related topics in the encyclopedia article on "Geometry," one touches upon Archimedes, a prototype of Krug, and the other refers to a manuscript promising the revelation of ultimate things—the key theme in the novel.[22]

We have discussed how "God" and "Geometry" in the "Game to Gunm" volume of the *EB* might relate to the novel. We must now pose the question of how they relate to each other. What connection, if any, exists between geometric figures and God? The connections are abundant. The followers of Pythagoras (who is glancingly referred to in *Bend Sinister*) believed that "the elevation of the soul and the union with God" takes place by means of mathematics.[23] Their doctrine that God orders the universe by means of mathematics is echoed by Plato in his dictum "God ever geometrizes."[24] More specifically, the circle figure has been the symbol for God, for the Infinite, for the Self, and so on, in many belief systems. Not atypical is the formulation attributed to Hermes Trismegistus, the Greek name for the Egyptian Thoth, the scribe of the gods: "God is a circle whose center is everywhere and the circumference is nowhere."[25] Although within the framework of *Bend Sinister*, the circle, as opposed to the gammadion, is obviously a positive symbol in that it marks Krug's affinity with the world of his creator, it is also the shape of his prison. We recall Krug's metaphor comparing his skull-encased mind to a circular dungeon, as well as the circular prison chamber in which he finds himself prior to his interrogation (155-56 & 188). The circle has a flaw as the novel's symbol-motif, for while it is in one sense perfect, it is, in another sense, circumscribed, self-limiting and even vicious.

We now turn to the question of how this identity of theological concept and geometric symbol relates to the two worlds, or, more accurately, the worlds-in-infinite regression scheme that is fundamental to *Bend Sinister*. For this we must return to Archimedes. Among Archimedes' numerous contributions to geometry there is a figure known as the Spiral of Archimedes which we give below:[26]

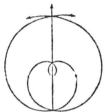

Perhaps by chance, or perhaps not, the Spiral of Archimedes stands as an admirable model of the auto-included regressive worlds at least partially sensed by Krug. Krug is the inmost circle (*krug*) living within the novel's circular prison world, the second circle of the spiral. He intuits, however, a controlling circumambient world—that of the author who creates his, Krug's world. The only direct point of contact with the deity's world is where the lines of the spirals intersect, i.e., "death." The consciousness defined by the middle circle is identically positioned with respect to the still larger circle (creative consciousness) that includes it. Like Archimedes' Spiral, the pattern continues on *ad infinitum*, i.e., on toward infinite consciousness.

In deriving our regressive fictional universe model for *Bend Sinister* we have moved from Krugian circles to the Archimedean Spiral. Is there further justification for our proposal apart from the Krug/Archimedes parallel and the narrative structure of the book itself? Such justification may be found not in *Bend Sinister* but in Nabokov's autobiography, *Speak, Memory*, his next major work after *Bend Sinister* and, like it, conceptually based on a curved figure, the rainbow's arc. *Speak, Memory* provides a further link between the self-contained circle of restricted consciousness and the transcendent spiral toward infinite consciousness. In the autobiography Nabokov writes that he sees his life as a "colored spiral in a small ball of glass." "The spiral," he goes on to say, "is a spiritualized circle. In the spiral form, the circle, uncoiled, unwound, has ceased to be vicious; it has been set free" (275). We cannot say whether or not Nabokov had the model of the Archimedean Spiral in mind when he created the worlds of his novel, but the concept of the spiral, the circle set free, is indisputably central to his vision not only of *Bend Sinister*, but also of his own life.[27]

## SOLUS REX AND THE "ULTIMA THULE" THEME

Nabokov's unfinished novel, *Solus Rex*, composed in Paris during the winter of 1939-40, was the final flowering of the author's "last season of Russian prose writing."[28] The novel was abandoned following Nabokov's emigration to America in May of 1940. Nabokov apparently intended to resume work on it, for in a letter of April 29, 1941, to his new friend, Edmund Wilson, he remarked that he had "left Europe in the middle of a vast Russian novel which will soon start to ooze from some part of my body if I go on keeping it inside."[29] There was no resumption, however.

The two completed chapters, each of thirty-odd printed pages, were published separately under the titles "Solus Rex" and "Ultima Thule." The former appeared in the final issue of the Parisian émigré journal, *Sovremennye zapiski*, and the latter in the first issue of Mark Aldanov's New York émigré journal, *Novyi zhurnal*.[30] The two chapters show virtually no interrelation and it had been reasonably assumed that the publication dates reflect the intended order of progression in the completed work. Only with the appearance of the English translations in 1973 did Nabokov affirm that "Ultima Thule" is chapter I and "Solus Rex," chapter II. Nabokov had earlier informed his German bibliographer, Dieter E. Zimmer, that *Solus Rex*, used as the title of the separately published second chapter, was intended as the title of the entire novel.[31]

*Solus Rex*, presumably because of its fragmentary nature, has attracted little critical attention. Such study as it has received has for the most part focused on the relationship of the "Solus Rex" chapter, which tells of political intrigue in a remote, mythical, Northern island kingdom, to the 1962 English novel *Pale Fire*. Here we shall examine *Solus Rex* first in its own terms, and then in relation to *Bend Sinister*, the English novel undertaken following the abandonment of *Solus Rex*. *Bend Sinister* grows thematically (albeit not in plot or setting) from the earlier work and sheds a good deal of light on the central mystery of *Solus Rex*, most specifically on the "Ultima Thule" chapter. *Solus Rex* can be viewed as a crystalization of a central Nabokovian theme that emerges in *Invitation to a Beheading* (1938) and *The Real Life of Sebastian Knight* (1941) and then assumes a dominant position in *Bend Sinister* (1947) and *Pale Fire* (1962), as well as in other of the later English novels. The "Ultima Thule" theme, as we shall term it, is that of death and the hereafter.

"Ultima Thule," the opening chapter of *Solus Rex*, takes the form of an imaginary letter from the narrator, one Sineusov, an émigré Russian artist staying on the Riviera, to his late wife. Although his wife has been dead for nearly a year, all of the artist's thoughts and activities continue to revolve around her. Sineusov's single obsession is to learn whether or not he can hope to establish contact with his wife either now or in the hereafter. Such hopes are darkened by the artist's mocking distrust of spiritualists and his deep suspicion of religion.

In his "letter" Sineusov recalls many details of their life together, including the last harrowing months in which the pregnant wife is dying of tuberculosis of the throat. Among his memories is a scene in which his bedridden wife, no longer able to speak, writes on her small slate that the things she loved most in life were "verse, wildflowers and foreign currency" (E164/R291). This last is occasioned by a commission which Sineusov receives to do a series of illustrations for an epic poem entitled "Ultima Thule." The poem is written in a strange Nordic tongue, and the poet has such a negligible command of French, their sole common language, that the artist has only the haziest impression of the work he is to illustrate. In so far as Sineusov can ascertain, the epic tells of an unhappy, unsociable king who rules a remote, melancholy and strife-torn island kingdom set in the mists of the far north. After making some preliminary sketches which seem to please the poet, the artist starts work, but the author suddenly disappears, leaving the project suspended in a void. Sineusov, grief-stricken by his wife's illness and death, continues his illustrations simply to distract himself.

Sineusov's letter, mentally composed on a lonely beach, has a more immediate point of departure than memories of his marriage. It is triggered by his recent encounter with Adam Ilyich Falter, his boyhood mathematics tutor in Russia. The artist reminisces to his late wife about their brief visit with Falter, the gifted son of an alcoholic restaurant cook in St. Petersburg, who after emigration had become the manager of a Riviera resort hotel.[32] This visit took place shortly before the onset of the wife's prolonged illness, and Sineusov had forgotten about it until he encounters Falter's brother-in-law, who tells the bereaved artist a strange story. Not long after their visit Falter had been traveling and stopped for the night at a small village hotel. A short while after he retired, the night air was rent by sounds resembling "the paroxysmal, almost exultant screams of a woman in the throes of infinitely painful childbirth—a woman, however, with a man's voice, and a giant in her womb" (E158/R284). The screaming, seemingly endless, paralyzed all who heard it, and some time elapsed before the manager gained access to the room where the silent Falter stood vacuously. Not responding to questions, he walked out of the room, urinated copiously from the top of the stairs, returned to his bed, and fell into a deep sleep.

Falter's sister and brother-in-law bring home the madman whose behavior continues to be bizarre but harmless. Falter's case attracts the attention of a fashionable Italian psychiatrist staying at the resort hotel. The doctor, Bonomini, is the originator of a form of therapy involving historical, costumed psychodramas which lead to a cure by reenacting the ancestral etiology of the patient's psychosis. This promising method is of little avail in Falter's case for almost nothing is known of his more remote antecedents. Consequently, the psychiatrist takes a more direct approach and asks Falter about the cause of his nocturnal screams. After some prodding, Falter confides in the good doctor, who promptly suffers massive heart failure. At the inquest, Falter, no less mad than before, tells the authorities that he, Falter, has solved "the riddle of the universe" (E163/R290) and that the shock of the imparted secret has been too much for the psychiatrist.[33]

At the time of his chance encounter with Falter's brother-in-law Sineusov is on the point of returning to Paris to lose himself in his aborted "Ultima Thule" commission for, as he says, "that island born in the desolate, gray sea of my heartache for you, now attracted me as the home of my least expressible thoughts (E165/R292). On hearing of Falter's experience, however, the narrator realizes that his former tutor's revelation may answer his question about possible reunion with his dead wife. To this end he arranges a meeting with Falter, who refuses to impart his lethal secret to his former student, although the latter promises either a vow of silence or, if Falter prefers, immediate suicide (E168/R296). A long Socratic dialogue ensues in which Sineusov is permitted to probe the periphery of the ultimate revelation by asking Falter about the existence of God and, more central to his immediate concern, about the preservation of personal identity beyond the grave. Falter replies with a mixture of seeming inanities and tantalizing paradoxes. At length Sineusov breaks off the interview no wiser than before. To his surprise, a few days later he receives from Falter's brother-in-law a bill for his "consultation." Not only has the artist not found answers to his questions, but remains skeptical that his mad ex-tutor actually possesses, as he claims, "a key to absolutely all the doors and treasure chests in the world" (E172/R301). A short time later Sineusov receives a note from the now hospitalized madman informing him that he, Falter, will die on Tuesday and "that in parting, he ventured to inform me that—here followed two lines which has been painstakingly and, it seemed, ironically, blacked out" (E181/R313). All of the foregoing has been recounted in Sineusov's "letter" which is composed on the following day and which ends on the gloomy thought that perhaps his memories are the only guarantee of his wife's continued existence.

What Sineusov has failed to notice during his discussion with Falter is that in the course of illustrating a point about the nature of "an all-encompassing truth," the madman has made passing reference to "the poetry of a wildflower or the power of money," phrases more than vaguely reminiscent of the words of Sineusov's dying wife (E172/R301). Again, later in the conversation, Falter, in response to Sineusov's query as to why he appears less than omniscient (supposing the truth of his claim), replies

"...I act like a beggar, [a versifier] who has received a million [in foreign currency] but goes on living in his basement, for he knows that the least concession to luxury would ruin his liver" (E173/R302). The bracketed words, absent in the Russian original, have been inserted into the English text by Nabokov in order to afford further sustenance to Falter's claim, but Sineusov again fails to recognize the evidence he so eagerly seeks.

"Solus Rex," the second chapter of Nabokov's unfinished novel, opens with the awakening of the king of a remote Northern island country. The ruler is referred to as Kr in the Russian version and K in the English, both alluding to the standard chess abbreviations for king. Through Kr's thoughts we learn the troubled history of his kingdom and the story of his accession to the throne some five years before through a coup against his libertine, homophilic cousin Adulf. Kr is a morose scholar-manqué who has little taste for either pomp or power. Apart from a mysterious allusion to the "no longer independent artist Dmitri Nikolaevich Sineusov" there is seemingly no connection between the characters and events of the "Ultima Thule" chapter and those of "Solus Rex" (E190/R9). Nabokov's introductory note to the English translation clarifies this anomaly. Sineusov has indeed returned from the Riviera, as he had planned, to his Paris apartment where he has immersed himself in his artistic recreation of Ultima Thule, that island born of heartache which has now become the home of his least expressible thoughts (E165/R292).[34] In his new imaginary kingdom, Sineusov, now transformed into Kr, is to be reunited with his late wife, now reincarnated as his Queen Belinda. Nabokov's note tells us that the reunion will be a brief one, however, for Sineusov's/Kr's wife is to die again that very day, a chance victim of an unsuccessful assassination attempt on her husband.

As we know, Nabokov, counter to his intention, did not return to his "vast" Russian novel-in-progress. Whether there were structural difficulties in coalescing the disparate sections of *Solus Rex* or whether the favorable critical reviews of Nabokov's first English-language novel, *The Real Life of Sebastian Knight*, encouraged the author to abandon Russian for English, is not clear. Nor is there anything to suggest that the author contemplated translating the completed portions and continuing in English. *Solus Rex* was abandoned—at least in the form its author had originally conceived it.

*Solus Rex* did not vanish without issue, however, for it left a substantial legacy in the form of two of Nabokov's English novels. The most evident line of descent is from the "Solus Rex" section of the uncompleted work to *Pale Fire*, written nearly twenty years after its progenitor. Andrew Field in his pioneering *Nabokov: His Life in Art* has admirably traced the complex interrelations of *Solus Rex* and *Pale Fire*. We shall here restrict ourselves to noting a few broad parallels of theme and fact. Foremost are the imaginary Northern island kingdoms, Ultima Thule and Nova Zembla, with their respective rulers, Kr and King Charles. The latter parallel is the more evident when it is realized that Kr, the Russian chess notation for *korol'* "king," etymologically derives from the Latin form of Charlemagne, *Karl Magnus*.[35] Seminal in both novels is the idea of a work of art, a poem, which, little understood by the heroes, becomes the springboard for the creation of a mythological kingdom ruled by the narrator. Both men, aliens to the lands of their residence, are driven to this fantasy ploy by personal tragedy: Sineusov—by the death of his beloved wife, and Botkin/Kinbote by madness of unknown origin. The parallel is established most pointedly when Kinbote urges upon Shade the title "Solus Rex" for his poem "Pale Fire." Although "Solus Rex"—a term referring to a type of chess problem in which Black has but a single piece, the king—has no relevance to the actual content of Shade's poem, it is an exceedingly apt title for the stories of both King Charles the Beloved of Nova Zembla and Kr of Ultima Thule.

The more immediate but less renown offshoot of Nabokov's unfinished Russian novel is the 1947 *Bend Sinister* which in concept proceeds directly from the "Ultima Thule" chapter of *Solus Rex*. Nabokov's last mention of *Solus Rex* to Edmund Wilson was in April of 1941. In November 1942, he wrote Wilson referring for the first time to a novel-in-progress called *The Person from Porlock*.[36] This was the first of a number of titles, *Solus Rex* among them, considered and rejected by the author before settling on *Bend Sinister*. The only obvious point of similarity between the "Ultima Thule" section of *Solus Rex* and *Bend Sinister* is that their protagonists, the artist Sineusov and the philosopher Krug, have recently lost their wives. Apart from this, the two works would seem to have little in common in terms of plot, setting or characterization. We shall see, however, that they share a common central theme and within that thematic context a number of subthemes and motifs. Since *Bend Sinister* is the more fully developed work we shall first identify our theme there and then backcast to the more elusive and fragmentary *Solus Rex*.

The theme of *Bend Sinister* is fairly explicit. As we know, Krug, the master of creative destruction, has eschewed the traditional philosophical quest for the True Substance, "the Diamond suspended from the Christmas Tree of the Cosmos" (152). It is only after the death of his wife that he turns to "the greatest mystery of all," i.e., infinite consciousness (168). Krug's ultimate revelation comes the night before his death when he is visited by the mind behind the mirror, the novel's anthropomorphic deity who renders him mad (210). The tormented philosopher suddenly understands that he and his entire world are merely fictional creations in the mind of their creator in his own "real" world. Hence nothing matters. The horror, the anguish, the pain are not real. At the instant of death, Krug is gathered up into the "real" world of the author-persona, the anthropomorphic deity. Put somewhat differently, Krug's revelation is that the limited consciousness of his world which makes it seem self-contained and "real" is merely an enclave, a closed circle, within the (relatively) infinite consciousness of its creator, the author, in *his* world. Krug has discovered the secret of his universe and, with it, the meaning of death and the hereafter.

Let us now return to "Ultima Thule." Falter, like Krug, comes into possession of the "secret of the universe" and is not strong enough to withstand the revelation. He too goes mad. There can be only one ultimate secret, and it is obvious that Falter's revelation is the same as Krug's: the solution to the mystery of consciousness. The crucial issue is whether consciousness is inherently limited, somehow circumscribed, or whether it is infinite. Within the fictional world in which the characters dwell, it is finite. For denizens of that world, Ultimate Enlightenment, the Absolute Truth means breaking through the confines of that circumscribed consciousness in which they reside and merging with the (relatively) infinite consciousness of their creator in his own "real" circumambient universe. The point of contact between the two worlds is death. This aesthetic cosmology and the "ultimate" question that leads to its revelation, we have termed the Ultima Thule theme.

This cosmogonic theory is of import not only in itself, but also because it contains the answer to a corollary question of more immediate consequence to Sineusov, who asks Falter: "Is there even a glimmer of one's identity beyond the grave, or does it all end in ideal darkness?" (E176/R306). Falter gives an evasively paradoxical reply touching vaguely on the idea of consciousness. For a more explicit answer we must turn again to the cosmology posited in *Bend Sinister*. The answer would seem to be as follows: if consciousness is infinite, then personal identity may survive beyond the grave; if consciousness is limited, then death is ultimate darkness. Death, at least for authorial favorites, is simply the transition point between limited and infinite consciousness. This is of burning moment to both Sineusov and Krug, who are obsessed with their deceased wives (and sons). It is the motivation for their search for the riddle of the universe—the Ultima Thule theme.

The two mad Adams, Falter and Krug, have been bereft of their senses by the same revelation, and both have attained the same ultimate enlightenment. Further parallels, which go well beyond what we have thus far indicated, are somewhat downplayed by the differing emphasis of the two works. Although both Sineusov and Krug are brought to their fundamental inquiry by the deaths of their wives, the consciousness theme and its two-world corollary are developed differently . Sineusov's probings are motivated almost entirely by his loss and the hope of bridging that terrible chasm. To him the primary issue is the survival of personal identity (hers, his) after death. The question of consciousness is for him more abstract and less immediate. For Krug, the professional philosopher, the loss of his wife, while no less soul-rending, entails a consideration of the more fundamental, more abstract issue of consciousness. All else flows from that. Ultimately, however, both of these matters are adjunct to the issue at the core of the Ultima Thule theme, i.e., the meaning of death.

Identity of major theme is perhaps not sufficient grounds to assert a direct genetic tie between the "Ultima Thule" chapter of *Solus Rex* and *Bend Sinister*. Our preceding argument about the nature of Falter's revelation is based on a backcasting from *Bend Sinister* to *Solus Rex*. We shall now advance a line of evidence running in the opposite direction—from *Solus Rex* to *Bend Sinister*. When in the midst of their discourse Sineusov expresses his doubt about Falter's claim to omniscience, to absolute wisdom, the madman replies that he does not claim to know all, just everything that he might want to know. He then continues: "Anyone could say that—couldn't he?—after having leafed through an encyclopedia; only, the encyclopedia whose exact title I have learned (there, by the way—I am giving you a more elegant definition: I know the title of things) is literally all-inclusive" (E172-3/R301-2). This "title" trope comes up again in a discussion of the relationship of the idea of God to Falter's revelation. When Falter rejects the posited relationship as irrelevant, Sineusov infers that if the secret, the thing sought, is not linked to the concept of God and "if that thing is, according to your terminology, a kind of universal 'title,' then the concept of God does not appear on the title page" (E174/R304), and no God exists. Falter continues to disallow the association. Sineusov makes one last vain attempt to force an answer by posing the question in negative form: "One cannot, then, seek the title of the world in the hieroglyphics of deism?" (E175/R305).

This Borgesian discussion of absolute omniscience in terms of encyclopedia and title has a ghost echo in *Bend Sinister*.[37] We have already remarked that *Solus Rex* was among the tentative titles for *Bend Sinister* considered by Nabokov. Another, much more mysterious, was *Game to Gunm*, the title of volume X of the *Encyclopedia Britannica*. As we have seen, two entries in that volume, specifically those on "God" and "Geometry," are particularly germane to the theme and its realization in *Bend Sinister*. The entire texture of the novel is permeated with (sometimes quite literally) cryptic allusions and patterns manifesting "a mind behind the mirror" that manipulates Fyodor's terror-ridden world. This anthropomorphic deity is the author of the encyclopedia, and Krug, like Falter, has learned the title of one of the encyclopedia volumes.

A second series of allusions found in *Bend Sinister* is also faintly foreshadowed in "Ultima Thule." One of the archetypes for Krug, whose name means "circle" in Russian, is the Greek geometer Archimedes, to whom the oft-quoted phrase *Noli disturbare meos circulos!* is attributed. This is but one of the associations between Krug and mathematics, particularly geometry. We have previously proposed that the very model of the two worlds of *Bend Sinister*, that of Krug and that of his maker, and the connection between them, can be symbolized by the geometric figure known as Archimedes' Spiral. Thus in some metaphorical sense mathematics models the cosmological revelation sought and then obtained by Krug. The seeds of this "geometry" motif are sown in "Ultima Thule" when Sineusov recalls with pleasure how Falter would intermix his prosaic math tutoring "with unusually elegant manifestations of mathematical thought, which left a certain chill of poetry..." (E156/R281). Perhaps more important is Sineusov's mental re-creation of the events immediately preceding Falter's revelation. The artist tries to imagine Falter's random thoughts as the doomed man absently makes his nocturnal way back from a bordello to the fateful hotel room. Among these disparate and inconsequential thoughts is an "amusing mathematical problem about which he had corresponded the year before with a Swedish scholar" (E157-8/R283). This is, however, but one of the dissociated thoughts that apparently provide the combinational context for Falter's metamorphosis.[38]

Resonant with the "geometry" motif in the two novels is the preoccupation with circles and curves. Here again the figure is embryonic in *Solus Rex* and more elaborately developed in *Bend Sinister*. In their long dialogue Falter repeatedly warns his former pupil against logical deduction as a means of ferreting out the secret of the universe. Logical reasoning is adequate, Falter says, for "covering short distances, but the curvature of the earth, alas, is reflected even in logic" (E169/R297). Such logic simply brings one back to the point of departure "with a delightful sensation that you have embraced truth, while actually you have merely embraced yourself."[39] Other references to the distorting and self-defeating effect of the curvature of logical thought abound in *Solus Rex* (E174/R304 & E178/R308-9), and we have previously discussed the centrality of circle imagery to the worlds of *Bend Sinister* and Krug's attempts to break through the vicious auto-circumscribed circle of his own world to penetrate that of his maker.

This preoccupation with curvature links the two novels in yet another important way. The central characters, Sineusov and Krug, both seek gnostic knowledge in consequence of the death of their wives. Their kinship goes beyond this, however, and is even reflected in their names. Krug's name means "circle" and resonates with the basic conceptual configuration of *Bend Sinister*. Sineusov's name has similarly critical associations that prefigure those of Krug's name. The Russian meaning of Sineusov is "blue moustache," a meaning reflected in Falter's whimsical mode of addressing his former pupil as Moustache-Bleue.[40] Just as Krug's name has bilingual associations, so does Sineusov's for it evokes the Latin *sinus*, meaning "curve." The curve of Sineusov prefigures the fully developed circle of Krug. Both men, at least initially, are trapped in the circular dungeon of thought that debars their access to the secret they wish to learn. Other associations arise from the similarity of Sineusov to the Latin *sinister*, meaning "left, unfavorable, injurious." Sineusov, like Krug (and Falter & Paduk) is left-handed. It is perhaps this last that echoes faintly in Nabokov's final title, *Bend Sinister*, the heraldic term for bastardy and an apt name for a novel in which all is sinistral.

The above argument demonstrates the major lines of association between *Solus Rex* and *Bend Sinister*. There remain a number of minor carry-overs that, while not thematic in nature, testify to the close kinship of these temporally sequential, albeit superficially divergent, novels. Overlapping minor motifs include Dr. Bonomini's silly psychodramas and Dr. Amalia Wytwyl's ghastly play therapy that ends in the death of Krug's son; there is also Sineusov's dead son—unborn but still a source of anguish to the widower. Krug, like Sineusov, pens a letter to his dead wife (Ch. IX); the Kafkaesque beetle-shaped bootjack in the royal bedroom of Kr of Ultima Thule (E189/R8) migrates to Krug's study (30 & 175), and so on.

One further set of questions must be posed about the shared secret of the protagonists of the two novels. Are the revelations of Falter and Krug real or illusory within the context of each book? What reason is there for the protagonists to believe their revelations? This problem particularly plagues Sineusov, who repeatedly tries to force Falter to explain the nature of his proof for his unrevealed revelation. Falter asserts that its truth is self-evident, but nonetheless he inadvertently (or perhaps advertently) gives evidence of his omniscience with his passing allusion to the words of Sineusov's dying wife—something known only to the artist. Also germane is that Falter, apparently accurately, predicts the day of his own death. The proof of Krug's revelation is at once simpler and more complex. His creator, his author, deliberately and overtly reveals himself, but the revelation maddens Krug. This raises the question as to whether his insight is real or hallucinatory. The truth of his insight is affirmed by Krug's subliminal awareness throughout the narrative of the allusive footprints and configurations that bespeak the controlling presence of the novel's other world and its tutelary deity, the author-persona. Thus in both novels the solution to the mystery of the universe, the meaning of death, is found by the protagonists.

*Solus Rex*, Nabokov's last Russian prose work, posits a theme common to much of his writing. We have called it the "Ultima Thule" theme, the theme of the ultimate unknown, death. This theme can be observed in various guises in several, perhaps even most, of Nabokov's novels. In *Solus Rex*, Falter, to whom "the essence of things has been revealed" (E168/R296), has solved the riddle of the universe by stumbling upon "a Truth with a capital T that comprises in itself the explanation and the proof of all possible mental affirmations" (E172/R300). By virtue of this literally mind-shattering revelation, Falter has become superhuman and stands *outside* our world, in the true reality (E150/R274), i.e., in another world which proves to be that of an omnipotent author, an "anthropomorphic deity." In the unfinished *Solus Rex*, that Truth is not revealed to Sineusov (or the reader), although there is internal evidence that Falter has indeed solved the riddle of the universe. *Solus Rex* is a preliminary probing of the theme that finds its mature development in *Bend Sinister*.

The Ultima Thule theme and its attendant cosmology is central to much of Nabokov's mature fiction, but it assumes a dominant position in the late thirties and early forties. *Solus Rex* is the incomplete center panel of a triptych flanked on the left by *The Real Life of Sebastian Knight*, written in 1938, and on the right by *Bend Sinister*, composed between 1942 and 1946. The narrator of *The Real Life of Sebastian Knight* is the Russian half-brother of the recently deceased English writer Sebastian Knight. The narrator, who knows his half-brother only superficially, receives, after several years of silence, a letter from Sebastian asking that he visit him in the hospital near Paris where he is dying. That night, the narrator, known only as V., has a dream in which Sebastian seems to promise to solve a "monstrous riddle" (178). The narrator, obsessed with this secret throughout his journey, arrives at the dying man's bedside too late. Subsequently he decides to undertake a critical biography of Sebastian in an attempt to come to know him and to learn his secret. In his account, the making of which unfolds before our eyes, he recounts Sebastian's last novel, *The Doubtful Asphodel*, which deals with a dying man's confrontation with his own death. The hero goes through various mental stages. As the end draws near, "We feel," says the narrator, "that we are on the brink of some absolute truth, dazzling in its splendour and at the same time almost homely in its simplicity" (166). The secret, the absolute solution, "which would have set free imprisoned thought and granted it the great understanding" (168), is not, however, revealed. The hero of *The Doubtful Asphodel* dies before disclosing it. *Sebastian Knight* formulates the Ultima Thule theme: a death induces a character to pose and attempt to solve the riddle of the universe. The statement of the theme remains rudimentary, however, for no solution to the riddle is suggested, nor is the related subtheme of consciousness introduced, as it is marginally in *Solus Rex* and centrally in *Bend Sinister*.

The Real Life of Sebastian Knight is not the first of Nabokov's novels to treat the Ultima Thule theme. Its earliest major appearance is to be found in the 1934 *Invitation to a Beheading* which has obvious affinities in tone and theme with *Bend Sinister*. Cincinnatus, the protagonist of *Invitation to a Beheading*, is under sentence of death for the crime of "gnostical turpitude." Unlike his philistine neighbors, Cincinnatus has secret inklings of another "ideal" world peopled by beings like himself. In his prison journal he records his intimations of this other world which he intuits from dreams and the existence of various curcumambient patterns and allusions which represent "leaks" from the ideal world. Although Cincinnatus senses the falsity of this world in which he awaits death and intuits the presence of an ideal world, he is unable to formulate and articulate his vision. Nonetheless he insistently affirms that he alone possesses a secret, a sense of the "invisible umbilical cord that joins this world to something—to what I shall not say yet..." (E45-46/R63). Elsewhere he writes of his dream world that "it must exist, since, surely there must be an original of the clumsy copy" (E93/R93). Although Cincinnatus fears death, he suspects that it will mark the transition point between the terrible world in which he lives and an ideal world of beings like himself. His intuitions are seemingly confirmed when his mock-up world literally begins to disintegrate, and he arises from the headsman's block and moves "in the direction of beings akin to himself." The parallel to *Bend Sinister* is apparent. The hero, facing death, probes "the riddle of the universe" and has his intuition confirmed at the instant of death which proves to be a transition from a world of circumscribed consciousness to one of infinite consciousness. The treatment of the Ultima Thule theme here differs from its later formulation in that the controlling role of "an anthropomorphic deity" in an ideal world is not explicitly formulated. The idea is, however, latent in the scheme. Otherwise who is it that shatters the mock world of Cincinnatus as he mounts the scaffold?

We have remarked on *Pale Fire* as one of the two direct descendants of *Solus Rex*. That kinship is, however, more with the "Solus Rex" chapter of the unfinished novel than with the opening chapter that sets forth the Ultima Thule theme. An overall parallel exists, nonetheless, for Kinbote/Botkin uses John Shade's poem as the basis for his own fantastic creation, the world of Nova Zembla—just as Sineusov creates his own kingdom of Ultima Thule on the basis of a poem written in an incomprehensible language. In *Pale Fire*, however, it is Shade, the poet, and not Kinbote, the mad exegete, who is preoccupied with the Ultima Thule theme. In his poem, Shade examines his feelings arising from the suicide of his daughter and his own impending death. Like Cincinnatus and his other Nabokovian predecessors, he finds evidence of a higher consciousness in the existence of an intricate pattern of coincidence in the world around him. Thus Shade too has probed the ultimate mystery and finds solace in art, in detecting and mimicking the pattern-weaving of the creator of his world, the master artist who lives in his own world on the far side of death, a universe of infinite consciousness and perfect knowledge. This is, however, a secondary theme in *Pale Fire*, for the center of the novel is Kinbote's story, not Shade's.

Nabokov's last three novels also contain echoes of the Ultima Thule theme. In *Ada*, the events of the narrative take place on the world of Demonia or Anti-Terra. The hero, Van, devotes his professional life to probing the existence of a mysterious counter-world—an Ultima Thule known as Terra—the existence of which is inferred by the collation of dream data and the visions of mystics and madmen. In addition, certain patterns in the texture of Demonia hint at the existence of a controlling hand outside the limits of that world. Anti-Terra's Baron Klim Avidov, the "word-father" of Ada, Van, and Lucette, is the anagrammatic ambassador of Terra's Vladimir Nabokov. The underlying pattern of the novella *Transparent Things* is not dissimilar. The events of the tale are narrated by the already deceased novelist, Mr. R, who manipulates the wretched life of the protagonist, Hugh Person, his erstwhile editor, from a world beyond the grave.[41] The Ultima Thule theme may also be seen in Nabokov's last novel *Look at the Harlequins!* The narrator and hero, Vadim Vadimovich, vaguely senses that he himself is but a "parody, an inferior variant of another man's life, somewhere on this or another earth" (89). Near the end of the book, as Vadim lies paralyzed at the threshold of death, he realizes that he has been merely "a figment of somebody's—not even...[his] own— imagination" (249).

The Ultima Thule theme has a number of component parts. Central is that there are two (or more) worlds. Only one of these universes is, however, "real." Resident on this "real" world is an artist who conceives, creates and regulates a secondary fictional universe and all that happens in it. To most of the inhabitants of the secondary universe, their world seems to be the only world. It is hermetic. A chosen few, however, authorial favorites, sense certain patterns woven into the texture of their world that hint at the existence of a controlling presence. When these characters are confronted with death, either that of a loved one or their own, they undertake the search for Ultima Thule, that other world with its promise of immortality and reunion with their own. At the instant of their death, as their makeshift universes disintegrate, these favorites are rescued by their creator into his, the "real" world. The subtheme of consciousness has an important part in this conceptual cosmology that lies at the heart of so many of Nabokov's novels. The consciousness of the inhabitants of the secondary universe is limited. For them their world is the only world and often a terrible one. In this philistine universe only the chosen few, thanks to their aesthetic sensibilities, suspect the presence of a circumambient universe which, from the point of view of the secondary restricted universe, represents "perfect knowledge" and infinite consciousness. The relationship between the created universe, the object of art, and the creating universe, the world of the artist, is characterized by limited versus unlimited consciousness. Death, the transition point between the two worlds, marks the transition of the protagonist from circumscribed awareness to omniscience. Central to the entire scheme is the god-like role of the artist, the writer who proposes and disposes in his created world.

The Ultima Thule theme occupied a dominant position in Nabokov's writing for forty years. From the 1934 *Invitation to a Beheading* to the 1974 *Looking at the Harlequins!*, it provided a conceptual framework for many, but not all, of his works. It is not present in the early Russian novels, nor in the 1936 *Despair*. It is only marginally present in his best Russian novel *The Gift*. It is absent from *Lolita*. It is, however, to be found in all of the other novels, although different aspects of the theme are stressed in the different books. In *Invitation to a Beheading*, there is no explicit indication of the controlling presence of the other world's anthropomorphic deity, although his presence is obvious in the denouement. In *Ada*, *Transparent Things* and *Look at the Harlequins!* the image of the artist-creator remains latent, and only by careful detection can the reader discern his tacit presence and role. *Solus Rex* and *Pale Fire* differ in that their Ultima Thules are the creations of characters within the novels. They entail worlds within worlds within worlds, but their intrinsic schemes do not differ in principle from the simpler models.

The "Ultima Thule" chapter of *Solus Rex* and its immediate successor, *Bend Sinister*, have served as a springboard for our definition and elaboration of this central theme in Nabokov's work. They represent its "classic" statement with all of the above-mentioned ingredients. They explicitly pose the key question from which all else flows, i.e., the riddle of the universe. Death is at the center of much of Nabokov's writing—a statement nonetheless true for his having written two comic masterpieces—*Lolita* and *Pale Fire*. Death is invariably what precipitates the protagonist's search for a pattern affirming the existence of Ultima Thule. This is more than a purely aesthetic concern as attested by the opening pages of *Speak, Memory*, where the author writes of his quest to "distinguish the faintest of personal glimmers in the impersonal darkness on both sides of my life"—a quest that has included both trenchantly skeptical visits to spiritualists and the ransacking of dreams (20). These probings led Nabokov, like his creature, the doomed poet John Shade, to take solace and find ecstacy in the intricately patterned game of art. In Nabokov's mythology of Ultima Thule, the artist weaves the design of his own immortality.

NOTES

Section Six

1. Only the adjectival form *potustoronii* with the definition "unearthly, supernatural" is listed in Russian dictionaries. The etymological meaning of the derived noun form is, roughly, "on-that-side-ness." Note that the demonstrative pronoun *tu* in the middle of the word is the accusative feminine form of *tot* (as in *tot svet* "that world") which in opposition to *etot* (as in *etot svet* "this world") plays a critical role in the cosmology of *Invitation to a Beheading*.

2. In addition to "I Still Keep Mute," Vera Nabokov cites "Evening on a Vacant Lot," "How I Love You," and "Fame" as expressive of the theme of the "hereafter." Parallel Russian and English texts may be found in *Poems and Problems*, pp. 22, 68, 78, and 102.

3. *The Nabokov-Wilson Letters: Correspondence between Vladimir Nabokov and Edmund Wilson 1940-1971*, edited, annotated and with an introductory essay by Simon Karlinsky (New York, 1979), pp. 85-86. Henceforth textual citations will be identified by letter date; footnote citations by *Letters* plus the page number.

4. The titles *Solus Rex* and *Game to Gunm* are given in *Letters*, pp. 136 and 169. The title *Vortex* is found in a list of manuscripts presented by the Nabokovs to the Library of Congress on December 10, 1958. Stephen Jan Parker, "Some Nabokov Holdings in the Library of Congress," *The Vladimir Nabokov Newsletter*, 3 (Fall, 1979), pp. 16 & 19.

5. These annotations are reprinted in the 1973 McGraw-Hill edition and as a separate essay in *Nabokov's Congeries*, selected, with a critical introduction by Page Stegner (New York, 1968), pp. 239-46. Our page citations for both "Introduction" and text are from the Time Reading Program Special Edition, New York, 1964. For an example of Nabokov's deliberate use of his Introductions to misdirect readers, see our earlier discussion of *The Defense*.

6. The only critical study that approaches the novel from this angle of vision is Richard F. Patteson's "Nabokov's *Bend Sinister*: The Narrator as God," *Studies in American Fiction*, 5 (1977), pp. 241-53. Another good general treatment of the novel is Susan Fromberg Schaffer's "*Bend Sinister* and the Novelist as Anthropomorphic Deity," *The Centennial Review*, 17 (Spring), pp. 115-55.

7. The person from Porlock (an English village) was a tradesman who interrupted Samuel Coleridge just after he had begun transcribing his poem "Kubla Khan" which had come to him in an opium dream. When the poet returned to his desk the inspiration was beyond recovery. *A Treasury of Great Poems: English and American*, ed. Louis Untermeyer (New York, 1955), p. 684.

8. The puddle that joins the two worlds was a real one which formed after every rain outside of the Nabokov apartment on Craigie Circle in Cambridge, Massachusetts. Andrew Field, *Nabokov: His Life in Art*, p. 201. The puddle is also the locus of the vortex which supplied the second working title of the novel.

9. A more recent example is Gilbert Sorrentino's *Mulligan Stew* (New York, 1979) in which the characters, some borrowed from avant-garde classics such as Flan O'Brien's 1939 *At Swim-Two-Birds*, discuss the novelist-hero at length. Sorrentino's novel includes some marvelous Nabokov skits and allusions.

10. Andrew Field, *Nabokov: A Bibliography* (New York, 1973), p. 87.

11. Beams of light are Nabokov's standard fixture indicating intercourse between worlds. Vadim Vadimovich's transitions between worlds in *LATH!* are also marked by a slanting ray of light (16 & 250). Perhaps more explicit is the 1934 poem "How I Love You" which Vera Nabokov singles out as an example of the theme of the "hereafter:" "The beams pass between tree trunks; . . . Stand motionless under the flowering branch, / inhale—what a spreading, what

flowing!— / Close your eyes, and diminish, and stealthily / into the eternal pass through" (*PP* 81).

12. Krug is linked with apples in yet another passage. After being permitted to view his son's body, the crazed Krug rushes out but is restrained by a "friendly soldier" who says "*Yablochko, kuda-zh ty kotishsa* [little apple, whither are you rolling]?" This line is used again by Nabokov in *LATH!* (10). The phrase is the beginning of a four-line *chastushka* that was enormously popular in the early years of the Russian Revolution. The *chastushka* form is a sort of ditty, often humorous and epigrammatic (and at times vulgar), which is usually socio-political in content. This particular *chastushka* had a multitude of variants among both Reds and Whites. One version current in Southern Russia where Nabokov spent the early years of the Civil War was "*Oy, yablochko, / Kuda kotishsya? / Na Chrezvychayku popadyosh', / Ne vorotishsya!* (Oy, little apple/ Where are you rolling? / If you get to Cheka headquarters [the dread political police] / you won't come back!) D. Zelinin, "Das heutige russische Schnaderhüpfl (*chastushka*)," *Zeitschrift für Slavische Philologie*, 1, 1925, p. 360.

13. The Archimedes reference was first called to my attention by Linda Nelson: *The Home Book of Quotations*, ed. Burton Stevenson (New York, 1967), p. 273. Other information is drawn from the *Encyclopedia Britannica*.

14. Associations of toads and evil are also relevant here. In Milton's *Paradise Lost*, for example, Satan appears as a toad in the Garden of Eden. *Milton Encyclopedia*, ed. William B. Hunter, Jr., (Lewisburg, 1978), VII, p. 68.

15. The ego-I of Krug, the philosopher, is appropriately stored in the midst of Descartes' "*cogito ergo sum.*" The chess-Mephisto presumably refers to Wolfgang Kempel's Automaton Chess Player built in Vienna in 1769. The automaton was a life-size figure in Oriental costume seated behind a cabinet-like affair with a chess set on top. The moves were actually made by a man ingeniously concealed in the cabinet. H.J.R. Murray, *A History of Chess* (Oxford, 1969), pp. 876-77.

16. An interesting article on the languages of the novel may be found in Antonina Filonov Gove, "Multilingualism and Ranges of Tone in Nabokov's *Bend Sinister*," *Slavic Review*, 32, 1, pp. 79-90.

17. Other characters participate in elaborate networks of allusion that give resonance to their roles. Among Krug's friends, we might mention Hedron, the mathematics professor, and Ember, the translator. Hedron, whose name is the Greek suffix referring to geometrical forms, is included in Krug's world by his custom of amusing David with conjuring tricks and by drawing circles for him. Ember, Krug's translator, is in a sense his alter ego for his name is the Hungarian word for "man" just as Krug's "Adam" is the Hebrew word. Of the characters in Paduk's camp the richest in allusion is Mariette, the police spy who works as Krug's house- and nursemaid. She is enveloped in allusions to Morgianna, the hero's servant girl in "Ali Baba and the Forty Thieves," Mérimée's *Carmen*, Cinderella of the vair slipper, Lesbia, to whom Catullus addressed his "*Da mi basia mille,*" and, most importantly, the nymph of Mallarmé's "*L'Apres-Midi d'une Faune.*"

18. A number of these references have been identified by L.L. Lee in his *Vladimir Nabokov* (Boston, 1976), pp. 108-12.

19. A survey of the theatrical aspect of the novel may be found in Julia Bader, *Crystal Land: Artifice in Nabokov's English Novels* (Berkeley, 1972), pp. 96-106.

20. *Letters*, p. 136.

21. Such was the case for the 1937 edition and all subsequent editions at least through 1959.

22. Not all of Nabokov's information was drawn from the article in question. Neither the crucial "Don't touch my circles," nor the promise of the Rhind papyrus to disclose "all secrets, all mysteries" is to be found in it. Although Nabokov's source for the Rhind papyrus

information remains unknown, it is of interest that he discussed it in a letter to Edmund Wilson dated December 2, 1944 (*Letters*, pp. 145-46).

23. B.L. Van der Waerden, *Science Awakening* (Gronigen, 1954), p. 93. Van der Waerden also provides a good summary of Archimedes' life and work (208-28). Of particular interest is his reproduction of the mosaic "Death of Archimedes" depicting the scene in which he is said to have spoken his last words here quoted as "Fellow, don't touch my figures" (210). The mosaic is given as Plate 24a opposite page 217.

24. E.T. Bell, *Men of Mathematics: The Lives and Achievements of the Great Mathematicians from Zero to Poincaré* (New York, 1965), p. 21.

25. *An Illustrated Encyclopedia of Traditional Symbols*, ed. J.C. Cooper (London, 1978), pp. 36-37.

26. The figure is adapted from the 1959 printing of the *Encyclopedia Britannica*, vol. VI, p. 894, where it appears in the article on "Curves." The Spiral of Archimedes (*Arkhimedova spiral'*) seems to have somewhat greater prominence in standard Russian reference works where it is accorded its own alphabetic entry in the classic Brokgauz-Efron *Entsiklopedicheskii slovar'*, ed. I.E. Andreevskii, elsewhere cited by Nabokov, as well as in the *Malaia Sovetskaia Entsiklopediia*, ed. B.A. Vvedenskii, 3rd ed., (Moscow, 1958), vol. 1, and in the *Bol'shaia Sovetskaia Entsiklopediia*, ed. S.I. Vavilov, 2nd ed. (Moscow, 1950), vol. 3.

27. An extended treatment of this theme may be found in L.L. Lee, "Vladimir Nabokov's Great Spiral of Being," *Western Humanities Review*, XVIII (Summer, 1964), pp. 225-36.

28. *A Russian Beauty and Other Stories* (New York, 1973), p. 147. This volume also contains the English translation of the two published chapters of *Solus Rex*.

29. *Letters*, p. 44.

30. *Sovremennye zapiski*, 70, (1940), and *Novyi zhurnal*, 1 (1942). "Ultima Thule" was reprinted in Vladimir Nabokov (Sirin), *Vesna v Fialte i drugie rasskazy* (New York, 1956). All Russian citations are to the *Sovremennye zapiski* and *Vesna v Fialte* versions; all English citations are to the versions indicated in footnote 28.

31. Field, *Nabokov: His Life in Art*, pp. 292 & 353.

32. Falter's father, Ilya, is the subject of one of the numerous puns in what promised to be one of Nabokov's most verbally playful novels: *povar vash Ilya na boku* "your cook Ilya is on his side," i.e., too drunk to stand upright (R278). The Russian phrase is a punning surface translation of *pauvres vaches, il y en a beaucoup* "poor cows, there are many of them." *Letters*, pp. 47-48. There is also a latent reference in *na boku* "on his side" to author Nabokov.

33. The riddle of the universe is a recurrent motif in Nabokov's novels as we have illustrated in the introduction to our chapter. Other examples are cited below.

34. *A Russian Beauty*, p. 147. The artist has entered into Ultima Thule, the island kingdom of the poem he is illustrating. The only clue to his transformation into the character Kr occurs in a passage in which the thoughts of the king momentarily seem to blend with those of "the no longer independent artist Dmitri Nikolaevich Sineusov" as he gazes at a ruby-lettered neon sign RENAULT (190). In the Russian text, the word GARAGE is in Latin script (9). This fleeting reference is the only firm link between the two chapters. More tenuous is an association between a friend of Sineusov referred to as "poor Adolf" who may or may not have been transformed into the overthrown and murdered Prince Adulf (E152/R281 & E191/R11). In his preface to the English translation Nabokov remarks that he modelled the physical aspect of Adulf on S.P. Diaghilev, the impressario of the Ballet Russe. Adulf is, Nabokov says, one of his "favorite characters in the private museum of stuffed people that every grateful writer has somewhere on the premises" (148). One last faint inter-echo is that the author of the epic poem describes its setting to Sineusov as "a melancholy and remote island" (E164). In the "Solus Rex" chapter the island kingdom is described as that *"île triste et lointaine"* (E192). The Russian texts use the identical wording *"grustnyi i dalekii"* in both occurrences (R291 & 12).

35. Maks Fasmer, *Etimologicheskii slovar russkogo iazyka*, II (Moscow, 1967).

36. *Letters*, pp. 44 & 85-86.

37. Jorge Luis Borges' story "Tlön, Uqbar, Orbis Tertius" also offers the thematic conjunction of knowledge of an alternate world and an encyclopedia volume. The story may be found in Borges' *Labyrinths: Selected Stories & Other Writings*, (New York, 1964).

38. Note that the name Falter means "butterfly" in German. The butterfly, due to its metamorphic transformations (egg, caterpillar, cocoon-like pupa and butterfly) is a traditional religious symbol of immortality of the soul and has often been so used by lepidopterist Nabokov. For a particularly clear-cut example, see the 1924 story "Christmas" in *Details of a Sunset and Other Stories*. In Russian as *Rozhdestvo* in *Vozvrashchenie Chorba: rasskazy i stikhi*. A survey of butterflies as intermediaries from the "other" world may be found in W.W. Rowe *Nabokov's Spectral Dimension* (Ann Arbor, 1980), p. 113. It is curiously apt that Falter, who has completed the metamorphic cycle, is both the past and present tutor of Sineusov, who is his pupil. The word "pupil" and "pupa", the cocoon-like stage of metamorphosis, are close cognates.

39. Nabokov via Falter rounds off this discussion of circularity with a bit of word play which is striking in English but stunning in Russian. Cf. the English "logical development inexorably becomes an envelopment" (196) and the Russian *razvitie rokovym obrazom stanovitsia svitkom* (297) "Development inexorably turns into a scroll." The verbal root *vit* means "twist, turn."

40. Falter's use of "Moustache-Bleue" (E175-76) is restricted to the English version. A number of changes have been introduced into the treatment of proper names in the translation. In the original, Falter's brother-in-law and sister and the Italian psychiatrist all remain nameless. In the translation the couple become Mr. and Elenora L., while the doctor becomes Bonomini in another of Nabokov's ritualistic aspersions on psychiatrists. The name Sineusov is drawn from a list of names of extinct Russian noble families supplied to Nabokov by a historian friend in the thirties. Field, *Nabokov: His Life in Art*, p. 200.

41. See Rowe, p. 13.